AF552861

CULTURE AND CIVILIZATION SERIES

BUDDHISM AND INDIAN CIVILIZATION

Edited by
Dr. R.K. Pruthi

DISCOVERY PUBLISHING HOUSE
NEW DELHI-110002

First Published-2004

ISBN 81-7141-866-X

Published by

DISCOVERY PUBLISHING HOUSE
4831/24, Ansari Road, Prahlad Street,
Darya Ganj, New Delhi-110002 (India)
Phone: 23279245 • Fax: 91-11-23253475
E-mail:dphtemp@indiatimes.com

Printed at :
ARORA OFFSET PRESS
Laxmi Nagar, Delhi-92.

PREFACE

In the sixth century B.C, India witnessed the commencement of a great revolution. Her ancient religion had degenerated. The religious instinct, the grateful emotions which had inspired the composers of the vedic hymns were dead; vast ceremonials, dead forms, remained.

Gautama of the sakya race was versed in the Hindu learning and religion of the age. He rebelled against the unrightious distinctions and dead ceremonials.

Inspired by his love of purity Gautama eschewed the rites of the vedas. He insisted only on self culture, on benevolence, on practice of virtue. This is what made Buddhism a living and life-giving religion which in the course of a few centuries became the prevailing faith not of a sect or a country but of the continent of Asia.

Aim of the book is to place before the readers some aspect of Buddhism which is a unique feature of Indian civilization.

In preparing this work we incurred indebtness of the esteemed scholars and many friends who have helped in many ways. My publisher and his staff have worked hard in its publication. They deserve my readers patronage.

R.K. Pruthi

Contents

	Preface	*v*
1.	Life of Buddha	1
2.	Buddhism	8
3.	Buddhist Thought	36
4.	Buddhist Ethics	44
5.	The Doctrines of Buddhism	73
6.	Buddhism Persecuted	83
7.	Theravāda Buddhism	100
8.	The Buddhist Doctrine of Karma and Development of Indian Civilization	160
9.	Contribution of Buddhism to Art	180
10.	Some Sayings of the Buddha	189
11.	The Stability of Societies	207
	Chronology	240
	Glossary	245
	Bibliography	285

1

Life of Buddha

The Buddha as a Man: We may now attempt an estimate of the greatness of the Buddha as a man, and not as the founder of a religion followed by more than a fifth of the human race. We can make an estimate of that greatness on the basis of some of the sayings attributed to him, or anecdotes told about him in the texts compiled after his death.

Stages in His life: The Buddha was married at sixteen, His only son was born after more than twelve years of married life. He renounced the world when he was enjoying it most, at twenty-nine. He spent six years in a life of uttermost austerities, achieving Buddhahood of Enlightenment at thirty-five . From thirty-five up to his death, at eighty, for a period of forty-five years, he gave himself completely to active social service and ministry.

Initial Weaknesses: The Buddha, like the lotus, blossomed into perfection out of the ordinary conditions of life. He was not initially above the ills which flesh is heir to. He did not, like ordinary men, find renunciation and asceticism at all easy. He himself confessed: "I also, ye monks, before I had attained Enlightenment...myself subject to birth, growth and decay, sickness and death, pain and impurity, sought after what also is subject to these, viz. wife and children, slaves, male and female, goats and sheep, fowls and swine, elephants, cattle, horses, mares, gold and silver... How if I seek the birthless, ageless, diseaseless, deathless, and the stainless incomparable surety, the extinction of illusion! And, ye monks, after some time, while still in my first bloom, shining, dark-haired, in the enjoyment of happy youth, in the first years of manhood, against the wish of weeping and wailing parents, with shorn hair and beard, clothed in ragged raiment, I went with forth from home to homelessness." And again: "Before my full Awakening. I clearly perceived the wretchedness of desires but not finding happiness or aught better outside of desires and evil things, I knew not to turn away from following after them."

Mendicant's Meal: His first meal as mendicant he could hardly eat. "His stomach turned and he felt as if his inwards were on the point of coming out by his mouth, for in that existence he had never before so much as seen such fare," till by self-admonition he overcame his feeling of "distress at that repulsive food."

Fear of Solitude: His next problem in this new life was its solitude and the fear of it. He himself thus describes it: "How hard to live the life of the lonely forest dweller...to rejoice in solitude. Verily, the silent groves must bear heavy upon the monk who has not yet won to fixity of mind!.... He is seized with mortal fear and terror ``to overcome which he would" go forth to the lonely tombs in the woods, out under the trees and abide the night through in those places of horror and affright... And, as I tarried there, a deer came by, a bird caused a twig to fall, and the wind set all the leaves whispering; and I thought: `Now it is coming—that fear and terror'...but I neither stood still, nor sat, nor lay down until, pacing to and fro, I had mastered that fear and terror."

Paul Dahlke well remarks (*Buddhist Essays,* p. 15): "Never before did founder of religion speak like this. One who thus speaks needs not allure with hopes of heavenly joy. One who speaks like this of himself attracts by that power with which the Truth attracts all who enter her domain."

Daily Routine: His life of ministry of for nearly half a century was a life of strenuous work following a strict time-table of daily duties. Rising early morning, washing and dressing himself, he meditated and then went out for alms, bowl in hand, alone or with his followers. Taking his meal with some hospitable host, he gave a discourse and returned to his retreat, waiting to her if all his disciples and had taken their meals. Then be would suggest to them topics for meditation and retire for "Meditation during the noon-day head". The afternoon was given to public discourse followed by evening bath, meditation, discourse to his monks, and retirement for meditation and sleep. *(From account of Buddhaghosha as given in Rhys Davids' American Lectures.)*

A Beggar Before Whom Kings Bowel: He behaved like an ordinary monk all through his life. "In the days when his reputation stood at its highest point, and his name was named throughout India among the foremost names, one might day by day see that man, before whom kings bowed themselves, walking about, alms-bowl in hand, through streets and alleys, from house to house, and without uttering any request, with downcast look, stand silently waiting until a morsel of food was thrown into his bowl (Oldenberg). Once at Alavi, in the simsapa forest, he was found resting on a cattle-path upon a couch of leaves in deep meditation, while it was bitterly cold winter and frosting: "rough is the ground trodden by the hoofs of the cattle; thin is the couch of leaves; light the monk's yellow robe; sharp the cutting winter wind," and yet the Master said: "I live happily, with sublime uniformity." (From a Sutta of the *Anguttara*).

Superhuman in Humility: His humility, utter and sincere, was itself superhuman. Once, "at the annual final Assembly of the monks, before the time of wandering began, the Exalted One looked round over the silent company and said to the monks: 'Well, ye disciples, I summon you to say whether you have any fault to find with me, whether in word or in deed'." Again, when a Brahmana asked him: "Does the honoured Goutama permit sleeping in the day-time?" The Buddha's frank answer was: "In the last month of summer after the meal when one has returned from the begging round, I confess to lying down upon the right side, upon the cloak, folded in four, and, with collected senses, falling asleep." He is always careful to disclaim any superhuman virtues: once he says to his disciples, "It is lack of understanding and insight into the Four Holy Truths that is to blame, O Brothers, that we—both you and I—so long have travelled the dreary road of *samsara*." We irresistibly feel: "This is the highest; farther can no man go!" (*Dahlke*).

Detesting Divination: Thus, as we have already seen, he did not permit exhibition of superhuman powers by his monks. "It is because," says he, "I perceive danger in the practice of mystic wonders that I loathe, and abhor, and am ashamed thereof" (*Kevaddha-Sutta*). All kinds of "divination sooth-saying, foretelling, or forecasting," he condemns as "low arts" (*Brahmajala-Sutta*).

More Anxious for Truth Than Followers: Therefore he was anxious that the Truth should spread and not that his followers should increase. He was anxious that "the bad things should be put away, things that are corrupting, entailing birth renewal, bringing suffering, resulting in ill making for birth, decay and death in the future; that the things that make for purity shall grow, so that full and abounding insight may be attained even here and now"—"and not because I wish to gain pupils." Thus he could say to an intending convert: "Let him who is your teacher be your teacher still." He asked Uruvela Kassapa, revered by "all the people of Anga and Magadha", and the leader of 500 Jatilas at Rajagriha, "to go first and inform them of his intentions" before changing to Buddhism (*Mahavagga*). Before permitting the Lechchhavi general, Siha, to be his disciple, he desired him not to withdraw his support from his quondam co-religionists, the Nataputtas or Nirgrantha Jains, lest they should be left helpless.

Impatient of Praise by Pupils: He could not stand his own praise by his disciples, however devoted and sincere. Once his favourite pupil, Sariputta, burst out: "Such faith have I, Lord, that me thinks there never was nor will be nor is now any other greater or wiser than the Blessed One." The Buddha replied to this emotional outburst in his usual quiet and humorous manner: "Of course, Sariputta, you have known all the Buddhas of the past?" "No, Lord," said Sariputta. "Well then, you know those the future?" "No, Lord." "Then at least you know me and have penetrated my mind thoroughly." "Not even that, Lord." "Then why, Sariputta, are your words so grand and bold?"

Unmoved by Slander: He was equally unmoved by blame or slander. The Lichchhavi chief, Sunakkhatta, "unable to live the holy life under the Buddha," deserted the Order and went about Vaishali "proclaiming to all and sundry that the Blessed One has no knowledge of the things that lie beyond the ken of ordinary mortals, that his doctrine was a product of mere reasoning, a thing of his own wit's devising," and so forth (Majjhima). Sariputta reported this to the Buddha who only said that Sunakkhatta "had said this thing only of his anger". His teaching was: "Who doth not, when reviled, revile again, a two-fold victory wins." "Abuse that is not answered is like the food rejected by the guest which reverts to the host." His one thought was how to make people realise the Truth that would end all suffering. He used to say: "Let a man of intelligence come to me, honest, candid, straightforward; I will instruct him....and if he practises according as he is taught, then to know for himself and to realise that supreme religion and goal, for the sake of which clansmen go forth from the household life into the homeless state, will take him only seven days."

Control Over Assemblies: The Buddha's greatness is also brought out in the debates and discourses marking every day of his ministry. There was perfect order in his Assemblies. King Ajatashatru, led by his physician, Jivaka, to one such Assembly prolonged into a full moon night, fearing its silence said: "You are playing me no tricks, Jivaka? You are not betraying me to my foes? How can it be that there should be no sound at all, not a sneeze, nor a cough, in so large an Assembly, among 1250 of the brethren?" Looking on the assembly seated in silence, calm as a clear lake, the King sighed: "Would that my son, Udayi Bhadda, might have such calm!"

Superiority in Debate: His controversial method was to put his opponent on the defensive. Nigrodha, the leader of 3000 disciples, tried to outwit him, thinking that for his seclusion "his insight was ruined, he is not at home in conducting an Assembly, nor ready in conversation, but occupied only with the fringes of things", and asked him to expound his doctrine, The Buddha said it was difficult "for one of another view without practice or teaching, to understand" it, but, "come now, Nigrodha, ask me a question about your own doctrine. By this question, Nigrodha was dumbfounded. The Buddha himself said: "That in disputation with anyone whatsoever I could be thrown into confusion or embarrassment—there is no possibility of such a thing; and, because I know of no such possibility on that account it is that I remain quiet and confident." And to Sariputta he further said: "And, when ye shall carry me hither upon a bed, the intellectual vigour of the Perfect One will remain unabated."

Greatness at Death: The truth of his remark is amply borne out by the scenes at his death-bed. To weeping Ananda he calmly said: "Be of good cheer, Ananda. Do not weep. Have I not told you oftentimes that this is the regular course of things that we must part from all that is precious and dear to us?"

Last Words: Great in life, the Buddha was greater in death. The founder of a System found no place in it for himself. When questioned in his dying moments by Ananda for instructions for the Order, he answered: "The Tathagata thinks not that it is he who should lead the brotherhood or that the Order is dependent upon him. Why then should he leave instructions in any matter concerning the Order?" And then came his classical declaration:

"Therefore, O Ananda, be ye lamps unto yourselves. Be ye a refuge to yourselves. Betake yourselves to no external refuge. Hold fast to the Truth as a lamp. Hold fast as a refuge to the Truth . Look not for refuge to any one besides yourselves."

And then when the question of honouring his memory arose, he said in the same spirit: "The brother or sister who continually fulfils all the greater and lesser duties, who is correct in life, observing the precepts—it is he who rightly honours him with the worthiest homage." And when Ananda asked the dying Buddha, "What are we to do, Lord, with the remains of the Tathagata?" He answered: "Hinder not yourselves, Ananda, by honouring the remains of the Tathagata. Be zealous, I beseech you, Ananda, in your behalf! Devote yourselves to your own good! Be earnest, be zealous, be intent on your own good! And after I am gone, let the Truths and Rules of the Order which I have set forth and laid down for you all be the Teacher to you."

A Contemporary Opinion: The contemporary opinion about him is thus summed up by the Brahmana, Sonadanda, in a public speech:

"Truly, sirs, the venerable Goutama is well-born on both sides, of pure descent, and with no reproach in respect of birth.

"He has gone forth into the religious life, giving up the great clan of his relations, much money and gold, and treasure.

"He is handsome, pleasant to look upon, inspiring trust, gifted with great beauty of complexion, fair in colour, fine in presence, stately to behold.

"He has a pleasant voice and pleasing delivery, gifted with a polite address, distinct and not husky, suitable for making clear the matter in hand.

"He is the teacher of the teachers of many, one who puts righteousness in the forefront of his exhortations to the Brahmana race.

"To him people come right across the country from distant lands to ask questions, and he bids all men welcome, is congenial and conciliatory, not supercilious, accessible to all, not backward in conversation.

"Whereas some Samanas and Brahmanas have gained a reputation by all sorts of insignificant matters (such as by wearing the clothes, etc.), his reputation comes from perfection in conduct and righteousness.

"And he is trusted, honoured, and venerated by the King of Magadha, Seniya Bimbisara, King Pasenadi of Kosala, and even by the leading Brahmana teacher Pokkarasadi, with their children and wives, their people and courtiers or intimates" (*Sonadanda-Sutta*).

2

Buddhism

The religion known as Buddhism is the religion which has the largest number of adherents in the world. Despite all difficulties of accurate statistics we may take it that about one-third of the human race follow the teaching of the Buddha, and in the West a very large amount of attention has been drawn to these teachings by the devoted work of a number of Orientalists who have been fascinated by the charm of the Buddha himself, by the purity, by the elevation of his teachings. For many reasons into which I cannot now go in detail, Buddhism has greater attraction for the Western mind than either Hinduism or Zoroastrianism—Buddhism especially in the form in which it is taught in the southern Church. The northern Church—Buddhism as it is found in Tibet and China—is so closely allied to Hinduism in its teaching as to the gods, as to the continuing Ego, as to the life after death, as to rites and ceremonies, as to the use of Sanskrit mantras, that it has less attraction for the Westerner. For you must remember that the Westerner has a mind which s essentially practical rather than metaphysical, and that he is inclined to be repulsed by much talk about the invisible world, and by much teaching which refers to the more mystic side of religion. In the southern Church this mystic side in course of time has apparently disappeared to a very great extent, at least so far as the translations are concerned that the Europeans possess. Books which deal with the more mystic side are not yet translated, and therefore are not before the Western[1] public. What they recognize as Buddhism is a system of wonderful ethics, couched in the most beautiful and in the most poetical language; they recognize in it these moral teachings coupled with rare liberality of thought, with the constant appeal to the reason, with the constant attempt to justify and render intelligible the foundations on which the morals are built; and this appeals very strongly to the minds of many Westerners, who have turned aside from the cruder presentments of religion that are current in Europe, and who seek in Buddhism a refuge from the complete scepticism to which otherwise they would feel themselves doomed.

Now with regard to the teachings of Buddhism, I shall found myself on the Buddhist scriptures themselves, for that is the fairest way of dealing with a faith; and then, as always, looking at these in the light of occult knowledge, I shall try to show you how consistent they are with the noblest teachings of other faiths, with the essential truths of religion, and how it is very largely owing to misconception, to misrepresentation, to the small extent,. we may say, to which some of the later disciples have expounded the teaching of the Buddha—it is largely in consequence of these misconceptions and omissions that in the land which was his birthplace, amongst the people to whom by race he belonged, his doctrines are now looked upon with so much of suspicion, and scarcely any are found to accept his teachings, or willing to call themselves by his name. Daughter of Hinduism, Buddhism most undoubtedly is, daughter of the ancient faith, born in comparatively modern times, and if rightly read the Buddhist Scriptures are the echo of the Hindu Scriptures, and the teachings—though often thrown into a less metaphysical and a more directly practical form—are teachings that are penetrated with the Hindu spirit, as indeed you might expect, remembering the lips that spake them. The form into which they were thrown is specially adapted for spreading these truths outside the limits of India itself, a form which, by the foreknowledge of the Buddha, was made to carry the teachings of the purest Hindu morality into many a country outside the limits within which Hinduism would be taught, intended to spread it through populations less keenly metaphysical and less intellectual than those of the Hindu people. We find here, the fundamental verities, though the form into which they are thrown is simpler, and is in many ways perhaps more directly practical. The mission of the Buddha—while it began in India with the hope perchance that the whole work might go on in harmony and without disruption—was intended to carry the fight of truth to other peoples, a mission that has been triumphantly fulfilled, and that, we may hope, will continue to be fulfilled for many an age to come.

Now the essential teachings of the Buddha are contained in the three great divisions of Buddhist sacred literature, the three Pitakas, or baskets, as they are called. The first of this is the Vinaya, and contains all the rules laid down for the monastic order that he established, the famous Sangha, the guardian and repository of His religion. In addition to the rules of discipline, we have also in the Vinaya a large number of teachings given by the Buddha, more mystical in their character than those of some of the other volumes; being specially intended for the training of the monastic order, specially intended for the teaching of the disciples, these books speak out more plainly as to the visible world than do some others; they give out more fully what is regarded by the materializing West as the legendary side of Buddhism; but this is really a true and essential part of Buddhist teaching, and, as was said long afterwards by Nāgārjuna: "Every Buddha has both a revealed and a mystic doctrine.' The exoteric is for the multitude of new disciples. The esoteric is for the Boddhisattvas and advanced pupils, such as Kāshyapa. It is not communicated in the form of definite language, and could not, therefore, be transmitted by Ānanda, as definite doctrine among the Sūtras. Yet it is virtually contained in the Sūtras. For instance, the Fa-hwa-king, or 'Sūtra of the Lotus of the Good Law', which is regarded as containing the cream of the revealed doctrine, is to be viewed as a sort of original document of the esoteric teaching, while it is in form exoteric."[1] When the Buddha was seventy-one years of age, he expounded the esoteric doctrine in answer to the questions put to him by his great disciple Kāshyapa, and although, as J. Edkins says, this doctrine could no be fully put into language—for always the esoteric doctrine, being spiritual, is beyond intellectual language—none the less can it be deduced from the Sūtras.

The second of these three Pitakas consists of Sūtras, or Suttas, as they are generally called—because the Buddha is supposed to have spoken in Prākrit, the common dialect derived from Sanskrit, which is now called Pāli. The Suttas form that part of the Buddha's teachings which were given to the people, his ethical teachings, and discussions, disputations, questionings, explanations, arising out of them, and out of circumstances that he met with in his daily life. Here are the great records of the life and teachings of the Buddha, showing that life as it was lived in India, and those teaching as they fell from his sacred lips. The third Pitaka is the *Abhidhamma*, of which very little is known at present in the West. It is said to be full of mysticism, and to contain the Buddhist philosophy as apart from the Buddhist ethics But that I must leave on one side, as unreachable by us, and there is plenty of matter in the other two Patakas to take up very up very much more than all the time at our disposal.[2]

In considering how I should lay this great teaching before you, what would be the form which would make it at once most attractive and most instructive, I decided that it would be best to put it in the way that we may say originally came to the people who listened to the Buddha himself, for his teaching is so interwover with his life, its beauty and its fascination depend so largely on the One who uttered it, and on the marvellous perfection of that many-sided life, that to describe it as a mere dry system, a apart from the life of the Blessed One, seems to deprive it of its inspiring force, to deprive it of its greatest influence over the lives of man.

Let me remind you, at the very outset, of the way in which the Buddha is looked upon, alike by his own disciples, by every occultist, and by every one who knows anything of the invisible world, and of the way in which the position of a Buddha is gained. Many a hundred incarnations went before that final incarnation in which the illumination of the Buddha was attained. Step by step he climbed up the long ladder of existence; life after life of self-sacrifice and devotion led him from earthly manhood to divine humanity, from divine humanity to the position of a Bodhisattva, from the positior of a Bodhisattva to that of a Buddha. The Buddha is said to have perfected His vow *Kalpa* after *kalpa.* Immeasurable ages of innumerable lives lay behind him here he was born in the town of Kapilavastu, in the palace of the King, born for his last birth upon this planet, born to reach the perfect illumination, and to become one of the series of supreme Teachers of Gods and men.

In the velley of the Ganga, about a hundred miles to the north-east of the sacred city of Vārānasī, this child was born, and it is said, and truly said, that all nature rejoiced over his birth-hour, knowing the work he had come to accomplish in the world. It is said that Devas showered flowers on the mother and the child, that the rejoicing shook all the worlds of Gods and men, for the child that was born was to be a mighty teacher, the instructor of myriads and myriads of the human race. The date of his birth is put by the Sinhalese at 623 B. C.; at 685 B.C. by the Siamese.[3] He was named by his parents Siddhārtha, "He who has accomplished his purpose"; that name was given because of a prophecy made by a great Brāhmana soon after his birth, that the child should be a mighty teacher and an enlightener of the nations of the earth. He grew up during his youth apparently in ignorance of his mighty destiny. It is a strange problem that has pressed on many minds how it is that with some of the greatest who are born into the world, the knowledge of their own greatness is for a time veiled. You may remember it was the same with Rāma. He did not in his early days show any knowledge that he was an Avatāra of the Supreme; he was taught by Vashishtha, and from him received in his then body the knowledge of true Yoga. So also with the Buddha; as we trace him through the beautiful life he led as a boy, as a youth, up to the date of his marriage with his cousin, and for still a year or two afterwards, we see him leading indeed a noble, a beautiful and a pure life, but a life that did not apparently recognize its own greatness, with the mind turned to the invisible world but not yet realizing its mission nor the part it had to play.

We read how his father, longing that he should be the King of earth rather than the monarch over millions of minds of men in the spiritual world, tried to keep back from him the knowledge of the suffering that was going on in the world around. He environed him on all sides with all that was fair and delightful, in order that the knowledge of the sorrow of the world might be shut out from his eyes. We read how, by the guiding of a Deva, he was led to go forth from his place and the pleasure-garden that surrounded it, and driving in his chariot he met four men who gave him the first touch of the awakening. First, he met a man who was aged, and up till this time he had never seen but the young; he asked what was this man, half-blind, tottering, and palsied, with a wrinkled face, with weakness in every limb; and his charioteer answered, he was an aged man, and that to all that were born into the world age must come in time. He met a man suffering from horrible disease; he had seen nothing but health and beauty, and he asked what was this; the charioteer told him, this is disease, under which many of the children of men must suffer. He saw a corpse, he who had seen nothing but the living, and he asked what was this; and the charioteer said, it is death, to which all who are living must come. And lastly he met an ascetic, calm, serene, and peaceful, full of happiness, full of peace, and he asked how it was that in a world where there were disease and death this man could walk through the world serene. He was answered that this man had a life beyond the life of men, a life fixed in the eternal; hence his peace, his serenity, his calm in the midst of sorrow.

Going back to his palace the prince reflected, and from his lips broke forth the cry: "Full of hindrance is this household life, the haunt of passion; free as the air is the homeless state. "That idea fastened on him—the contrast between the haunt of passion and the homeless man; until at last, rising in the night when wife and child were sleeping beside him, he bent over the young wife, beautiful in her sleep, and over the babe that lay beside her in the first tenderness of its youth, and touching them not, lest he should awaken them and their cry should shake his purpose, he went forth from the palace of his father, he called his faithful charioteer to bring his horse, and went through the silent sleeping city, through the quiet streets of the deserted town, until, coming to the gates of the city, he dismounted from his horse, gave it to the charioteer and bade him lead it back to the palace. He then stripped off his princely garments, cut off his fair, and went forth alone, homeless, to seek for the cause of human sorrow and for its cure. He who was to be the Buddha could not live in joy and happiness in the palace of the King, while men outside were suffering, were agonizing and were dying; he went out to seek the cause of the suffering, and the cure which he might bring to human woe.

Then we trace him in the search he made after divine wisdom. First going to greate recluses, to Arāda Kalāma and Uddaka, he tried to learn from them the secret; they were learned in philosophy, in religion, and he sought to learn from them the cause and the cure of sorrow. He studied the mysteries of philosophy, he sat at their feet learning all the intricacies of metaphysics, and at last, despairing, he arose, feeling that not there was the cure of sorrow, not by mere intellectual learning should the salvation of men be found. Going onwards, he met five ascetics, and for six years he gave himself to the ascetic life, practising penances greater than any other practised, reducing his food at last to a mere grain a day, until finally he fell, emaciated, fainting and helpless, worn out by the rigour of his austerities. A passing girl, Nandā, brought him rice and milk He took the food and arose refreshed, and when his comrades saw that he had taken food, they turned from him, saying: "This ascetic is going back to the world, he is weary of austerity and is unworthy of the sacred vocation." And they left him, and again he went forth alone, to find in solitude the secret of human woe.

As he was wandering on his ways, the time approached when illumination was to be found. Reaching Gayā, he sat down beneath the sacred Ashvattha tree, saying that he would never rise from his seat until light had dawned upon his spirit and the secret of sorrow was found. He sat there patiently and all the hosts of Māra, the evil ones, assailed him with temptations of pleasure and with threats of pain; all the Asuras gathered round him, seeking to shake his constancy and to modify his determination. He sat, clad in the garment of pure resolution, untouched, unshaken, even when the image of his weeping wife appeared before him, with outstretched arms pleading that he would turn his face backward to the world again. At last in the silent hour the illumination came. As he sat beneath the sacred tree, there dawned on him the light which he had been born into the world to discover. There came to him that mighty awakening which made him the Enlightened, the Buddha, which told him of sorrow, of the cause of sorrow, of the cure of sorrow, of the path which leads beyond it. Buddhahood was achieved, a Saviour of the world was there. And then there broke from his lips the song triumphant, that must be familiar to many amongst you: "Looking for the maker of this tabernacle, I shall have to run through a course of many births, so long as I do not find (him); and painful is birth again and again. But now, maker of the tabernacle, thou hast been seen; thou shalt not make up this tabernacle again. All thy rafters are broken, thy ridge-pole is sundered; the mind, approaching the Eternal, has attained to the extinction of all desires."[4]

That was the secet of the Buddha—that by the extinction of desires man rises to peace. Under the tree of wisdom he had seen the sorrow of the world, its cause in desire, its end in the ending of desire, and the noble eightfold path which led out of it into peace eternal. Seeing it for himself and for the race, he passed into Nirvāna, the uncreated, the passionless, the all-embracing. And when the Blessed One had thus entered into Nirvāna, he sat beneath the Bodhi tree for seven days, "enjoying the bliss of emancipation."[5]

During the night closing the seventh day, he "fixed his mind upon the chain of causation" and traced the evolution of the universe, expressing it in the twelve Nidānas, the succession of which shows the order of the stages, until we reach the suffering we find around us; the first is *avidyā*, "ignorance," i.e. limitation, the primary cause—because without this limitation in All-Consciousness, by the action of the Supreme, no universe, no variety, can arise. From *avidyā* come the *samkhāras*, from these consciousness, then name and form, then the six powers of perception, from these contact, from contact sensation, from sensation desire, from desire attachment, from attachment "Existence"—i.e. personality—from this birth, and from birth decay, with all the sorrows of life.[6] These form the evolutionary chain, and, properly understood and unfolded, contain the whole philosophy of the evolving universe, and its returning path.

Arising from his seat under the Bodhi tree, the Buddha sat under a banyan tree for another seven days, at the end of which, in answer to a Brāhmana, he spoke words that explain his whole attitude to Brāhmanas: "That Brāhmana who has removed (from himself) all sinfulness, who is free from haughtiness, free from impurity, self-restrained, who is an accomplished master of knowledge [or of the Veda], who has fulfilled the duties of holiness, such a Brāhmana may justly call himself a Brāhman, whose behaviour is uneven to nothing in the world.[7]

For the more periods of seven days each, the Buddha sat under two other trees, and then he took food from two merchants, who became his first disciples. Returning to his seat under the banyan tree, a strange scene occurred. "In the mind of the Blessed One, who was alone, and had retired into solitude, the following thought arose; 'I have penetrated this doctrine which is profound, difficult to perceive and to understand, which brings quietude of heart, which is exalted, which is unattainable by reasoning, abstruse, intelligible (only) to the wise.[8] This people, on the other hand, is given to desire, intent upon desire, delighting in desire. To this people, therefore, who are given to desire, intent upon desire, delighting in desire, the law of casuality and the chain of causation will be a matter difficult to understand; most difficult for them to understand will be also the extinction of all *samkhāras,* the getting rid of all the substrata [of existence], the destruction of desire, the absence of passion, quietude of heart, Nirvāna. Now if I proclain the doctrine and other men are not able to understand my preaching, there would result but weariness and annoyance to me.' And then the following...stanzas, unheard before, occurred to the Blessed One: 'With great pains have I acquired it. Enough! Why should I now proclaim it? The doctrine will not be easy to understand to beings that are lost in lust hatred. Given to lust, surrounded with thick darkness, they will not see what is repugnant [to their minds], abstruse, profound, difficult to perceive and subtle.'[9]

At this crisis Brahmā Sahampati (the third Logos of our chain) intervened, seeing that "the mind of the Tathāgata, of the holy, of the absolute Sambuddha inclines itself to remain in quiet, and not to preach the doctrine." He tells the Buddha that some will understand and reminds him of the suffering earth: "Look down, all-seeing One, upon the people lost in suffering overcome by birth and decay, thou who hast freed thyself from suffering! Arise, O here, O victorious One! Wander through the world, O Leader of the pilgrim band,[10] who thyself art free from debt. May the Blessed One preach the doctrine; there will be people who can understand it!" And so he looked on the world, with the eye of a Buddha, full of compassion, and saying: "Wide open is the door of immortal to all who have ears to hear; let them send forth faith to meet it. The Dhamma sweet and good I spake not, Brahmā, despairing of the weary task, to men."[11]

He then arose, and whither did he go, to commence his beneficent mission? He went to the sacred city whence spiritual missions have ever started in India; he went to Kāshi, to the holy spot whence the spiritual life of India has ever taken its rise; and there in Isipatana, in the deer-park of the city of Vārānasi, he set rolling the wheel of the Law. Here were dwelling the five ascetics who had turned their backs on him. To them he went, and announcing himself as Sambuddha, he told them that the two extremes of self-indulgence and of constant self-mortification were alike profitless, and that, avoiding these, he had trodden " the middle path, which leads to insight, which leads to wisdom, which conduces to calm, to knowledge, to the sambodhi,[12] to Nirvānā." This middle path is the holy or noble eightfold path, the fourth of the "Four Noble Truths." It is: Right Belief, Right Aspiration, Right Speech, Right Conduct, Right Livelihood, Right Endeavour, Right Memory, Right Meditation. He then expounded to them the other three Truths He had seen under the Bodhi tree: "This, O Bhikkhus, is the Noble Truth of Suffering: birth is suffering; dacay is suffering; illness is suffering; death is suffering; presence of objects we hate is suffering; separation from objects we love is suffering; not to obtain what we desire is suffering. Briefly, the fivefold clinging[13] to existence is suffering. This, O Bhikkhus, is the Noble Truth of the cause of suffering: thirst that leads to rebirth, accompanied by pleasure and lust, finding its delights here and there; [this thirst is threefold] namely, thirst for pleasure, thirst for existence, thirst for prosperity. This, O Bhikkhus, is the Noble Truth of the cessation of suffering; [it ceases with] the complete cessation of this thirst—a cessation which consists in the absence of every passion—with the abandoning of this thirst, with the doing away with it, with the deliverance from it, with the destruction of desire."

When the " supreme wheel of the empire of Truth" was thus set rolling, it is recorded that all the Devas, beginning with those of the earth and passing to the seventh, of highest, world, shouted with joy, and cried that none could ever again turn back the wheel.[14]

Yet further he explained to them the difference between the Self and the not-Self, in words that should for ever have made impossible the contention that he taught that there was no continuing life in man: "The body [rūpa], O Bhikkhus, is not the Self... Sensation, O Bhikkhus, is not the Self... Perception is not the Self... The *samkhāras* are not the Self... Consciousness is not the Self." Defining each more fully, he declares of each that it "is not mine, is not, me, is not my Self; thus it should be remembered by right knowledge according to the truth." And he concludes: "Considering this, O Bhikkhus, a learned, noble hearer of the word becomes weary of body, weary of sensation, weary of perception, weary of the *samkhāras*, weary of consciousness. Becoming weary of all that, he divests himself of passion; by absence of passion he is made free; when he is free, he becomes aware that he is free; and he realizes that rebirth is exhausted; that holiness is completed; that duty is fulfilled: that there is no further return to this world."[15]

From this time forth, the Lord Buddha preached his doctrine, and men and women became enlightened, obtaining, as he taught, "the pure and spotless Eye of the Truth," the knowledge that all that has a beginning must have an ending; then they surrendered all worldly things and became Bhikkhus, mendicants, putting on the yellow robe, carrying the alms-bowl, taking refuge in the Buddha, in his doctrine and his Order. And the Order grew and multiplied, and after a while the Lord sent out his disciples to teach, and gave them authority to admit to the Sangha (the Order) those who sought entrance, on the triple declaration thrice repeated; "I take my refuge in the Buddha. I take my refuge in the Dhamma. I take my refuge in the Sangha."[16]

Dr. Rhys Davids—who is so fascinated by the ethical life of Buddhism, and who so utterly and so strangely resents its inner spirits, and declares that in Buddhist teaching there is no continuing Ego, no development of the eternal and spiritual nature of man—gives us from Buddhagosha's commentary on the first of the Dialogues a most attractive picture of the daily round of that holy life. "The Blessed One used to rise up early (i.e. about 5 A.M.), and out of consideration for his personal attendant, was wont to wash and dress himself, without calling for any assistance. Then, till it was time to go on his round for alms, he would retire to a solitary place and meditate. When that time arrived, he would dress himself completely in the three robes (which every member of the Order wore in public), take his bowl in his hand and, sometimes alone, sometimes attended by his followers, would enter the neighbouring village or town for alms, sometimes in an ordinary way, sometimes wonders happening," recounted at length. Then people would come out and pray him to accept his food from them, and he would sit down and eat. "Then would the Blessed One, when the meal was done, discourse to them, with due regard to their capacity for spiritual things, in such a way that some would take the layman's voe, and some would enter on the paths, and some would reach the highest fruit thereof. And when he had thus had mercy on the multitude, he would arise from his seat and depart to the place where he had lodged. And when he had come there, he would sit in the open verandah, awaiting the time when the rest of his followers should also have finished their meal." Then standing at the door of his room, he would speak a few words of exhortation, and at the request of any disciple would "suggest a subject for meditation, suitable to the spiritual capacity of each."

The disciples departing to meditate, the Buddha would rest a while, and "when his body was rested he would arise from the couch and for a space consider the circumstances of the people near that he might do them good. And at the fall of the day, the folk from the neighbouring villages of town would gather together at the place where he was lodging, bringing with them offerings of flowers. And to them, seated in the lecture hall, would he, in a manner suitable to the occasion, and suitable to their beliefs, discourse on the Truth." Dismissing them, at the close of the day, he would sometimes bathe, and then sit alone, "till the brethren, returned from their meditations, began to assemble. Then some would ask him questions on things that puzzled them, some would speak of their meditations, some would ask for an exposition of the Truth. Thus would the first watch of the night pass, as the Blessed One satisfied the desire of each, and then they would take their leave. And part of the rest of the night would be spend in meditation, walking up and down outside his chamber: and part he would rest lying down, calm and self-possessed within. And as the day began to dawn, rising from his couch, he would seat himself, and calling up before his mind the folk in the world, he would consider the aspirations which they, in previous births, had formed, and think over the means by which he could help them to attain thereto."[17]

Into the framework of this noble, simple life, the jewels of the Buddha's teachings were set. In order to appreciate them, we need to remember this environment, to remember that the Buddha was a Hindu speaking to Hindus on matters largely familiar to them, using religious and metaphysical terms in their ordinary accepted meanings, raising no opposition as a heretic—as he assuredly would have done had his teaching been materialistic, as it become later among some non-Hindus, ignorant of the connotation of the terms employed—a Teacher, distinguishable from other teachers of his time by his contemporaries only by the incomparable purity, compassion and wisdom that breathed from his every look, his every word. Dr. Rhys Davids, regarding Buddhism as "diametrically opposed" to Hinduism, regards it as an evidence of wonderful toleration that he was allowed to teach so peacefully. "It is even more than that. Wherever he went, it was precisely the Brahmins themselves who often took the most earnest interest in his speculations, though his rejection of the soul theory and of all that it involved was really incompatible with the whole theology of the Vedas, and therefore with the supremacy of the Brahmins. Many of his chief disciples, many of the most disintinguished members of his Order, were Brahmins."[18] It is more reasonable to suppose, and the supposition is borne out by his recorded sayings, that he met with no opposition just because he did not reject the soul theory with all that it involves; and when some of his followers committed this terrible blunder, Buddhism became extinct in India, for never will Hindus accept any so-called religion that casts aside belief in the gods and in the immortality of man. As Dr. Rhys Davids says: "We should never forget that Gotama was born and brought up and lived and died a Hindu. His teaching, far-reaching and original as it was, and really subversive of the religion of the day, was Indian throughout. Without the intellectual work of his predecessors his own work, however original, would have been impossible.[19] He was no doubt the greatest of them all; and most probably the world will come to acknowledge him as, in many respects, the most intellectual of the religious teachers of mankind. But Buddhism is essentially an Indian system. The Buddha himself was, throughout his career, a characteristic Indian. And, whatever his position as compared with other teachers in the West, we need here only claim for him, that he was the greatest and wisest and best of the Hindus."[20]

How continually he spake as Hindu to Hindus, his similes and teachings often show, being drawn from the ancient scriptures. Take, as illustrations, the three controls of actions, speech, mind and body,[21] drawn from Manu; the sentence: "he who holds back rising anger like a rolling chariot, him I call a real driver; other people are but holding the reins," and the reference to the senses as well-broken horses, recalling the teaching of Yama in the Kathopanishad.[22] The play on the higher and lower self,[23] drawn from the Bhagvad-Gitā. "All that we are is the result of what we have thought; it is founded on our thoughts, it is made up of our thoughts,"[24] from the Chāndogyopanishad. "It is good to control the mind, which is difficult to hold, unstable, and which goes where it pleases,"[25] a reminiscence of the Bhagavad-Gitā. But it is useless to multiply instances. Enough that the great teacher carefully re-echoed the ancient writings, not as needing them himself—he who knew all—but lest the ignorant should be caused to stumble, and turn away from the faith of their fathers.

Let us now turn to the mass of teachings that confrotns us, and learn from examples something not only of his precepts, but of his methods. To a remarkable degree they were pointed, they were practical, and addressed to the consciences of his hearers; he never for one moment hesitated to speak in plainest language, in clearest terms, of the faults into which we are betrayed, of the mistakes into which men are constantly falling. For the Buddha was a Teacher indeed, a Teacher whose words illumined the minds. Strong and practical, then, and for the most part it seems as if some passing incident gave the opportunity for a parable or a story bearing an ethical lesson. His Bhikkhus were quarrelling, and as each man quarrelled with his neighbour returned the quarrel, and hatred ruled where peace ought to have been. Then the Budha called them to him; and he told them a story; the story of a king of Kāshi who made war against the king of Koshala, a small kingdom, and drove him away from his kingdom and took it to himself. The dispossessed king and his wife went and lived in a poor hovel, and there a son was born to them. The barber of the dispossessed king, seeing his former master, and desiring to curry the favour of the conqueror, betrayed to him the fugitive, and the king sent forth and seized the fugitive and his wife and gave them over to the executioner. As they were being led to the place of death, the son, who had been sent away for safety, came and saw his father and mother on their way to execution, and he pressed through the crowd. The father whispered: "My son, be not long, be not short; hatred ceases not by hatred; by non-hatred it ceases"; and he then went on to death; and the son pondered over the father's words, he understood them not. Presently he took service under the king who had slain his mother and father, after reducing them to beggary, and, attracting the king's attention, he was taken as his personal attendant. The king loved the youth, and used to sleep with his head in his lap. As he slept there one day the young prince thought "This king is in my power; he has slain my father and mother; he has reduced me to misery; he is helpless, I will slay him"; and he drew out his sword. But his father's words came to his mind: "be not short", and he knew it meant: "be not hasty in your action"; he put the sword back and remembered the other words, that hatred ceases not by hatred. The king awoke and said he dreamt that the prince he had dispossessed had slain him, and the youth, drawing his sword, revealed himself and told him that his life was at his mercy. The king prayed for his life, and the prince answered him: "Nay, O king, I have forfeited my life by this threat, and thou must give me back my life and thy pardon." So he gave the king his life, that he could have taken, and the king pardoned the offence and gave him also his life, and then the prince told him of his father's dying words: "My father taught me that I must not be long—I must not keep hatred; I must not be short—I must not be hasty in action. That hatred ceases not by hatred at any time, but hatred ceases by love. For if I had slain thee, thy friends would have slain me in return, and my friends would then have slain thy friends, and so hatred would not have ceased; but now we have each given to the other his life, and thus hatred ceased by love." Then the disciples became at one amongst themselves, and peace was restored within the Order.

The weeping mother, with dead babe clasped to bosom, is told her child shall be restored to her if she can bring some mustard seed from a house where none has died; the gentle lesson sank more deeply than a hundred sermons.

A man abused him vehemently as he was preaching the great doctrine: "A man who foolishly does me wrong I will return to him the protection of my ungrudging love; the more evil comes from him, the more good shall go from me." While a man reproached him, "Buddha was silent, and would not answer him, pitying his mad folly." The man having finished his abuse, Buddha asked him, saying: "Son, when a man forgets then rules of politeness in making a present to another, the custom is to say, keep your present. Son, you have now railed at me; I decline to entertain your abuse, and request you to keep it, a source of misery to yourself. For as sound belongs to the drum, and shadow to the substance, so in the end misery will certainly overtake the evil doer." Buddha said: "A wicked man who reproaches a virtuous one, is like one who looks up and spits at Heaven; the spittle soils not the Heaven, but comes back and defiles his own person. So again, he is like one who flings dirt at another, when the wind is contrary; the dirt does but return on him who threw it. The virtuous man cannot be hurt; the misery that the other would inflict comes back on himself."[26]

Sometimes a gleam of humour flashes out, and it is not difficult to picture the scene between the anxious disciple and the gentle, slightly amused, Master: "How are we to conduct ourselves, Lord, with regard to womankind?" "Don't see them, Ananda." "But if we should see them, what are we to do?" "Abstrain from speech, Ānanda." "But if they should speak to us, Lord, what are we to do?" "Keep wide awake, Ananda."[27] Keep wide awake; notice what you are doing, guard your thoughts. A long sermon as to the wisdom of guarding himself from being led astray would not have been half as effective as that single sentence, "Keep wide awake, Ananda."

Among the striking characteristics of his teachings we find the occult fact that evil can only be put an end to by its opposite good: "Let a man overcome anger by love; let him overcome evil by good; let him overcome the greedy by liberality, the liar by truth.[28] A man must be strong and purposeful: "Earnestness is the path of immortality (Nirvāna), thoughtlessness the path of death. Those who are in earnest do not die; those who are thoughtless are as if dead already."[29] Causation is unbroken: "If a man speaks or acts with an evil thought, pain follows him, as the wheel follows the foot of the ox that draws the carriage... If a man speaks or acts with a pure thought, happiness follows him, like a shadow that never leaves him.[30] "He who has done even a little good finds in his world and in the other happiness and great profit; it is like a seed that has well taken root... He who has done what is evil cannot free himself of it; he may have done it long ago or afar off, he may have done it in solitude, but he cannot cast it off, and when it has ripened he cannot cast it off."[31] Above all, desire must be got rid of, as the root of all sorrow: "From desires comes grief, from desires comes fear; he who is free from desires knows neither grief nor fear... It is hard for one who is held by the fetters of desire to free himself of them, says the Blessed One. The steadfast, who care not for the happiness of desires, cast them off and do soon depart... As the shoe-maker, when he has well prepared his leather, can use it to make shoes, so when one has cast off desires, he has the highest happiness... Desires are never satiated; wisdom affords contentment... Not even in the pleasures of the gods does the disciple of the perfect Buddha find pleasure; he rejoices only in the destruction of desires.[32] The teaching is pithly summed up: "Avoid doing all wicked actions; practice most perfect virtue; thoroughly subdue your mind; this is the doctrine of the Buddha."[33]

Most important is the teaching of the Buddha on "the subjugation of all the Āsavas." of the outgoings of the life in man towards objects of desire. Of these there are seven classes, to be abandoned respectively: (1) by insight–insight into the four noble truths, destroying the delusion of self, hesitation—the five senses and the mind; (3) by right use—clothes, alms, and abode, to be used, not delighted in; (4) by endurance—cold and heat, hunger and thirst, gad-flies, mosquitoes, wind, sun, snakes, abusive words, bodily suffering, pains; (5) by avoidance—obvious dangers, improper places and companions; (6) by removal—evil thoughts; (7) by cultivation—the higher wisdom. When all this is done, "he has destroyed that craving Thirst, by thorough penetration of mind he has rolled away every Fetter, and he has made an end of Pain."[34]

His ethical teaching was pointed and direct to a rare degree; take for instance this: "This fault of others is easily perceived, but that of oneself is difficult to perceive, a man winnows his neighbours's faults like chaff, but his own fault he hides, as a cheat hides the bad die from the gambler. If a man looks after the faults of others, and is always inclined to be offended, his own passions will grow, and he is far from the destruction of passions."[35]

The Buddha was fond of forcing his questioners to answer their own questions. Instead of answering a question, he questioned the questioner. Instead of laying down a doctrine or truth in answer to a question, he gradually led the man stage by stage to answer that question for himself—one of the wisest ways of teaching and the most likely of all ways to make a man realize the truth. Thus, when a young Brāhmana, by name Vāsettha, asked him whether certain learned Brahmanas shows the right way of reaching union with Brahmā, the Buddha replied by a series of questions, the answers to which showed that the Brāhmanas neither knew Brahmā nor were like him, that while versed in the Vedas they were "omitting the practice of those qualities which really make a man a Brāhmana, and adopting the practice of those qualities which really make men not Brāhmanas," and at this point the Buddha summed up: "that these Brāhmanas, versed in the Vedas and yet bearing anger and malice in their hearts, sinful and uncontrolled, should after death, when the body is dissolved, become united to Brahmā, who is free from anger and malice, sinless, and has self mastery—such a condition of thigns has no existence." He then tells the youth that when the Tathāgata was asked the way that leads to the world of Brahmā, he could give the answer: "For Brahmā I know, Vāsettha, and the world of Brahmā, and the path which leadeth unto it. Yes, I know it, even as one who has entered the Brahmā world, and has been born within it." "He, by himself, thoroughly undestands, and sees, as it were, face to face, this universe—the world below with all its spirits, and the world above, of Māra and of Brahmā—and all creatures, Samanas and Brāhmanas, Gods and men, and He then makes His knowledge known to others." When a man is attracted by the truth, and leaves his home, going forth into "the homeless state" and leading a noble and pure life, pervades the whole world "with heart of Love, far-reaching, grown great and beyond measure," such a man is approaching union with Brahmā; and that he "should after death, when the body is dissolved, become united with Brahmā, who is the same—such a condition of things is every way possible".[36]

Here we have the key to all his teachings with regard to the Brāhmanas. Over and over again he says that they are to be treated with respect, that they are to be treated with reverence; but over and over again he also says that he does not call that man a Brāhmana who is vicious, who is uncontrolled, who is greedy, who is full of the vices of the world. So also he says as to his own Bhikhus, that he does not call that man a Bhikshu who wears a yellow robe and whose passions are uncontrolled. For the Buddha was not deceived by outward appearance, nor by the mere look of the outer appearance, nor by the mere look of the outer man; he looked at the heart and only when the heart was clean would he admit that the man had the right to bear a sacred name. He demanded, as every great teacher has demanded, that those who bear a sacred name should honour that name by the life they lead, and not bring scandal and discredit upon it by being full of passion and lust, anger and greed. His testimony to what they had been is full of interest. Asked by some Brāhmanas whether the Brāhmanas of his day were like the ancient Brāhmanas, he replied in the negative, and proceeded: "The old sages were self-restrained, penitent; having abandoned the objects of the five senses, they studied their own welfare. There were no cattle for the Brāhmanas, nor gold, nor corn, (but) the riches and corn of meditation were for them, and they kept watch over the best treasure... Inviolable were the Brāhmanas, invisible protected by the Dhamma, no one opposed them (while standing) at the doors of the houses anywhere. For forty-eight years they practised juvenile chastity; the Brāhmanas formerly went in search of science and exemplary conduct. The Brāhmanas did not marry (a woman belonging to) another (caste), nor did they buy a wife." They did not kill cows, "our best friends, in which medicines are produced," but sacrificd the gifts made to them. "They were graceful, large, handsome, renowned, Brāhmanas by nature, zealous for their different works; as long as they lived in the world this race prospersed. But there was a change in them." They began to covert wealth, they began to slay cows; "there were formerly three diseases: desire, hunger, and decay, but from the slaying of cattle there came ninety-eight". So things went from bad to worse, till "Dhamma being lost, the Suddas and the Vessikas disagreed, the Khattiyas[37] disagreed in manifold ways, the wife despised her husband. The Kshattriyas and the Brāhmanas and those others who had been protected by their castes, after doing away with their disputes on descent, fell into power of sensual pleasures."[38]

How lofty was the opinion held by the Buddha of the true Brāhmana may be read in the closing shlokas of the *Dhammapada*, in which, after giving the characteristics of the true Brāhmana he concludes: "Him I call inded a Brāhmana whose path the Gods do not know, nor spirits (Gandharvas), nor men, when passions are exitinct, and who is an Arhat (venerable). Him I call indeed a Brahmana who call nothing his own, whether it be before, behind, or between, who is poor, and free from the love of the world. Him I call indeed a Brāhmana, the manly, the noble, the hero, the great sage, the conqueror, the impassable, the accomplished, the awakened. Him

I call indeed a Brahmana who knows his former abodes, who sees heaven and hell, has reached the end of birth is perfect in knowledge, a sage, and whose perfections are all perfect."[39] The Buddha re-affirmed the ancient ideal, the essence of caste consisting in spiritual development, and if he declared that "a man does not become a Brāhmana by his plained hair, by his family, or by birth,"[40] he only declared what Manu had taught when the caste-system was ordained. Similarly he declared of his own monks: "A man is not a mendicant (Bhikshu) simply because he asks others for alms; he who adopts the whose law is a Bhikshu, not he who only begs. He who is above good and evil, who is chaste, who with knowledge passes through the world, he indeed is called a Bhikshu." "Many men whose shoulders are covered with the yellow gown are ill-conditioned and unrestrained; such evil-doers by their evil deeds go to hell."41 In the *Udānavarga* the Tibetan recension of the *Dhammapada*, a chapter is devoted to the Brāhmana, and he is described, leading a life of holiness, (Brahmacharya), who neither harms nor kills any living thing." He "has reached the perfection (set forth in) the Vedas," he "is on the way to Nirvāna," he "has now a body for the last time," he "is tolerant with the intolerent," he "he has crossed the stream."[42]

There is the ideal of the Brāhmana taught by the Buddha. There is the description of what the name should carry with it; and I appeal to the ancient Hindu Scriptures which endorse that contention. I appeal to such books as the *Māhābhārata,* which contain exactly the same line of thought, and to the words of Manu, that the Brāhmana without the qualities of the Brāhmana was like "an elephant of wood and antelope of leather," the mere outward appearance of the thing, and not the reality. It is no more reasonable to speak of the Buddha as antagonistic to the Brāhmanas than the speak of Manu in exactly the same words; for both taught the same truth, that a man must have the inner life before he was worthy of the name. And if it be said, as I hear Hindus say, that he desired to abolish the Brāhmana caste because he thus pointed out the evil lives of Brāhmanas, then we shall have to argue that he wished to abolish his own order of Bhikshu, because he decalred that the yellow robe did not make the Bhikshu, but that there must be self-restraint, pure life, and the absence of worldly wealth. To represent the Buddha as an enemy of Brāhmanas and as seeking to destroy them as a caste, when all that he did was to hold up the ancient ideal and to reproach those who lives dishonoured it, is a perversion of facts. Had he succeeded in purifying the caste, he would thus have restored it to its ancient splendour; but he failed, alas! and its own poor ideals are hurrying it towards a self-chosen extinction. The occultist can but hold up the immortal ideal, and if men, rejecting it, perish, they perish.

Touching the gods, the Buddha did not take the position often ascribed to him, a position impossible to One who knew all worlds. He says that he himself has visited all the worlds of the Gods, and therefore that he knows the way to them and is able to guide men along the parth. And on one occasion when he was asked the way to the world of Brahmā. He answered by asking the man whether he did not know the way to his own village, and whether he could not direct thither the wayfarer. The man answered that he was born there, and knew the way that led to it; so also, replied the Buddha, did he know the world of Brahmā having visited it and being familiar with it.[43]

We find frequent references to the gods, endorsing the beliefs of the Hindus he addressed: "By earnestness did Maghavan[44] rise to the lordship of the Gods." "The disciple will overcome the earth, and the world of Yama, and the world of the Gods." "The gods even envy him whose senses, like horses well broken in by the driver, have been subdued." (Note the simile taken from the *Kathopanishad*). "Le tus live happily then, though we call nothing our own. We shall be like the bright Gods, feeding on happiness." "Speak the truth, do not yield to anger, give if thou art asked for little; by these three steps thou wilt go near the Gods."[45] In the Southern Church the belief in the Gods seems to have disappeared, but man's ineradicable need to worship re-appears in the adoration paid to the Buddha himself. In the northern Church, less injured by materialism, the worship of the gods survives, and they are worshipped under their Hindu names. There also we find the Trimāti re-appearing under Buddhist names: Shiva represented by Amitābha, the Boundless Light, Vishnu by Padmapāni, otherwise Avalokiteshvara; the thrd being Manjushri, "the representative of creative wisdom, corresponding to Brahmā."[46]

Closely allied to the conception of the great hierarchies of gods, are the ideas of "heaven" and "hell," regions of the world invisible through which man passes when out of the physical bodydevachan and part of Kāma Loka, the Theosophist calls them. The Buddha by no means ignored these states; in fact, we find him describing both at length; many hells are mentioned in some detail by him in the *Mahāvagga*, in connection with the post mortem fate of one of his

Bhikshus; again in the *Mahā-parinibhāna-sutta,* he declares of the wrong-doer: "on the dissolution of the body, after death, he is reborn into some unhappy state of suffering or woe," while the well-doer, under similar conditions, "is reborn into some happy state in heaven."[47] The northern Church scriptures have very full accounts of the invisible words: there is the Kāma Loka, consisting of the earth and the four lower heavens, the abodes of Devas, Asuras, demons, beasts and men (the physical and astral planes); then comes the abode of Māra (astral) and the eighten heavens of the Rūpa Loka (Rūpa Devachan or Svarga); and beyond these the Arūpa Loka of four heavens, "an ecstatic state of real existence; here dwell those disciples of Buddha who have not attained the imperishable nature." Beyond this is Nirvāna.[48] In regard to this, as with regard to some other of the more occult truths, the scriptures of the northern Church seem to be fuller than those of the southern; the traditions of the Arhats, to whom the Buddha gave in His old age the secret teachings, were carried into Tibet and China when the Buddhists fled away from India, and were there faithfully preserved.

His view of the so-called miraculous powers is recorded in the *Surangama Sūtra,*[49] where the Buddha is recorded to have said that by practising Samādhi without any reliance on Bodhi—i.e. seeking the Siddhis rather than Jñāna[50]—men attained the power of flying through space, of invisibility, etc., and attained various degrees of sublime knowledge but not reaching wisdom, they were still bound to the whel of transmigration.

Much controversy has arisen over the apparent denial, by the southern Church, of a continuing Ego, passing from life to life. Such Orientalists as Dr. Rhys Davids insist on it, and much of the popular Hindu distrust of Buddhists arises from the general belief that they do not believe in the Ego. The teachings of the Buddha himself, however, are clear enough. Thus, when asked about some of his disciples who had died, "where has he been reborn and what is his destiny?"—He answered that one had reached emancipation; another "has become a Sakadāgāmin, who on his first return to this world will make an end of sorrow;" another was "no longer liable to be reborn in a state of suffering:" in all these cases, a persisting individuality is obviously taken for granted. A disciple may say of himself: "Hell is destroyed for me; and rebirth as an animal, or a ghost, or in any place of woe. I am converted; I am no longer liable to be reborn in a state of suffering, and am assured of final salvation."[51] So also he said that those who died while "they with believing heart, are journeying of such pilgrimage, shall he reborn, after death, when the body is dissolved, in the happy realms of heaven."[52] The doctrine of the Self from the Vinaya has already been quoted. And we find him saying, like any other Hindu: "For Self is the lord of self; Self is the refuge of self"[53] a sentence meaningless if there be no Self.

In fact the whole teaching loses its reasonableness and falls into ruins, if the fundamental teaching be withdrawn of an Ego that passes from birth to birth in the cycle of reincarnation, and emerges in the Self when emancipation is gained. This is the Hindu teaching, and the Buddha built his teachings on its universal acceptance among his hearers. In the northern Church the doctrine remained unchallenged of the "true man without a position"; the Lin-tsi School teaches: "Within the body which admits sensations, acquires knowledge, thinks and acts, (compare the statement regarding the Self in the Vinaya) there is the 'true man without a position,' Wu-weichenjen. He makes himself clearly visible; not the thinnest separating film hides him. Why do you not recognize him? The invisible power of the mind permeates every part... This is Buddha, the Buddha with you."[54]

Next should be considered his teaching of "the parth," which depends entirely upon the continuity of life. The Path, in Buddhism, has the same stages as those given by Shri Shamkarācārya, both as to the preliminary path and the path itself. The Buddha asks from his disciples, as the first qualification, that opening of the mind which is identical with discrimination, or *viveka,* discrimination between the permanent and the impermanent; the second step is that regarding action, which teaches indifference to the fruits of action, and is identical with *vairāgya;* then follow the six qualities of the mind, the same six recounted in speaking of the same path as taught in Hinduism; fourthly, the deep longing for liberation, the same as *mamukshā;* and lastly, the *gotrabhu,* the same as the *adhikāri,* when the man is ready for Initiation. After Initiation comes the parth itself, traced in the following quotation, which begins at the highest stage and follows it backward. "Buddha said: The Rahat (Arhat) is able to fly through the air, change his appearance, fix the years of his life, shake heaven and earth. The successive stages towards this condition of being are: The Anāgāmin, who, at the expiration of his life (years) ascends in a spiritual form to the nineteen heavens, and in one of these completes his destiny, by becoming a Rahat. Next, is the condition of a Sakridāgāmin, in which, after one birth and death, a man becomes a Rahat. Next, the condition of a Srotāpanna, in which, after seven births and deaths, a man beocmes a Rahat. These are they who, having entirely separated themselves from all desires and lusts, are like branches of a tree, cut of and dead."[55]

Thus the Buddha taught his disciples, as the scriptures still record, and we have the right to use these scriptures against the misconceptions of those who, materialized in their own thought, are impatient of the verities of the world invisible.

Arhatship was the last step before attaining complete liberation, and gaining the Nirvānic consciousness. The teaching of the Buddha as to Nirvāna is, perhaps, the clearest on record, being positive instead of, as is usual, negative. Having said that the Bhikshu should concentrate within himself all his mental faculties. "as the tortoise draws its body into its shell," the Lord proceeds to tell of Nirvāna: "Bhikshus, the uncreated, the invisible, the unmade, the elementary, the unproduced, exist (as well as) the created, the visible, the made, the conceivable, the compound, the produced; and there is an uninterrupted connection between the two. Bhikshus, if the uncreated, the invisible, the unmade, the elementary, the unproduced, was nonentity, I could not say that the result of their connection from cause to effect with the created, the visible, the made, the compound, the conceivable, was final emancipation... The impermanency of the created, the visible, the made, the produced, the compound, the great torment of subjection to old age, death, and ignorance, what proceeds from the cause of eating; (all this) is destroyed, and there is found no delight in it; this is the essential feature of final emancipation. Then there will be no doubts and scruples; all sources of suffering will be stopped, and one will have the happiness of the peace of the Saṃskāra... This is the chief (beatitude) of those who have reached the end, perfect and unsurpassable peace, the destruction of all characteristics, the perfection of perfect purity, the annihilation of death."[56] Such is the description of a state in which he ever dwelt, whether in or out of the body; yet we find people who instead of believing in the annihilation of death, believe in the annihilation of life in Nirvāna. I know no scripture in which the truth as to Nirvāna is put as plainly as it is here. It is existence, and not non-existence; it is reality, and non-existence; it is reality, and not non-reality; it is permanency, and not transitoriness. What is meant by "Nirvāna," by the "going out" implied in the name, is, he declares, the going out of all these impermanent things; these disappear, and then man attains his final emancipation.

For forty-five years did the Lord Buddha wander over Northern India, teaching, until his work was done and he came to the laying aside of his body. A strange story is attached to his outgoing, significant enough in the old days, but read in a literal sense in these modern days, by those who eat pigs. Chunda, a worker in metals, shortly after the Buddha had announced his approaching departure, offered him his daily meal and prepared dried boar's flesh, sweet rice and cakes. The Lord bade Chunda serve him only with the boar's flesh, giving the rice and cakes to the disciples, and bade him bury what of the boar's flesh remained; for "I see no one, Chunda, on earth, nor in Māra's heaven, nor in Brahmā's heaven, no one among Samanas and Brāhmanas, among Gods and men, by whom, when he has eaten it, that food can be assimilated, save by the Tathāgata."[57] Surely such word are enough to show that the "boar's flesh" was not physical food, such as men who live on flesh assimilate without difficulty. After eating, he taught and then sickness fell on him and great pain; he bore it calmly, and recovering, went on his way. That same day his skin was observed to shine with exceeding splendour, and he told Ānanda that it was the sign of his departing that night, and lying down, he rested for awhile, arising, went to the Sāla grove of the Mallas and lay between the twin Sāla trees, with his head to the north; the trees showered on him their flowers, and heavenly flowers fell, and heavenly music sounded in homage to the dying Lord, but he spake to Ananda and said that while such homage was due to him, yet worthier was the homage paid by the pure and noble man or woman who obeyed his law. All the Devas of the world gathered, and crowds of men came to pay their last homage, and the Buddha made his last Arhat, the mendicant Sabhadda; five hundred disciples stood round him at the ending and he spake his last words: "Bohold now, brethren, I exhort you, saying: Decay is inherent in all component things. Work out your salvation with diligence." Then silence fell, and he passed into deepest meditation, and returned not.

As a king of kings, his body was prepared for the burning, and laid on a pyre of all fragrant woods; it left no ash, but the bones remained. These were divided as sacred relics, and carried away in eight portions, each to be placed under a Thūpa, and a ninth Thūpa was erected over the vessel in which his body had been burned, and a tenth, by the Moriyas, over the embers of his funeral pile. So ended the noblest life yet lived by one of our humanity, the first who on this globe has attained Buddhahood. "Bow down with clasped hands! Hard, hard is a Buddha to meet with, through hundreds of ages!"[58]

There is no time to trace the later growth of Buddhism; the development of its different schools of philosophy, the arising of noble teachers trained in its wisdom, the materializing of the faith that followed its introduction among less developed and less metaphysically inclined people, and its maintenance in its original purity in its esoteric schools. Enough has been said of the saying of the Buddha himself to substantiate my position as to the identity of the teachings and the training in Hinduism and Buddhism, and to justify my plea for love and amity between the two faiths that belong to the Hindu people, and are the glory of the Hindu race. This teaching of the Buddha, of the Mighty, of the Enlightened One, who, first of all in our humanity climbed the ladder of Buddhahood, is the ancient teaching reproclaimed. There are hatred and division too often between Hinduism and Buddhism; there are suspicion and doubt and antagonism, which have made a great gulf between the two mighty religions, and men will not try to bridge it either on the one side or on the other. Yet the Teachers of both belong to the same Brotherhood; the disciples of both are going towards the same Brotherhood; there is not difference there between the Hindu Master and the Buddhist Master, for both teach the same essential verities, and have come along the path common to both religions. Born on Indian soil, speaking with Indian lips, reproducing the noblest moralities of the Hindu Scriptures, recognizing the Hindu Gods, the Buddha is still rejected by the Indian people as a Teacher, though inconsistently worshipped as an Avatāra by many of the orthodox Hindus.

Why should there be enmity instead of brotherhood, why should there be suspicion and hatred instead of peace? This mighty religion that moulds so many million minds, this noble philosophy that trains so many million intellects, this life—the most perfect in its details of which there is any record amongst the histories of men, evolved in our land—why should you exclude them from your sympathy, why withold from them your reverence and your love? The Buddha comes to you, a man of your own country, the glory of the Hindu people, born in the Kshattriya caste, belonging to the Aryan people, teaching the ancient truths in a new form, and making them ready for the training of vaster multitudes. He is ours, as he is also the world's greatest among its teachers, purest and fairest of all the blossoms of humanity, this flower flowered on the Indian soil, this teacher spake the Indian tongue, and loved the Indian people. He taught them, he worked for them, he healed them, instructed them; and then his compassion flowed outwards, overflowed the worlds. Then surely we may reverence him, the Blessed One, the Lord, the Teacher. He is admitted to the Teacher among the Gods; he may well also be done homage to as Teacher among men.

Hinduism and Buddhism would do well if—mother and daughter—they rushed together again in a motherly and filial embrace, and forgot in that embrace the history of their estrangement, forgot in that embrace the history of their long separation. Then would the Indian home again be at one, one roof-tree covering mother and daughter alike, thus able to influence the western world with one lip and with one tongue, helping forward the redemption of that humanity of which the Buddha was born, and for which he lived. Let all re-echo the words which close the account of his departure: "Bow down with clasped hands! Hard, hard is a Buddha to meet with through hundreds of ages!"

—*Annie Besaut*

References

1. Chinese Buddhism, by Rev. J. Edkins, p. 43.
2. Dr. Rhys Davids says: "The books, as we have them, were put into their present shape... in the century or two after the death of Gotama" (*Buddhism*). At the Council of Rajagriha under Kāshyapa and Ānanda, held immediately after the death of the Buddha, "Buddhism" may be said to have been organized. At the second Council, that of Vaishāli, under Yashas and Revata, held 377 B.C., the dissentients rejected the Abhidhamma, but the disputes it was called to settle were merely on certain points in the Discipline of the Sangha. The third Council, under Ashoka, at Pātaliputta in 242 B.C., again left the Pitakas unchallenged, so that we may fairly take them as representing accurately the doctrines of the great Teacher.
3. Dr. Rhys Davids say, it "may be fixed approximately at about 600 B.C." *Buddhism*, p. 20.
4. *Dhammapada*, 153, 154. Sacred Books of the East, Vol. 10, translated by Max Müller.

5. *Mahāvagga,* I. 1. 7. The account of this period may be read in the Sacred Books of the East, Vol. 13, *Vinaya Texts,* translated from the Pāli by Drs. Rhys Davids and Oldenburg. Or, as regards the teaching of the Bhikkhus, it will be found in Vol. 11, *Buddhist Suttas,* translated by Dr. Rhys Davids, in *Dhammachakka-ppavattana-sutta.*
6. Ibid., 2.
7. Ibid., II. 2.
8. Yet people fancy that Buddhism is a simple ethical system, founded wholly on reason, and capable of being grasped in its entirety by the unspiritual!
9. Ibid., V. 2, 3.
10. The hosts of reincarnating Egos, held in debt by Karma.
11. Ibid., 4-10.
12. All-knowledge.
13. Clinging to the five elements of existence which make the transitory self, the five sheaths.
14. The absurd modern idea that a Buddha could deny the existence of the gods had not then been born, and all the early records are full of their co-operation and rejoicings.
15. Ibid., VI. Every student will recognize here the *koshas* of the Vedanta, noting that the *samkhāras* represent the Pranamayakosha, sensation and perception the Manomayakosha; the fifth Ānāndamayakosha, is not mentioned, for that film of bliss is not lost even in the Turīya state, obtaining which a man returneth not.
16. Ibid. XIII. 3. 41.
17. *Buddhism,* pp. 108-12.
18. Op, cit., p. 115.
19. How then can we be asked to wrench the terms he uses away from all their previous connotations?
20. Op. Cit., pp. 16, 117.
21. *Dhammapada,* 281.
22. Ibid., 222, 94.
23. Ibid., 380.
24. Ibid., 1.
25. *Udānavarga,* 31. 1.
26. *The Sūtra of the Forty-two Sections,* translated by S. Beal, from the Chinese. *Catena of Buddhist Scriptures,* pp. 193, 194.
27. *Mahā-parinibbāna-Sutta,* 23. Sac. Bks. Of the East, Vol. 11.
28. *Dhammapada,* 223.
29. Ibid., 21.
30. Ibid., 2.
31. *Udānavarga,* 28. 25, 30.

32. Ibid., 2. 2, 6, 12, 14, 18.
33. Ibid., 28. 1.
34. *Sabbāsava-Sutta.* Sac. Bks. of the East, Vol. 11.
35. *Dhammapada,* 252, 253, Sac. Bks. of the East, Vol. 10.
36. *Tevijja Sutta. Sac.* Bks. of the East, vol. 11. Here again we notice how the Buddha endorses the occult teachings as to the existence of the gods, instead of pushing them aside, as the popular view often asserts. Of course, no one with knowledge could take up the modern materialistic idea now fathered on Buddhism.
37. Shūdras, Vaishyas, and Kshattriyas.
38. *Brahmanadhammikasutta,* in the *Sutta-nipāta,* trans from the Pāli by V. Fausboll. Sac. Bks. of the East, Vol. 10, pt. 2.
39. *Dhammapada,* 420-23.
40. Ibid., 393
41. Ibid., 266, 267, 307.
42. Op. cit., 33. Trūbner's Oriental Series, trans. from the Tibetan by W. W. Rockhill.
43. See *ante,* the answer to Vāsettha.
44. Indra.
45. *Dhammapada,* 30, 43, 24, 197, 224.
46. Sanskrit-Chinese Dictionary, Eitel, *sub voce.*
47. Op. cit., 1. 28, 42.
48. *Catena of Buddhist Scriptures.* Summarized from Chinese: Scriptures. pp. 89-91.
49. Ibid., pp. 30-31.
50. Seeking powers rather than wisdom.
51. *Mahā-parinibbāna-suttā,* 2. 6-10.
52. Ibid., V. 22 The Pilgrimage is to any one of the four places at which the Buddha was respectively born, reached illumination, founded the kingdom of truth, and died.
53. *Dhammapada,* 380.
54. *Chinese Buddhism,* pp. 163, 464.
55. *Sūtra of the Forty-two Sections. Chinese Buddhism,* 191.
56. *Udānavarga,* 26. 1, 21, 22, 24, 31.
57. *Mahā-parinibbāna-sutta,* 19.
58. The closing words of the *Mahā-parinibbāna-sutta,* from which the above account of departure is summarized, any passage in inverted commas being textual quotations.

3

Buddhist Thought

The period of our study marks the heyday of Buddhist philosophy. The words of the Buddha now begin to be conned carefully and to receive elaborate comment. Varied interpretations of the words of the Master give rise to various schools of thought. The first great schism in original Buddhism is said to have taken place about one hundred years after the *parinirvāṇa* of the Buddha. It was a schism of Buddhism into the Mahāsaāṇghika and Sthavira schools. These schools subdivided themselves into a number of minor sections. Twenty of them are mentioned by Vasumitra in his '*Treatise on the points of contention by the different schools of Buddhism*' referred to by Suzuki in his *Outlines of Mahāyāna Buddhism*'. The main schism arose out of a controversy regarding the theory and practice of *vinaya,* or rules for the order. The conservative party came to be called 'Sthaviras' or Elders, and the dissenters Mahāsānghikas or members of the great congregation.[2]

This reference to the early schools is here introduced merely to underline the fact that the later divisions of Buddhism known as Hinayāna and Mahāyāna are only a development of the incipient division of doctrine first manifested among the Mahāsaṇghikas and Sthaviravādins. The Sthaviravāda school developed into Hinayāna and the Mahāsānghika school into Mahāyāna.[3]

Apart from his words, the personality of Buddha himself is now made the subject of varied interpretation.[4] Was he a man among men or was he a superhuman being entering the world of men to save souls, erring and suffering souls, out of compassion? Being the Lord of Compassion the solicitude he feels for erring humanity endears him to mankind. Humanity in its helpless condition lifts up its hands in prayer to the Buddha. Buddha is the refuge. Self-surrender (*saraṇagamana*) and adoration (*panipāta*) mark the attitude of the *upāsaka*. Buddha, whose very essence is wisdom and love, becomes the saviour of mankind, a Bodhisattva, and a pattern for all to follow who strive to attain Buddhahood. The Bodhisattva waits and watches patiently for every man to approach him in a spirit of humility and self-surrender. '*Buddaṁ śaraṇam gachchhāmi*'—'I resort to the Buddha', becomes the cry of every soul longing for liberation from pain and sorrow. Buddha is the healer and the consoler and takes up the burden of man's salvation on himself. A religion that had forsworn a personal God makes of Buddha a God and places him on the throne which had lain vacant for nearly two centuries. The metaphysical agnosticism professed by the Buddha now yields to a theistic cult known as the Mahāyāna Buddhism which was elaborated by some of the best minds that India ever produced.

Speaking of the emergence of Mahāyāna as a new development in Buddhism, Radhakrishnan says: 'The Hinayāna protests against the Mahāyāna as an accommodation of the pure teaching to the necessities of human nature. Anyway, while it stands as an example to the world of realising the highest through knowledge, the Mahāyāna requires us to take part in the world, evolving new social and religious ideals. The absence of the supernatural and the consequent lack of any scope for imagination, the morbid way of solving the central problems of life, the reduction of Nirvāṇa to extinction and ethical life to a monastic asceticism, made the Hinayāna a religion for the thinking and the strong in spirit, while a new development had to arise for the emotional and the worshipful.[5]

It is mainly on points of religious doctrine that Buddhism divided into the two schools of Hinayāna and Mahāyāna. This fission brought about a further explication in the light of a fresh interpretation of some of the basic concepts of Buddhism, of which the concept of Nirvāṇa was one.

The death of the Buddha is called Nirvāṇa. The term 'nirvāṇa' literally means 'the state of a fire blown out'. It connotes the extinction of something. When a fire is blown out, nothing is left to be seen. What is it that is extinguishing? It is perhaps the ego, the 'I' which is the source of the possessive 'mine'—the source of lust (*rāga*), wrath (*dosa*) and greed (*moha*)—that is finally extinguished. With this, all *dukkha* will cease. Such a simple interpretation as this is in consonance with the 'four noble truths' (*chatvāri ārya satyāni*) of original Buddhism. The four principles as paraphrased by Stcherbatsky are: life is a disquieting struggle, its origin is in the evil passions, eternal quiescence is the final goal, and there is a path by which all the energies co-operating in the formation of life become gradually extinct[6]. But a further question arises now. Is the individual to be concerned with the extinction of his own misery, that is only *his* salvation or is it also his obligatory duty to help others to find *their* salvation too? The Hinayāna interpreted the words of the Master 'Be a lamp unto yourselves' to mean that each individual is the architect of his own deliverance. Nirvāṇa is to be sought for in order to put an end to the individual's own miseries. The Mahāyāna school, however, held that the condition of one's own salvation was to work for the salvation of others. The object of Nirvāṇa, in this school of thought, is to obtain perfect wisdom (*prajñā pāramitā*) with which the liberated can strive for the salvation of all beings in misery. It is very difficult to say which view truly represents the view of the Buddha. As Suzuki suggests, 'The probability is that Buddha himself did not have any stereotyped conception of Nirvāṇa, and, as most great minds do, expressed his ideas outright as formed under various circumstances, though of course they could not be in contradiction with his central beliefs, which must have remained the same throughout the course of his religious life.'[7]

The unintentional ambiguity of the original verbal gospel of the Buddha occasioned one striking result deeply significant for the development of philosophical thought in India. Some of the most acute thinkers, mainly in the interest of religion, applied themselves to investigations into the realm of mind which yielded a Logic, a Psychology and a Metaphysic of no mean order. Out of the Hinayāna arose the metaphysical schools of Buddhism known as the Sautrāntika and the Vaibhāshika schools, and out of the Mahāyāna the Mādhyamika or Śūnyavāda school and the Yogāchāra or Vijñānavāda school. Sautrāntika, Vaibhāshika, Mādhyamika and Yogāchāra are thus the most prominent of the systems of Buddhistic thought. In the chronological order the Vaibhāshikas arose in the third century after the *parinirvāṇa*, the Sautrāntikas in the fourth. The Mādhyamika school came into existence five hundred years after the *parinirvāṇa*, while Asaṅga, the founder of the Yogāchāra school, is as late as the third century of the Christian era.[8]

Both the Sautrāntika and the Vaibhāshika schools are regarded as *Sarvāstivāda* schools, i.e. schools of Buddhist Realism. They maintain that all things mental and non-mental are real. Our perception of external objects depends on the actual existence of those objects outside of us. If it were not so, we could perceive anything at any place at will. The difference between the two schools is expressed by the terms *bāhyānumeya vāda* and *bāhya pratyaksha vāda*. *Bāhyānumeya vāda,* which is the Sautrāntika view, maintains that we infer the existence of an external object through the idea or representation of it we have in our minds. This view may be called Representationism. *Bāhyapratyaksha-vāda* of the Vaibhāshika school is the view that external objects are directly perceived by us as they are. If objects are not capable of being directly perceived by us, to infer their existence through the ideas that we have of them would not be possible. This view may be described as Naive Realism.

As Stcherbatsky sums it up 'the standpoint of the Hinayāna is thoroughly realistic' the 'roughly speaking a real external world is assumed in Hinayāna, denied in Mahāyāna and partly reassumed in the logical school.'[9] Stcherbatsky suggests, following the Buddhists themselves, that the history of Buddhism in India may be divided into three periods, and the period under review here being the second one, the philosophy of the Mahāyāna school must occupy the central place.[10] This is the period of Buddhistic Idealism. The foremost thinkers belonging to this school are Aśvaghosha, Nāgārjuna, Asaṅga and Vasubandhu. Of them Zimmer says, 'Nāgārjuna (c. A.D. 200), the founder of the Mādhyamika school of Buddhist philosophy, which is the supreme statement of the Mahāyāna view, was by no means a vulgarizer but one of the subtlest metaphysicians the human race has yet produced. While Asaṅga and his brother Vasubandhu (c. A.D. 300), the developers of the Yogāchāra school of the Mahāyāna, likewise merit the respect of whatever thinker sets himself the task of really comprehending their rationalization of Nāgārjuna's doctrine of the Void. And Aśvaghosha, the haughty contemporary of Kanishka (c. A.D. 100), can have been no truckler to barbarians even though his epic of the life of the Buddha, *Buddhacharita,* is graced with many unmonkish charms.[11]

The Mādhyamika or Śūnyavāda (Doctrine of the Void) school is illusionism pure and simple. According to this school everything is unreal. Both mental and non-mental phenomena are illusory and unreal.

According to Nāgārjuna, 'There is neither being, nor cessation of it; there is neither bondage nor escape from it.' The Yogāchāra or Vijñānavāda school resembles the subjective idealism of the West. Berkeley's formula *esse est percipi,* to exist is to be perceived, would find ready assent among the Yogāchāras. Reality of an external world apart from its being perceived is unthinkable. The only thing real is mind. The so-called external world is an idea of the mind. While the existence of the external world can be denied, it is impossible to deny the existence of mind. It would lead to self-contradiction. The very existence of thought as an activity of mind proves the existence of mind. Nāgārjuna's doctrine of the Void (*śūnya*) is paradoxically stated by him thus: 'It cannot be called void or not void or both or neither, but in order to indicate it, it is called the Void.'

Nāgārjuna's notion of the Void was not the end of the whole story. He had a deep metaphysical purpose concealed in it. This was an attempt to discover the nature of Ultimate Reality. The phenomenal world as we know it cannot be real. It is riddled with self-contradictions. Whatever is real must be free from self-contradiction. The categories known to our frame of thinking as space, time and causality and the division of subject and object of knowledge appear to be self-stultifying. They may serve a pragmatic purpose. The business of transitory life may require it. *Saṁsāra* has only an empirical reality and cannot be ultimately real. Subject to constant flux the world of our pragmatic need is and yet is not. Nothing is there permanent to which one can hold. To perish perennially is of its very texture, could be ascribed to it all. This is *saṁsāra.* Nirvāṇa is an escape from this momentariness. It is a quiescence where the fret and fever of life will cease. But it can only be described in negative terms. We can only go to it by the *vis negativa.* As no positive description can be given of it, it is for all practical purposes void, sheer emptiness. But when one attains it, what seemed unreal so long would come to be the real of reals. It is an ineffable and incommunicable state. That is why Buddha remained silent. His silence was not the silence of ignorance, but the silence where no speech can possibly intrude. This is the experience that Buddha received under the Bodhi tree. He was the awakened, for he woke up from the slumber of *saṁsāra.* This is a state that everyone can reach provided he treads the path of the Buddha. Discipline of the senses and discipline of the mind are the stepping stones to it. He who is attached to Nirvāna must detach himself from everything else. Nirvāṇa is a jealous mistress. All earthly fetters must be shaken off before one can embrace her.

This line of thought, which has continued in the later philosophers who started with the premises of Nāgārjuna, landed Buddhism in mysticism. Logic became futile in the face of this. Discursive Reason showed its feet of clay. To quote Stcherbatsky: 'The only source of true knowledge is the mystic intuition of the Saint and the revelation of the new Buddhist scriptures in which the monistic view of the universe is the unique subject. This is a further outstanding feature of the new Buddhism, its merciless condemnation of all logic, and the predominance given to mysticism and revelation.'[12]

On the side of religion, Mahāyāna Buddhism led to a theistic system very similar to the theistic systems of Śaivism and Vaishnavism, preaching a loving devotion to personal God whom the devotee loves with all his heart and whose spontaneous grace he awaits. On the metaphysical side it led to a school of thought closely akin to the conception of an Absolute with regard to which all determination would prove to be negation. The mind is unable to grasp it and words fail to express it. Reason and language only apply to the finite and nothing can be said of the infinite.

Personal verification alone can convince one of the reality of such a Nirvāṇa. 'Come and See' (*chipassiko*) is the motto of this philosophy. This interpretation of Nirvāṇa is borne out by a passage from *Netti Pakarana* quoted by B.C. Law in his *Concepts of Buddhism* (pp. 76-7). 'Well expounded by the Master is the doctrine which bears the desired fruits here and now which has "come and see' for its motto, which assuredly leads to the goal, the truth whereof is to be experienced by the wise, each individually for himself, namely, the one which consists essentially in subduing the haughty spirit, the perfect control of thirst, the upsetting of the very storage of creative energy, the arrest of the course of *saṁsāra* as regards the fate of an individual, the rare attainment of the state of the void, the waning out of desire, the dispassionate state, the cessation of all sense of discordance, the *nibhāna*.'

As to this condition the Buddha speaks the language of all the mystics of the world when he says: 'This condition is indeed reached by me which is deep, difficult to see, difficult to understand, tranquil, excellent, beyond the reach of mere logic, subtle and to be realized only by the wise (each individually for himself).[13]

In the Buddhism of this period, Reality acquires a new definition. This definition is expressed in the concept known as *pratītya samutpāda* or Dependent Origination. The very interdependence of elements in this universe is a denial of the ultimate reality of the elements accepted by common sense as real. But as Stcherbatsky states: 'the new Buddhism did not repudiate the reality of the empirical world absolutely, it only maintained that the empirical reality was not the ultimate one. There were thus two realities, one on the surface, the other under the surface. One is the illusive aspect of reality, the other is reality as it ultimately is.[14]

Nāgārjuna confesses in the *Mādhyamika Śāstra* that 'the teaching of the Buddha relates to two kinds of truth, the relative, conditional truth, and the transcendent, absolute truth.[15]

Another characteristic feature of the Buddhist philosophy of this period is the concept of *ālaya-vijñāna* or the 'store-house consciousness'. It is a Yogāchāra doctrine. Asaṅga and Vasubandhu attempted to evolve a complete system out of it. The concept of *ālaya vijñāna* opens up a realm of Buddhist depth-psychology. It has much in common with the Freudian 'unconscious' and represents the 'fantasy-making' and the projection of one's own subjectivity into an external world. According to this view what we call an objective world is really a projection or illustive manifestation of the mind called *ālaya-vijñāna*. The concept of *ālaya-vijñāna* is based on a study in the inner workings of the human mind calculated to help us to realize the forces and conditions that lie within us, that either favour or retard our progress towards the final goal of Nirvāṇa.

The Buddhism of this period is an interwinding of the strands of religion, philosophy, psychology and ethics. Anagarika B. Govinda well puts it: 'If therefore, we speak of Buddhist philosophy, we should be conscious that this is only the theoretical side of Buddhism, not the whole of it. And just as it is impossible to speak about Buddhism as a religion without touching upon the philosophical aspect, in the same way it is impossible to understand Buddhist philosophy without seeing its connection with the religious side. The religious side is the way which has been established by experience (just as a path is formed by the process of walking), the philosophy is the definition of its direction, while the psychology consists in the analysis of the forces and conditions that favour or hinder the progress on that way.

Referencs

1. *CHI* I. p. 161.
2. See Yamakami Sogen, *Systems of Buddhistic Thought*, p. 99.
3. For a full treatment of the subject see Ryukan Kimura, *A Historical Study of the Terms Hinayāna and Mahāyāna and the Origin of Mahāyāna Buddhism.*
4. The Doctrine of Trikāya in Mahāyāna Buddhism.
5. *Indian Philosophy,* I. p. 592.
6. *Buddhist Logic,* I. p. 7.
7. D.T. Suzuki, *Onlines of Mahāyāna Buddhism.* pp. 49-50.
8. The historical order of the rise of these schools here accepted is based on Yamakami Sogen's *Systems of Buddhistic Thought.*
9. *Buddhsit Logic,* I p. 525.
10. Ibid, p. 7.
11. H. Zimmer, *Philosophies of India,* p. 510.
12. *Buddhist Logic,* p. 10.
13. B.C. Law, *Concepts of Buddhism,* p. 77.
14. *Buddhist Logic,* I. p. 90.
15. Quoted by Radhakrishnan, *Indian Philosophy,* I. p. 658.

4

Buddhist Ethics

Scope of the Study of Ethics

The term 'Ethics' derives from the Greek *ethikos,* that which pertains to *ethos*, character. It is also called 'Moral Philosophy', from the Latin custom. Popularly, 'ethics' is described as 'the science treating of morals' but since precise definition of the term is lacking it is necessary to state the ground which a consideration of 'Ethics' is intended to cover. G.E. Moore, in his *Principia Ethica,* refusing to take as adequate a definition of 'Ethics' as dealing with 'the question what is good or bad in human conduct', proceeds to declare; 'I may say that I intend to use "Ethics" to cover more than this—a usage for which there is, I think, quite sufficient authority. I am using it to cover the general enquiry into what is good.'

A more detailed description is given by Rev. H. H. Villiams: 'In its widest sense the term "ethics" would imply an examination into the general character and habits of mankind, and would even involve a description or history of the habits of men in particular societies living at different periods of time.' Observing the exceptionally wide field that would be so covered, the author concludes: 'Ethics then is usually confined to the particular field of human character and conduct so far as they depend upon or exhibit certain general principles commonly known as moral principles. Men in general characterize their own conduct and character and that of other men by such general adjectives as good, bad, right and wrong, and it is the meaning and scope of these adjectives, primarily in their relation to human conduct, and ultimately in their final and absolute sense, that ethics investigates.'

We are therefore concerned with a consideration of certain terms as used in a particular connection and also with their meaning in the absolute sense. In conjunction with these aspects the opinion of Professor Muirhead may also be borne in mind: 'We have two kinds of sciences...those concerning themselves with the description of things as they are, and those which concern themselves with our judgments upon them. The former class have sometimes been called "natural", the latter "normative", or, as is better, "critical" sciences. Ethics is critical in the sense explained. Its subject-matter is human conduct and character, not as natural facts with a history and causal connections with other facts, but as possessing value in view of a standard or idea.

The various ethical systems are therefore more likely to show divergence when one comes to consider the standard or ideal which furnishes the value of human conduct rather than with the prescriptions for the conduct itself. For example, killing, thieving, lying are in general considered to be evils, though whether they are at any time justifiable will depend on the terms of the ideal; on the other hand, happiness in invariably associated with good.

The study of Ethics as a particular discipline contributing to philosophical enquiry as a whole was due originally to Aristotle, since he distinguished between 'first principles', or the investigation of the ultimate nature of existence as such, and the subsidiary disciplines which, though having the same purpose, were of themselves able to deal with only a particular approach to it. Ethics constituted one such approach, and, of the many hundreds of Aristotelian writings, three major works on Ethics have come down to us. Aristotle maintained throughout the fundamental doctrine of Socrates and Plato that 'Virtue is Happiness', a doctrine with which Buddhist thought would, in general, be in agreement, and on two occasions was inspired to poetry concerning this tenet. In the Elegy to Eudemus of Cyprus he praised the man who first showed clearly that a good man and a happy man are the same, and in the Hymn in memory of Hermias he begins: 'Virtue, difficult to the human race noblest pursuit in life.' Two of the successors of Plato at the Academy showed the same belief in the necessity of virtue, division of opinion occurring only with the view as to what good is. Some two centuries earlier, a learned and eminent brāhman, having expounded his teaching as to what qualities are essential to the character of a 'true' brāhman — 'brahman' here representing the ideal—and having reduced them to morality and wisdom, was asked by the Buddha what that morality and wisdom are. The brāhman answered: 'That is the farthest we have advanced,

Gotama. It would indeed be well if the esteemed Gotama would clarify with regard to these words.' The lengthy exposition with which the Buddha replied constituted a standard basis for development of his teaching and will be referred to in detail in the course of the present text.

Returning to Aristotle, the theory that Happiness is Activity is contained in two of his most authoritative works, the *Metaphysica* and the *De Anima,* as well as in the three ethical treatises, the *Nicomachean Ethics,* and *Eudemian Ethics,* and the *Magna Moralia,* these proceeding on similar lines up to this point. The *Nicomachean* then continues to the theory 'that the highest happiness is the speculative life of the intellect....but that happiness as human also includes the practical life of combining prudence and moral virtue; and that, while both lives need external goods as necessaries, the practical life also requires them as instruments of moral action. The treatise concludes with the means of making men virtuous; contending that virtue requires habituation, habituation law, law legislative art, and legislative art politics. Ethics thus passes into Politics'.[4] The *Eudemian Ethics* and *Moralia* continue to considerations of good fortune and gentlemanliness, the latter being regarded as perfect virtue, containing all particular virtues.

Herein lie no indications of an ultimate or transcendental state, and for these one must look to later developments of the science of ethics, whether they arise in logical continuity or exist merely as arbitrary attachments introduced for the sake of convenience. Only the former condition would provide justification for considering ethics as a genuine contribution to the science of philosophy proper. In this article on Ethics in *Encyclopaedia Britannica,* 1951 edition, Professor Wolf has this to say of the study: 'ethics is not a positive science but a *normative* science—it is not primarily occupied with the actual character of human conduct but with the ideal. Many moral philosophers, indeed, have stated explicitly that the business of ethics merely consists in clearing up current moral conceptions and unfolding the ultimate presuppositions involved in them, and that it is not its function to discover any new moral ideas. It may be remarked that even the ethics of Aristotle attempted no more, although he was not bound by anything like this authority and the traditions of the Christian church.' Professor Wolf then states that he main problems of ethics 'turn chiefly on the following conceptions: (i) The highest good of human conduct, or its ultimate ideal aim, which may serve as the ultimate standard of right conduct; (ii) the origin or source of our knowledge of the highest good or of right or wrong; (iii) the sanctions of moral conduct; (iv) the motives which prompt right conduct. Another problem discussed by moral philosophers is that of Freedom of the will....'

In a consideration of Buddhist ethics these problems may be rearranged with advantage for two reasons. In the first place, according to Buddhist and other Indian thought the highest state is one which lies beyond good and evil. In the second place, according to Buddhism there is no break between the moral teaching and that which pertains directly to the ideal state; humanity, sufficiently advanced in the practice of the moralities, rises and continues to rise above the common limitations, of time and space whether these terms are interpreted from the point of view of the physical sciences or with reference to historical and geographical location. The first of the main problems set forth by Professor Wolf, namely, the ultimate ideal aim which may serve as the ultimate standard of right conduct, relates, according to Buddhist thought, to the supramundane or *lokuttara* state, and the connection between the moralities of everyday life and this *lokuttara* state is one which is entirely covered by the Buddha's teaching. It is, in fact, that which is known to Buddhists as *mārga, magga*, the Path, the Road, along which each person must travel for himself beginning with the practice of the common moralities up to the supramundane state beyond good and evil. From this point of view Buddhism can be said to provide the complete ethical study.

Following on certain introductory remarks which should serve to clarify the position taken up by Buddhist thought, the present consideration will be made under four main headings: (I) Origin and Source of Knowledge of the Highest, (II) The sanctions of Moral Conduct: The Three Refuges; The Precepts, (III) Moral Principles as possessing Value in View of a standard or Ideal, (IV) the Ultimate Ideal Aim which may serve as the Ultimate Standard, namely: The Realization of the Four Noble Truths.

Indian Thought in the Sixth Century BC

It must be emphasized at the outset that recognition of a state beyond good and evil in no way implies that a person who has performed a number or 'good' deeds may then relax morally and do anything he pleases; it merely hints at a state described by the Buddha when he was asked: 'Where do the four primary elements, earth, water fire the air, entirely cease?" He replied that it was not so that the question should have been put. It should have been thus:

> 'Where do after, water, fire, air, find no place?
> Where do "long and short", "fine and coarse",
> "Pleasant and unpleasant", not occur?
> Where are mind and body, mental and physical states,
> entirely stopped?

And the answer to this is:

> 'Where the consciousness that makes endless comparisons is entirely abandoned,
> Here 'long and short", "pleasant and unpleasant" do not occur.
> Here are stopped name and form mental and physical states.
> Here with the dying away of consciousness these things have no place.'

In this description the terms 'long and short', fine and coarse', 'pleasant and unpleasant', carry their customary meaning; the significance of 'name and form, mental and physical states' is less obvious since the expression *nāmañ ca rūpañ ca* has a variety of associations. In the early *Upaniṣads,* 'Brahman' was the Absolute Reality, while the term *nāma-rūpa* stood for the things of common experience. According to the *niṣprpañca* ideal of Brahman, the things of common experience represent phenomena with Absolute Brahman as the noumenon; Brahman is here the mere round of subject and object. According to the *saprapañca* ideal, the things of common experience emerge from Brahman and are later re-absorbed into it. So far Brahman was not personified, but in early Buddhistic literature it is the personification that comes under discussion, sometimes as 'Brahma', though also on occasion as 'Brahman', while, while 'Brahmā' appears also in the early portions of the epic *Mahābhārata.* In the latter case, however, 'Brahmā' is frequently identified with *Prajāpati,* a much older concept than Brahmā, but who at one time represented the creative power of nature. Confusion arose since both *Prujāpati* and Brahmā were considered, at different times to be the ultimate sources of all. But in whatever form Absolute Brahman is presented, it is distinguished from the things of common experience which are *nāma-rūpa. Rūpa* is the specific form and nature of a phenomenon, while *nāma* is the word or name serving as its sign; taking the terms together, *nāma-rūpa* should be understood as the particularity or determinate character of individual things. A further connection between *nāma* and *rūpa* is indicated in *Bṛhadāranyaka Upaniṣad* where a triad is mentioned consisting of *nāma, rūpa* and *karma* (action), the implications of which are very considerable; consideration of them is therefore deferred. Excluding karma for the moment, in Buddhist teaching *nāma* is also a metaphysical term used as comprising the four mental groups, or khandhas, of feeling, perception, mental formations and consciousness. These, together with the material principle *rūpa,* make up the 'individual person' as distinguished from other 'individuals'. *Nāma-rūpa* thus becomes 'individual being' or 'individuality'. In the above quotation from the *Kewaḍḍha Sutta* we understand for *nāma-rūpa* 'mental and physical states', so that when these cease without remainder the consciousness that makes endless comparisons will also cease and the supramundane state be attained.

Still one point remains which may have been present in the first linking-up of *nāma* and *rūpa* and which is again prominent in present-day thought: this concerns the singling-out of any one phenomenon from the whole mass of phenomena, which act is in general called a 'discovery'. With *nāma* closely associated with *rūpa,* the singling-out is not entirely disconnected with those parts of the mentality of the discoverer which could hardly be classified as 'perception'; therefore he may look to recognize a closer union between *nāma* and *rūpa* than it has so far been possible to demonstrate.

If however Indian thought looked towards an ultimate state in which pairs of opposites did not figure, considerable distinction has always been drawn between the conventional 'right and 'wrong' of the present existence. The idea of a fixed physical law, as of uniformity of nature or he ordered course of things such as the alternation of day and night, was formed at a very early date, probably well before the separation of the Aryan migrants into Indian and Iranian contingents. In the *Ṛgveda* it was known as *ṛta,* but the word occurs in Persian proper names as early as 1600 B C in the form *arta*, and in the *Avesta* as *asha*. By the time of the Mantras *ṛta* has also taken on the significance of a moral order, and expressions such as *gopā ṛtasya,* guardians of *ṛta*, and *ṛtāyu,* practisers of *ṛta,* are frequently met with. The Vedic gods were therefore both maintainers of cosmic order as well as upholders of moral law. In course of time other views appeared, but he main line of development of Indian thought did not lie in a unity of godhead, to the reduction of many gods to one who would be assumed to make and guide the world; rather it lay in a monism which traces the whole of existence to a single source. In the meantime, though performance of sacrifices was often dominant, since they were taken to be essential to the satisfying of man's desires, the idea of morality was never superseded. There existed a triad of obligations (*ṛṇa-traya*) for the fulfilment of which sacrifice was only the first; the second lay in indebtedness for the culture inherited, this to be discharged by handing on the traditions to the rising generation, and the third lay in continuing the race. The ideal includes the practice of adherence to the truth, of self restraint and kindness. Benevolence was particularly praised and meanness deplored. 'He who eat by himself will keep his sin to himself,' says the *Ṛgveda.*

The earlier gods were upholders of the moral order to the extent of rewarding virtue with happiness in heaven in their company. There is no explicit reference to 'hell' in the *Rgveda,* though it is clear in the *Atharvaveda* and in the *Brāhmaṇas* where it is a place of eternal darkness from which there is no escape. The idea of *iṣṭāpūrta,* however, occurs in the *Rgveda, iṣṭa* standing for the sacrifice to the gods and *pūrta* the gifts made to the priests, the merit accruing from these acts preceding a person into the next world where it secured him happiness. This merit is not entirely ethical but may become so if the reference to sacrifice is excluded and if the results of both good and bad deeds are assumed to pass on to determine the circumstances and conditions of the next existence. In that case we have an elementary idea of karma. Moreover, in the scale of rewards and punishments corresponding to the good and evil deeds of the present life, the Brāhmaṇas include amongst their serious punishments *Punar-mṛtyu,* repeated dying, this is to take place in some other world; there is no mention of repeated births though obviously these must occur if there are to be repeated deaths. In the early Upaniṣads the whole conception was clarified by recognition of a series of births and deaths as taking place either in this world or in a realm of better or worse conditions according to one's record here. Concern was then principally with the natural fruits of good and evil deeds maturing either in the present life or in some future life, irrespective of deities. What, then, was the position of a 'God'?

The word *deva*, from *div*, to shine, in Sanskrit means 'God', it is cognate with the Latin *deus*. It points to an era preceding that of the settlement of the Aryans in India in which the conception of God was associated with the luminous powers of nature. The spirit of veneration with which the early Aryans regarded such powers is also indicated by *yaj*, worship, a root found in many European languages. We have the association with the Vedic *yaj*, to sacrifice, as in the title '*Yajurveda*'. But with the development of the idea of karma and consequent lack of authority of the deities over man, the value of *deva* is modified.

In Buddhism the rendering of *deva* as 'God' is acceptable only in the sense that the being indicated is of a type superior to the average human, and whereas the gods of mythology resemble largely the creations of poetic fancy, taking their status more or less in accordance with the importance of the natural phenomena with which they are associated, the *devas* exist in definite grades according to their condition of mental development. In the *kāmaloka,* or world of desire, there exist six grades of *devas;* in the *rūpaloka* or fine-material world there are four, and in the *arūpaloka* or immaterial world there are also four grades. Beings attain to these spheres in accordance with the doctrine of karma, the spheres corresponding to the degrees of mental concentration and one-pointedness of mind (*cittass'e ekaggatā)* which, from time to time, have been experienced temporarily in the present existence. In the Indian religions these mental states are known as the *Jhānas,* or *Jhānic* states. They are descsribed frequently in the Buddhist texts, notably in the *Pṭṭhapāda Sutta,* the ninth of the *Long Discourses of the Buddha,* otherwise, *Dīgha Nikāya,* where the sequence is complete, the theme being that with study and discipline states of consciousness arise and with study and discipline they pass away. The substance of the account is as follows.

Being well-practised in the Moralities, having attained to a state of mindfulness and awareness, and being accustomed to simplicity of life, the meditator retires to a solitary place. He must overcome, at least temporarily, sensual desire (*kāmacchanda*), ill-will and anger (*vyāpāda),* sloth and torpor (*thīnamiddha*), restlessness and worry (*uddhacca-kukkucca*), and doubt (*vicikicchā*). These are the Five Hindrances (*pañcanīvaraṇa*) to mental development and vision, and, having subdued them, he feels extremely happy. So is born joy, a calming of the body, ease, and the ability to achieve much concentration of mind. He separates himself from sensuous enjoyment but, continuing to apply and sustain his thoughts with regard to objects, external and ideational, attains to and remains in the joy and ease resulting from his detachment. This is the Jhānic state. The second is attained by his withdrawing his thought from the object, thereby attaining to the serenity of mind and singleness of purpose consequent thereon. Withdrawing his thought from joy he observes his mental states with equanimity (*upekkhā*), but always remains alert; this is the third Jhānic state. For the fourth he withdraws from all ease and dis-ease, so retaining only his equanimity and one-pointedness of mind. These four Jhānic states concern the consciousness of the world or sphere of form, *rūpaloka* or *rūpāvacara*. The meditator may now proceed to the Consciousness of the Formless, *Arūpāvacare Citta*, of which there are four states. In this case there is no gradual suppression of the factors of consciousness, these having already been reduced to the two mentioned. There is, however, progressive change of the plane of thought, and the meditator is always directing his own mind. The first stage is the Jhāna-consciousness dwelling on the Infinity of Space (*ākāsānañcāyatana*) or Non-Collision of Objects, the second on the Infinity of Consciousness (*viññāṇañcāyatana*) or Non-Collision of Ideas, the third on Nothingness (*ākiñcaññāyatana*), and the fourth that wherein cognition is so extremely subtle that it cannot be said whether it exists or not (*nevasaññānāññāyatana*).

Of the whole succession of Jhānic states, the first two may be wrongly assumed from causes producing a temporary joy and case which have no moral foundation whatever; if from such a state of mind it is not possible to proceed to the equanimity and alertness of the Third Jhānic state then the assumption that the joy and ease had any connection with *Jhāna* is entirely wrong and harmful in the extreme. With regard to the *Arūpāvacare Jhāna* consciousness, the third, Nothingness' has been reached, if one may judge by their descriptions, by practised meditators of a variety of theological beliefs, christian Mystics included, so that the progress through the Jhānas is genuinely one of increasing mental concentration and is independent of creed. But whatever values are attached to the Jhānic states, to the Indian mind they are connected with the general structure of their cosmology. The deva realms, for example, represented states or types of existence into which were born beings who in the present existence had attained to various of the Jhānic states. The five physical senses do not necessarily persist through all the grades of devas since presumably they are replaced by finer perceptions, the *Ābhassara* devas, for example, who correspond to beings with experience of Second *Jhāna*, restaining only sight and hearing. However, all devas are subject to birth and death. Therefore for Buddhism the highest state, which constitutes complete emancipation in beyond any of the devas; it is that of the Buddhas who are for ever tranquil and stable and who see all things *yathābhūtaṃ*, according to Absolute Truth. This view has been expressed in the following verse: 'There is no track in the sky, externally there is no recluse. Conditioned things are not eternal; there is no instability in the Buddhas.' At the other extreme, below the level of mankind, are the denizens of the Demon World (*asuranikāya*), of the Ghost Realm (*pretaloka*) the Animal creation (*tiracchānayoni*),a and Hell (*niraya*). The whole range represents, therefore, a structure of grades of intelligence extending one side and the other of the human state as we know it as present, the higher being dependent, in the final instance, on the putting away of the Five Hindrances to mental development and vision, which is to say, dependent on the Moralities. Over this mental development and vision of man the devas have no control; they merely represent states to which may aspire with increasing morality and developing intelligence but they can be no more than incidental, and to a person intent on the Final Goal are of little interest.

That the doctrine of karma was not known to the Vedas, but it wàs accepted in principle and had been so for some time before the Buddha's day is clear enough from the *Bṛhadāranyaka* and *Chāndogya Upaniṣads,* and since, according to much modern scholarship, these are the only two pre-Buddhistic *Upaniṣads,* further development of the karma concept may be due to either Brahman or Buddhist influence. Common to both, however, is the clear distinction between karma and karmic effects, for 'karma' literally means 'action' in the abstract, while karmic effects are effects of particular actions. In fact, the doctrine of karma was elaborated and developed by non-vedic traditions such as Jainism and Buddhism. Buddhism briefly defines meritorious and demeritorious volition (*cetanā*) as karma. The Buddha said: 'it is mental volition, O monks, that I call karma. Having willed, one acts through body, speech or mind' The expressions 'good karma' and 'bad karma', used frequently in the West, have therefore no logical significance, though obviously karmic effects may be either good or bad. Nor has karma anything whatever to do with 'Fate'. The outstanding karmic effect for all Indian thought lay in the round of rebirths, and with the postulated means of breaking these rounds were associated the various developments of religious and philosophic thought. If for the Brahmans the ideal came to be realization of the union of Ātman, the 'inner self' of man, with Brahman, the Absolute Reality or its personification, this as representing the impossibility of further rebirths, then stress would be laid on theories involving a transmigrating essence of the 'soul' nature, in other words the *jiva,* to take effect while the ideal remained urealized. Buddhism, on the contrary, though recognizing the karmic effect of the round of rebirths, developed the doctrine of karma in conjunction with the *anatta* doctrine, or absence of a permanent in-dwelling 'self, and so presented life and the series of lives as a stream of consciousness. The form of this presentation may be seen by study of the following *gāthās* taken from the anthology of the earliest Buddhist literature or teaching the *Dhammapada*.

The most elementary Buddhist exposition of karma reads as follows: 'He who speaks or acts from a mind defiled, that one suffering follows as a wheel the foot that leads it," and: 'He who speaks or acts from a pure mind that one happiness follows as his shadow that never leaves him.

Many passages exist in the Buddhist texts to the effect that for an evil-doer 'when his body is destroyed the food arises in hell, but the statement is merely a generalization in respect of words inferior to that of the present and indicates the nature of the relationship between action and the results of actions. More precise indication is given in the *Dhammapada* chapter or 'Pleasant Things' Just as a traveller who has been long absent and comes back safe and sound is greeted on his return by his kinsfolk, friends and comrades, in the same way when a man passes from this world to another after a life of merit, so his good deeds welcome him as dear kinsmen on his return.' Further: 'Therefore amass good deeds for this other world; for men, everything in the other world rests on merits.' Correspondingly we have: 'If in committing evil acts the fool does not awake to understanding, he is burnt by his own actions as by fire. These quotations represent the more specific attitude of Buddhism towards action and the results of actions, the indication being more a running-on of the deeds themselves than a distinct break as might be inferred from specifying an act and its results to the performer. The idea is expressed, in particular reference to hatred, in the early verses of the

Dhammapada: Surely in this world enmities at no time cease through hatred; they cease through lack of hatred. This is the primeval law. Not having formerly perceived "In this matter we touch the realm of death", those who perceive this connection thereupon cease from strife. Sanskrit *Dharmapada* Rockhill's translation from the Tibetan *Udānavarga* contain the first sentence of this; the second is peculiar to the Pali. Here we have the suggestion of the running-on of the action, the effect being continuity of that particular action.

The quotations immediately preceding represent, however, only the latter part of the chain of events relating to an act, and for its whole history the origin of the act must also be taken into account. Regarding the origin we have the first lines of the two *Dhammapada* verses just quoted in part. They are identical in both cases: 'mind precedes all things; all things have mind foremost, are mind-made.' Here we have the key to Buddhist Ethics and, in fact, to the whole Buddhist teaching, for Buddhism is essentially a mind-culture. Any improvement or retrograde step must occur initially in the mind of the person concerned whether it proceeds to external manifestation immediately or at a later date, so that the importance of being aware of, and of controlling, one's thoughts is continually stressed. Each of the *Dhammapadas* has its chapter on Mind, and each deals at length with the difficulty of achieving control. We have, for example, 'Just as the arrow-maker straightness his arrow, so does a wise man make straight his mind, which is Agitated, fickle, difficult to keep guard on, difficult to hold back.' The simile is a very old one in Indian literature and finishes the subject of a bas-relief at Bharhut. Here is shown an arrow-maker seated at the door of his house; he has heated an arrow in a pan of coals and has made it wet with sour rice-gruel; closing one eye he is looking down the length of the arrow and is making it straight. Standing by are a medicant, the ex-king Janaka of Banaras, and his former queen, Sīvalī, who has followed him contrary to his will. The ex-king asks the arrow-maker why he closes one eye, and is told that with both eyes open the vision is distracted whereas with one eye open the vision is true. The moral is that one's mind should be made pliable, subject to control, with the vision kept clear and concentrated on the main aim.

The Bharhut inscription and its theme of the king turned mendicant draws attention to another basic difference between the line of Indian thought and that of the later Greek ethics from Aristotle onwards, for where the *Nicomachean Ethics* allows external goods to be necessary in the practical life of combining prudence and moral virtue as instruments of moral action, and in the highest life of the intellect as a means of physical subsistance. Indian thought offered nothing accommodating. Though the value of the present life is emphasized as providing essential opportunities for realization of the ultimate truth—it is, in fact, a stage of development through which one is obliged to pass—it was taken by Indian thought that this truth lies beyond the present state and its not to be considered as merely an improvement on present conditions with those conditions persisting in principle. The renunciation of one's social status, as in the case of King Janaka of Banraras, was a natural preliminary step to the renunciation of the whole round of rebirths. From earthy days, even when the *brāhmaṇas* were in process of compilation, certain people had left their homes to live in the forests; vivid pictures of the life are given in the *Rāmāyana* and other facts concerning the hermits are found in the *Dharma Sūtras*. By the time of the early *Upaniṣads* there were several classes of people who had adopted the homeless life, some because they objected to the authority of the *Vedas*, some because they wished to conduct their enquiries for the Truth with as little disturbance from the outside world as possible, and others who were said to have already attained to the Truth. Originally the hermits were known as *vaikhānasas*, from *Vikhanas* the traditional originator of the Rule, but later the term *vānaprastha*, forest-dweller, came into use. In course of time the leaders of the homeless life were wanderers (*parivrājakas*,), wearers of matted hair (*jaṭilas*) or finders of subsistence (*ājīvikas*). Extreme forms of asceticism were often resorted to, but the Buddha, from his own experience of them, considered them to be useless or even harmful unless they were accompanied by, or came as the result of, a very high degree of mental development. Still, detachment from the things of the present life formed an essential part of his teaching.

Returning to the question of breaking the round of rebirth, if for Buddhism there was to be no Brahman, no God, no inherent 'self', did the whole spell complete annihilation? This the Buddha repudiated entirely, classing a doctrine of annihilationism along with other speculations concerning the future, happy or otherwise. The Goal is completely unconditioned, and to attempt a description of it in terms of the conditioned state which we know at present is as future as to attempt a description of a 'happy' state. The point is illustrated in a conversation held by the Buddha with the well-known wandering mendicant of the day, *Poṭṭhapāda*.

'There are, Poṭṭhapāda, some samaṇas and brahmans who hold and expound the view: Certainly the self is completely happy and healthy after death. I went to them and said: "Venerable Sirs, I have heard that you teach the certainty of a happy and healthy self after death. In this so?" They acknowledged that it was so. I asked: "Is the world, as you know it and see it, completely happy?" "No," they said. I asked them: "Have you produced for yourselves complete happiness for one night or one day, or even for half a night or half a day?" They replied, "No." Then I asked: "Do you, Venerable Sirs, know a path or a method by which a realm of complete happiness may be reached?" They replied that they did not. "Have you heard of gods, who have arisen in a completely happy world, saying: 'There is a path, O Sirs, which, entered on and followed thoroughly and exactly, will lead to this world of complete happiness? We, Sirs, by following this path, have been reborn in a completely happy world. They replied: "No." The Buddha compared this state of affairs to that of a man who declared himself in love with a beautiful woman whom he had never seen and whose appearance and lineage he knew nothing whatever about; alternatively he likened it to that of a man building a flight of steps to a palace whose location and details of construction he did not know.

If then we have no details of the state of happiness, other than that it is 'happy', it remains only to consider what things give rise to unhappiness and to avoid them. Hence the Buddhia's teaching of the Four Noble Truths: 'Suffering, the Origin of Suffering, the Cessation of Suffering, and the Way to the Cessation of Suffering." Beginning with the seemingly simple practice of the ordinary moralities of everyday life, the teaching continues unbroken to the transcendental state known generally as *'Nirvāṇa'*. There is no modification for any particular person or class of persons, lay or otherwise, and, if the progress is sufficient. Nirvāṇa is obtainable in the present life. 'Cut out the love of self as you would an autumn water-lily with the hand; develop the way to peace, to Nirvāṇa, taught by the Happy One (the Buddha). There is no other training for the attainment.

The Enlightenment of the Buddhas

To the Buddhist the origin of the knowledge of the Highest State lies in the Enlightenment of the Buddhas, and the Buddhist's knowledge concerning this is derived from the teachings of Gotama Buddha. That these should be sufficient, if followed sincerely, is evident from the declaration made by Gotama Buddha to his devoted attendant Ānanda shortly before his passing away (*Parinibhāna*): 'I have expounded my doctrine throughout, in its entirety. Ānanda; the Tathāgata has not the closed fist of a teacher who holds back something of his Doctrine.'

Enlightenment consists essentially in knowing things in accordance with reality (*yathābhūtaṃ*) In seeing thus there are no misconceptions or mental projections regarding the appearance of a thing or a course of events; the seeing is entirely clear and according to absolute reality. Gotama Buddha describes the climax of the Buddhists's training thus: 'He comes to know what, in absolute truth, are the influxes (*āsavas*) their origin, their cessation, and the way to their cessation. From knowing thus and seeing thus, his mind is freed from the influxes and he knows "I am free." He knows: "Exhausted is birth; the Higher Life has come to perfection; that which should be done has been done; there will be no more of the present state."

Life of Gotama Buddha

The historic personage known to Buddhists as 'the Buddha' in Gotama Śākyamuni. He was born about the middle of the sixth century BC, probably in the year 566, in Lumbini Park in the neighbourhood of Kapilavastu in the north of the Gorakhpur district. A pillar, erected in 239 B.C. by the emperor Asoka, marks the place of his birth. Both his parents belonged to the Śākya clan, his father being a Chief. Astrologers had foretold that Gotama would become either a world-monarch or a great spiritual leader, and since it was taken for granted that in the latter case he would adopt the homeless life, his parent took every precaution to prevent his coming into contact with any form of unhappiness, surrounding him always with those things which, to them, seemed the best that life could offer. However, at the age of fourteen, one day in his father's garden, he did experience a state of mind in which he became aloof from his surroundings though still maintaining his faculties of observation and application of them. Many years elapsed before further developments occurred; Gotama married, had a son, and, to all appearances, led an existence suitable to a man of his rank. Then, in spite of all the precautions he encountered an aged man, a sick man, a corpse, and a man wearing the yellow robe of the wandering mendicant. Appreciating that old age, sickness and death are the lot of mankind, and that there existed persons who aspired to an existence where these did not figure, he resolved that he too would devote himself to finding the truth about life and the cause of all the suffering it entailed.

According to tradition, Gotama was twenty-nine years old when he left his father's house, his wife and child. One night he rode out with a single attendant beyond the city, dismounted, sent his horse back, and himself took to the homeless life of the forest. For some time he studied under famous teachers of the day but always found their doctrines deficient; the best of them could offer only a temporary, self-induced state of cessation of consciousness, and many relied merely on theorizing. Practising strenuous asceticisms he became so weak that he was hardly able to stand; then, finding that these served only to dull his thought, he abandoned them. With returning health he came to remember his early experience in his father's garden and to see that the only means of arriving at a solution of man's sufferings lay in his own meditation. One night he took up his position under the Bodhi tree (*Ficus regigiosa*), determined to remain there until he had reached complete understanding.

The Paṭiccasamuppāda

Canonical texts vary as to the hour at which Gotama reached this understanding and so became 'enlightened'; the *Udāna* gives in each of its first suttas of the Bodhivagga accounts of the process of reasoning connected with the Enlightenment, identical in every respect except that the first, second and third watches of the night, respectively are stated as the time of attainment. However, the main importance lies in the facts that the process of reasoning did immediately precede the Enlightenment, and that all the Buddhas attained to their respective Enlightenments by this process. It is known as the *Paticcasamuppāda,* or, more popularly, as the Nidāna Chain or Chain of Dependent Origination.

The *Mahānidāna Suttanta* contains an account of the *Paṭiccasamuppāda* as delivered by the Buddha, and he goes over it as in the *Mahāpadāna Suttanta.* As recorded in the latter, the occasion is given as that on which Venerable Ānanda remarked that the *Paṭiccasamuppāda* was easy to understand, the Buddha replying: 'Do not say so, ṭnanda; do not speak like that. Deep, indeed, Ānanda, is this *Paṭiccasamuppāda,* and it appears deep too. It is through not understanding this doctrine, through not penetrating it, these beings have become entrangled like a matted ball of thread, like a matted bird's nest, like *muñja* grass and rushes, subject to the round of rebirths (*Saṃsāra*) in a state of suffering.'

Nāgārjuna opens the *Mādhyamika-kārikā,* the textbook of the Mādhyamika school by the following dedication:

'The Perfect Buddha
The foremost of all Teachers I salute;
He has proclaimed
The Principle of Universal Relativity.

Indeed, so revered is this doctrine, that the well known Indian Mahāyanist scholar Śāntarakṣita offers his adoration to the Buddha in one of his treatises, the *Tatvasaṃgraha* as the 'Great Sage who taught the doctrine of *Paṭiccasamuppāda'*.

It must be remembered that unlike the majority of other religious philosophies, Buddhism has never given importance to the idea of the first cause, nor indeed to any form of cosmology. Theology did not develop in Buddhism as practical realization is expected of the Bhikkhu and not abstruse disputation. In any case, Buddhism does not recognize a conflict between religion and science as the former is, properly speaking, a practical spiritual application of the principles of the latter.

As the universe comprises the sum total of sentient life, there are, as one would expect, a multiplicity of causes which brought this entity into being. And in this connection, the doctrine of *Paṭiccasamuppāda* recognizes twelve distinct phases, links or divisions (*nidānas*) in cycle of causation, which, being interdependent, the whole doctrine can be termed that of 'dependent production'.

The abstract formula of the whole sequence of the doctrine has been schematized, showing the logic of it without the contents, as follows:

'Imasmiṃ sati idaṃ hoti;
imass' uppādā idaṃ uppajjati;
imasmiṃ asati, ideaṃ na hoti;
imassa nirodhā imaṃ nirujjhati.'

'That being thus this comes to be;
from the coming to be of that, this arises;
that being absent, this does not happer
from the cessation of that, this ceases.'

There is law in this process of causal sequence in which cycle it is impossible to point out a First Cause, simply because it forms a circle—the 'Wheel of Life' (*Bhavacakka*). Most people are accustomed to regard time as a line stretching from a finite past to a finite future. Buddhism, however, views life as a circle and life, reflected as such, is repeated over and over again, an endless continuum. Moreover, the whole series of phases must be taken in their entirety, the conception of the 'Wheel of Life' being in relation to space and time.

As recorded in the scriptures it is customary to begin the exposition of *Paṭiccasamuppāda* with the factor of (i) Ignorance (*Avijjā*). This ensures the continuation of death and remains a crystallization of the acts one performed during life. Ignornace, therefore, as an antonym of knowledge (*Vijjā*) or (*ñāṇa*), leads inevitably to (ii) volitional activities or forces (*saṅkhārā*) good and bad, or rather wholesome and unwholesome (*kusala akusala*), the effect of which leads to the motive for, or will to life. These two factors were regarded as the causes of thc past.

In the present life, the first stage is (*iii*) consciousness (*viññāṇa*) of mind or will towards life. When this taken upon itself (iv) material form or mind and body (*nāma-rūpa*), this action constitutes the second step. The third phase soon manifests itself as (v) the six sense organs (*salāyatana*), of which (vi) the sense of touch (*phassa*) predominates. The consciousness of the living being rears itself, followed quickly by (vii) feelings (*vedanā*) pleasurable (*sukʰa*), painful (*dukkha*) or neutral (*adukkham asukha*) associated with seeing, hearing, smelling, tasting, bodily and mental impressions.

In these stages the individual is formed, but he is not entirely responsible for his present condition due to complex past causes. The first of three causes which will ensure a future life for each individual is (viii) desire (*taṇhā*) which can be neutralized; but if joy, sorrow and the like are experienced, then (ix) attachment (*upādāna*) is produced, which in urn leads to one's clinging to the object of desire. The formation of another, (x) becoming (*bhava*) is ensured; (the latter term is preferable to that of 'existence' as this phase falls midway between this life and the next).

While the individual is enjoying the effects of his past, he is unaware of his creating the conditions for a future life. The whole process may be likened to that of the growth of an ordinary plumtree: its very existence depends upon fertile soil a suitable environment and favourable weather; next, after the elapse of a considerable period of time, when at last the tree has reached maturity and is blossoming, the fruit is finally born; but then, in no time at all, the fruit perishes and dies and the stones drop and are scattered, only to become seeds and produce trees in their turn. In the matter under discussion, therefore, (xi) birth (*jāti*), (xii) decay (*jarā*) and death (*maraṇa*) in themselves constitute the causes for renewed life.

In Buddhism, every stage is a cause (*hetu*) when viewed from its effect (*phala*) and there is nothing rigid or unalterable in this theory. The ignornace that remains after death is regarded as *kamma*—a dynamic manifestation of physical and mental energy. This latent energy is potential action, the motivating force behind the cycle of life. A living being determines his own action and as this cycle has been trodden over innumerable years, no beginning can be seen to this process.

Saṃsāra 'Constant flow' is the sum total of conditioned existence and as such has been likened to an ocean upon which the ripples of the waves denote each life, each one influencing the next. It follows from this analogy, that just as each life can only be influenced by the one preceding, so no outside power, such as a divine being, can possibly trespass and claim property rights!

Before closing the subject, it is noteworthy to recall that there are four kinds of *kamma* with regard to begetting future life: that having immediate effect in this life itself (*diṭṭhadhamma-vedanīya*), that having effect in the next succeeding life (*upapajja-vedanīya),* that having effect in some after life (*aparāpariya-vedanīy*) and that whose effect has completely lost its potential force (*ahosi*):

Finally, to sum up: there is only conditioned existence (*sahetudhanima*) with the necessary causes, the factors of which are considered as belonging to every individual. A fundamental doctrine of Buddhism is to regard everything in the universe as dynamic becoming but it is through this becoming that delusion increases and ignornace is prolonged. This fact, as Chandrakīrti says, is in existence everywhere in the universe:

> 'Nothing at all could we perceive
> In a universe devoid of causes,
> It would be like the colour and the scent
> Of a lotus growing in the sky.'

As associated directly with the Enlightenment of the Buddha the declaration of the *Paṭiccasamuppāda* would end with the actual enumeration of the links of the Nidāna Chain. This and the realization of other noble doctrine (dhammas) would constitute the aspect of the Enlightenment of the Buddha known as his *Mahāprajñā,* or Great Wisdom. However, before considering the bearings of these on the Buddhist's knowledge of the origin and source of knowledge of the Highest State, there remains, according to the *Mahānidāna Suttanta,* one more corollary declared by Gotama the Buddha in his instruction of Ānanda. This concerns the nature of the 'self'.

The Self and the Anatta Doctrine

The Buddha gives the current opinions concerning the self to be: (i) My self is small and has material qualities, (iii) My self is small and without material qualities, (iv) My self is limitless and without material qualities. Against there were persons who would make no declaration concerning the self.

The Buddha asks in what respects the self is perceived. It is seen thus: 'Feeling is my self'; 'Feeling is not my self, my self does not experience feeling'; 'Feeling is not my self, my self does not lack experience of feeling'; 'By my self are things felt, the thing that feels is my self.' To those who hold these views that feeling is my self, it should be said that feelings may be happy unhappy or neutral; any one of these three feelings, while it endures, excludes the other two. All of them are impermanent, conditioned, arising from other relations, things of decay, age, destruction, annihilation. If to a person experiencing any one of them it should seen. 'This is my self', then with the passing of that feeling it should also seen to him 'Gone is my self'. A person declaring 'Feeling is my self' is taking for the self impermanence, a mixture of happiness and suffering, a thing coming into existence and dying away here amongst the things of this world. Therefore the statement 'My self is feeling' is not acceptable.

On the other hand, to a person who declares 'My self does not consist in feeling, my self does not experience feeling', it should be said: 'Where there is entirely no feeling, can it be said "I am"?'

Again, whether it is claimed that 'my self does not consist in feeling, my self does not lack experience of feeling', or the converse, it may also be replied that it feeling should cease utterly, in every respect, could it be said there that 'I, this person, am?'

None of these statements concerning feeling and the self is therefore acceptable. The Buddha concludes: 'From the time Ānanda, that the bhikkhu ceases to regard the self as consisting in feeling, experiencing feeling, and does not maintain "my self experiences feeling, the thing that feels is myself," he grasps at nothing in the world, and, not gripping for support, does not long for anything. Not longing for anything, he attains to his final release for himself. He comes to know: "Exhausted is birth; the higher life has come to perfection; that which should be done has been done; there will be no more of the present state."

Concerning the existence of the Tathāgata after death, the Buddha said that any statements that he did or did not exist, or both, or neither, were 'foolish theories'. Why? 'As far as the contact of mind and mental objects and the range thereof, as far as language and the range thereof, as far as concepts and the range thereof, as far as intelligence and the roaming of intelligence, so far does there reach the cycle of rebirth and its turnings, having thoroughly understood that, the bhikkhu is freed, and, being so freed, does not know and does not see in the same way. To him the theories are not intelligent.'

From the direct statements of the *Nidāna* Chain, it is clear that 'life', in the usual interpretation of the term, move as a vicious circle continuously kept in motion by a drive of anxiety that it should do so. It is necessary to bear in mind that the term 'consciousness', as used in the Chain, refers to the general sense, as one might say that a person is 'conscious' if he does not. Having established contact with an object or event, one registers judgement on it; one may find it pleasant, unpleasant, or one may be indifferent to it. If the first two cases one wishes either to perpetuate the liaison or to destroy it; in the third one is merely not interested. Yet though in the main there are no fixed standards of pleasantness or unpleasantness, there are certain states which man, irrespective of time or place, dislikes, and certain others which he ardently desires. The outstanding example of the first is death, and of the second, life. Only the worst agonies to which man has been subjected have made him desire death, while dissertations on happy after-lives, Elysian fields, or whatever their appellation, have never superseded his desire to prolong the present existence. But the present existence has never shown any security of tensure, and to make it continue, or appear to continue, indefinitely, it has always been necessary to provide a support.

Yet in existence as we know it at present, life as followed by death, or a series of lives punctuated by deaths, how much of man has ever 'lived'? What is it of him that 'dies', and what is it of him that is 'reborn'? The sūtra and suttas quoted above supply the answer to the questions, and in the Buddhist teaching, far from living one single isolated life man lives a long series of lives connected with each other by a potential constituted by his previous actions. As one life draws to a close, the characteristics which would previously have been taken to constitute 'unconsciousness'—using the word in the general sense as previously—disappear. There remains a consciousness, sometimes referred to as the sub-consciousness, but which more accurately is the infra-consciousness, which is the potential mentioned above and which leads to a blind activity, the energy or effect of which is the will to live. At the moment of conception the first stage of the individual existence is that of the infra-conscious mind, or the blind will towards life. Its next stage of development lies in that of mental and physical states, the stage of pre-natal growth with the mind and body evolving in combination. From here onwards we have the development of the sense-organs, the making of contact with the outside world, and so on. But throughout these events, and throughout the existence just started is the undercurrent of potential, the result of past actions, which determines the personality of the individual in question and which is constantly making itself felt.

How far the individual can improve on this undercurrent will decide his circumstances and disposition in future lives, but there is no question of any organ representative of the individual, such as a jiva or soul, experiencing one existence only and fading out into some realm of happiness or misery, or with its potential lost in the general mass of the world's activity. Just as modern biologists tell us that there is no permanent part of the physical organism which sustains, or could possibly sustain, the whole process of life, but, on the contrary, that life consists in the processes of growth, nourishment, renewal, and such like which were once assumed to be the accompaniments to life, so there is o 'self' which stands at the centre of the mentality to which characteristics and events accrue and from which they fall away, leaving it intact, at death. The stream of consciousness flowing through many lives, is a changing as a stream of water. This is the anatta doctrine of Buddhism as concerning the individual being. Extended to all the phenomena of the universe we have a parallel in the Steady-

State Theory, or Theory of Continuous Creation as advanced by present-day astronomers, this is contrast to the former periodical creations as developing from Brahma or a primeval atom, or with the Creation once-and-for-all as put forward by the Zoroastrians and taken over by the Christians and other monotheistic religions.

Three Characteristics of Existence

The anatta doctrine is counted among the three characteristics of existence as put forward in the Buddha's teaching, the other two being Impermanence, or *anicca,* and Suffering, or *dukkha.* They are essentially present in all teachings claiming to rank as 'Buddhism'. The *Dhammapada* treats of them in a passage not presented identically, though often approximately, elsewhere in the Buddhist scriptures as we know them at present. According to the *Dhammapada* we have:

> "All mental and physical phenomena are impermanent." Whenever through wisdom one perceives this, then one becomes dispassionate towards suffering. This is the road to purity.
>
> "All mental and physical phenomena an painful." Whenever through wisdom one perceives this, then one becomes dispassionate towards suffering. This is the road to purity.
>
> "All things are without self." Whenever through wisdom one perceives this, then one becomes dispassionate towards suffering. This is the road to purity.'

Two points are of particular note in the translation of these verses. The first, 'is indifferent to suffering', is explained, both here and in the corresponding Sanskrit text, as 'a sense of difference to suffering arising out of a true knowledge of the real character of existence'. The meaning is due to Buddhaghosa and is also borne out in the Tibetan version. R.C. Childers, in an early translation of the Pali *Dhammapada,* gave the sense correctly as 'only does he conceive disgust for (existence which is nothing but) pain'.

The second point consists in the employment in the third verse of the world 'things as contrasted with the 'mental and physical phenomena' of the first and second. The corresponding Pali terms are *saṅkhāra* and *dhamma.* The meaning of *saṅkhāra* is more comprehensive here than in the previous case mentioned and now extends to all mental and physical phenomena which are *saṅkhada* (i.e. put together, compounded, conditioned). *Dhamma,* of which the corresponding Sanskrit form is *dharma,* carries a yet more extensive meaning. 'Dharma' derives from *dhr,* to hold, bear, so that the noun *dharma* would be 'that which is held to', therefore, figuratively, the 'ideal'. This to the Buddhas would be their Enlightenment, the Supreme Wisdom, *sambodhi.* To their followers it would be 'that to be realised', the seeing *yathābhūtam;* expressed in words dharma would be the Buddhas' teaching, the Moralities, Precepts, and general discipline of *magga,* the Road. But these meanings of dharma are not here applicable and are not intended, and dharmas in the everyday world as 'that which is held to' are the things, material or otherwise of everyday life. Used in this connection it is better not to translate 'dharma', but if translation is imperative 'thing' is the only possibility since it has no pretensions to being a scientific term. The rendering made by Stcherbatsky, 'elements of existence' is merely an aggrandisement which does nothing to clarify the meaning, for, as will be seen by the forthcoming classifications of dharmas, the world 'element' as used in the strict sense is not here applicable, while that which qualities for 'existence' from one point of view is 'nonexistent' from another. The term does not seem to have met with Stcherbatsky's entire satisfaction for we have from him shortly after: 'A Buddhist element is always a separate entity, it is neither "compound" nor "phenomenon", but is an element (*dharma*). The confusion becomes ever greater when one finds 'entity' to mean 'A thing complete in itself, its actual existence as opposed to qualities and attributes; something with a real existence of its own.' Rhys Davids was nearer the mark when he translated *diṭṭhe va dhamme* as 'in this very world', the context being to the following effect. An equirer having observed that craftsmen such as mahouts, horsemen, high-ranking military officers, cooks, bath attendants, confectioners, garland makers, accountants—many others were mentioned—were able, from the proceeds of their occupation, to support their families and enjoy themselves generally *diṭṭhe va dhamme,* asked if there accrues to a person who becomes a recluse any comparable result *diṭṭhe va dhamme.* Taking *diṭṭhe* as 'seen, perceived, understood', and *va* for *iva*, 'like, as', with *dhamma* 'that which is held to', we have for the whole expression 'that which is held to in everyday life'. Again, Rhys Davids and William stede in their Dictionary give for *diṭṭhe va dhamme* 'in the phenomenal world', as contrasted with *samparāyika dhamma*, 'the world beyond'. A.C. Banerjee, in his *Sarvāstivāda Literature,* gives for *dhamma* 'existent things', and for *dhammas* 'things'.

Taking the classifications of dharmas according to the Buddhist philosophical systems, *Sarvāstivāda* and *Vijñaptimātravāda* enumerate seventy-five and a hundred dharmas respectively. These divide into five groups entitled Mind, Mental Concomitants, Forms, Things not associated with Mind, and Things which are not put together. The first four groups are *saṃskṛta* dharmas, *saṃskṛta* corresponding to the Pali term *saṅkhata,* otherwise dharmas that are formed, prepared, put together, etc., while the 'fifth group contains the *asaṃskṛta* dharmas, things which are not formed, prepared, etc. The *Saṁskṛta* dharmas, which include the body and the four sense-organs of eye, ear, nose and tongue, include also the corresponding touch, form, sound, smell and taste, as well as the eye-consciousness, ear-consciousness, and so on. Amongst the mental concomitants which all systems treat with great respect, and feeling (*vedanā*), will (*cetanā*), vigilance (*appanāda*), while the class 'Things not associated with Mind' contain such various dharmas as birth (*jati*), number (*sankyā*), region (*deṣa*), time (*kāla*). The *asaṁskṛta* dharmas comprise space, modes of exhausting the life-process, and, in the *Vijñaptimātra,* that which transcends all specific characters and conditions, namely, *Tathatā*) Thusness, i.e. Truth, reality). Pali Abhidhamma condenses to four categories: Mind, Mental Concomitants, Form and the *Lokuttara* (supramundane).

According to the *Dhammapada* verses 277-9 quoted above, then, one turns away from, or becomes dispassionate towards an existence which by reason of the transitoriness of the phenomena brings only sufferings; further we are reminded of the lack of stability of all things.

Dukkha, here translated as suffering, may also represent misery unsatisfactoriness, or evil. '*Dukkha*' is the first of the Four Noble Truths, and figures in 'Feelings' to the extent that these may be painful or unpleasant as regards the physical and mental senses. 'Birth is painful, old age is painful, disease is painful, death is painful, grief, lamentation, suffering, misery and despair are painful, not to get what one wishes for is painful; in short, the clinging to the Five Khandhas is painful. Yet these five sensorial aggregates condition the appearance of life in any form, and in an existence that is essentially conditioned, even to the extent that it itself 'dists', we cannot know from our present standpoint anything that is unconditioned. Therefore we follow the Path pointed out by the Buddha, the Way to the Cessation of Suffering, so coming to a position from which, or in which, we may gauge that which is greater then happiness.

Mahākaruṇā of the Buddha

From the foregoing account of the Buddha's Enlightenment it is clear that the enlightening consisted primarily in the perceiving of the real nature of life as experienced in the present existence and the beings living it. Further there were the expectations of future more or less similar existences and the means of bringing about cessation of the conditioning of them all. But if the Buddha's teaching had been confined to these matters regardless of their application, though no doubt he would have drawn a considerable following of learned people throughout the ages, he would have come down in history as a great thinker and philosopher but as a theorist only. That this was not his intention, and that he took into consideration the estimate of the ordinary person as concerning himself, is clear from his exposition in the Pali *Brahmajāla Sutta* where, at the outset of this very comprehensive and profound discourse he remarks: 'An average worlding appraising the Tathāgata would speak of relatively small things, the things of this world, the Moralities. What would he sway?' The text continues to the effect that the average worldling would say that the Samaṇa Gotama does not take life, does not take that which is not given, and so on, enumerating the Moralities. Therefore, though he would not appreciate in detail the high attainments of the Buddha with regard to perfect wisdom and understanding, he could not fail to see the reflection of this in the Buddha's daily life of the present existence. Could the average person establish any connection between the supreme understanding and the ordinary moralities?

Many recent western writers have adopted the stand that original Buddhism consisted entirely in a reformatory movement amongst recluses, and that the laity were considered only in so far as they were necessary to the physical maintenance of the bhikkhus. 'Buddha's Church is a Church of monks and nuns,... He who cannot or will not gain this freedom (i.e., *leaving the home*) is not a member of the Church,' says Oldenberg, and continues: 'But while there was framed from the beginning for the monastic Church an organization, clothed with strict forms of spiritual procedure, there was no attempt made at creations of a similar kind for the quasi-Church of lay-brothers and lay-sisters.' Quotations adduced in support of these statements and other similar ones are drawn almost exclusively from Vinaya texts which, of course, deal essentially with the Rules of the Order. But making due allowance for the facts that Oldenberg published his work over eighty years ago, that the western nations had many centuries of strict Christian tradition behind them from which they were hardly beginning to get themselves free, and that such a term as 'Church' pertained strictly to their own terminology, the idea that Buddhism was entirely the property of monks and nuns, or bhikkhus and bhikkhunis, still persists. That the Sangha should form the nucleus where from the Buddha's teachings should be perpetuated is reasonable enough; for if with the vicissitudes of time the laity became estranged from Buddhist teachings, provided the Saṅgha remained true to its trust the populace could reform around it. History has shown that such vicissitudes did occur on more than one occasion and that the laity did so reform. If it is contended that the laity might have been more rigorously controlled so as to have been more independent of the Saṅgha, then it must be recalled that the strict control, religious or political, which has been such a feature of Western religions, was entirely contrary to the whole spirit of the Buddha's teaching. It cannot be argued that the laity was not adequately provided for at the outset of the teaching of the Buddha-dhamma, or that Buddhism represented merely a new doctrine for the consideration of recluses. That these and kindred notions are grossly incorrect is evident from a study of the events immediately following the Enlightenment itself.

It is a matter of extreme importance that the account of the Enlightenment of Vipassi Buddha as given by Gotama Buddha ends, not with an exposition of the *Paticcasamuppāda,* but with the conversation with the Great Brahmā. If the Enlightenment of the Buddha constituted his *Mahaprajñā,* the first result of this was his *Mahākuruṇā,* or Great Compassion. *Mahāpadāna Suttanta* gives: 'Then there occurred to Vipassi, the Exalted One, Arahat, and All-Knowing One: "What if I should now teach the Doctrine, the Truth?" But there also occurred to him: "I attained to this Truth, profound, difficult to discern, difficult to understand, of peaceful and excellent import, not of the order of logical education, subtle, which only the wise can appreciate. Yet this generation is attached to pleasure and delights in the attachment, and because of this it is difficult for it to understand the matters, namely, this causation and the Law of "This arises depending on That". These, too, are matters difficult to understand, namely: the calming of all mental concomitants, the forsaking of all substrata of rebirth, the destruction of craving, dispassion, quietude of heart, nibbāna. If I should teach the Dhamma and others did not understand it from me, that would be wearisome to me; that would be a vexation to me."

At that point, the Great Brahmā appeared to him, asking him to preach the Dhamma, for the reason that there existed beings with few defilements who, without knowledge of the Dhamma, would dwindle away. Vipassi replied that he had considered preaching the Dhamma and gave his reasons for deciding against doing so. The Great Brahmā asked him a second time and received a similar reply. On the request being made a third time, 'Vipassi felt compassion for all beings, and with his Buddha's vision, saw beings of various degrees of defilement, of sharpness and faculties, of various dispositions, of different capacities for learning, living in evil and fear, with small appreciation of a world beyond.'

Two gāthās follow this description, the first, due to the Great Brahmā, enlarges on this previous reason as to why the Buddha should preach the Dhamma.

> 'As a man who has climbed to the hill-top
> Looks down on the people below,
> So the Sage having reached to All-Vision
> Sees men as afflicted with woe.
> He considers their birth and decaying,
> And attaining to victory himself,
> A Leader, a man free from Grasping
> Who has broken the rounds of rebirth,
> Sees others possessed of ability—
> May he teach them the Dhamma himself!'

To this Vipassi replied:

> 'The doors of the deathless state are open wide.
> Let those who have ears abandon blind beliefs!
> Brahmā! Perceiving vexation is teaching,
> I did not declare my Dhamma to mankind.

Vipassi immediately set about his task of teaching the Dhamma, and, under similar circumstances, Gotama Buddha did likewise.

Though the incident may seem familiar to Buddhist readers, it contains one point which is often passed unstressed, namely, that as long as the prospect lay in teaching a few people in comparatively advanced states the Buddha refused to teach; but when he considered the whole heterogeneous mass of mankind and its sufferings he decided without hesitation that he would teach his Dhamma. Therefore, any statement to the effect that the Buddha Dhamma was intended for a select few only, of whatever nature that few might be assumed to be, is not in accord with the statement made by Gotama. Remembering the *Mahāprajnā* of the Buddhas, it is incumbent on one to remember their *Mahākaruṇā.* One may consider, in passing, the import of the presence of the Great Brahmā. Should it be taken that this super-being did present himself to the ocular vision of the Buddha? Or may one take it that the Buddha became conscious of that which the *Mahā-Brahmā* was popularly assumed to represent, namely, the Creator of the world and the living creatures in it? *Mahā-Brahmā* was not Absolute Reality; technically he was a *Rūpāvacara deva.* However exalted he may have been in his own particular realm, he still created in terms of form and was still subject to birth and death. The question 'Where do earth, water, fire and air entirely cease?' Has already been referred to in the present work as being put to the Buddha; it has been put immediately before to the *Mahā-Brahmā* who admitted that he did not know the answer and referred the question to the Buddha. From the Buddha's reply that the question should have been stated: 'Where do earth, water, fire and air not occur?' it is clear that the raising of the world from its present condition must be a matter for someone or something greater than its Creator. Hence the *Mahā-Brahmā's* request to the Buddha to preach his Dhamma here...

Therefore, in our consideration of the Origin and Source of Knowledge of the Highest State, we have to bear in mind the Great Compassion of the Buddha as inseparable from it. If after Enlightenment the doors of the deathless state were open wide, the Buddha, with the profound knowledge of mankind and its needs which his Compassion brought him was ready to show the way in.

5

The Doctrines of Buddhism

Having sat for seven long years under the Bôdhi tree, Gotâma opened his eyes and perceiving the world of Samsâra exclaimed: "Quod erat demonstrandum!" True, he had attained to the spotless eye of Truth and had become Buddha the Enlightened One; he had entered the Nothingness of Nibbâna, and had become one with the Uncreated and the Indestructible. And now he stood once again on the shore line of existence and watched the waves of life roll landwards, curve, break and hiss up the beach only to surge back into the ocean from which they came. He did not deny the existence of the Divine (how could he when he had become one with it?) but so filled was he with the light of Amitâbha, that he fully saw that by Silence alone could the world be saved, and that by the denial of the Unknowable of the uninitiate, the Kether, the Ātman, the First Cause, the God of the unenlightened, could he ever hope to draw mankind to that great illimitable LVX, from which he had descended a God-illumined Adept. He fully realized that to admit into his argument the comment of God was to erase all hope of deliverance from the text, and, therefore, though he had becomc The Buddha, nevertheless, in his selflessness he stooped down to the level of the lowest of beings and, abandoning as dross the stupendous powers he had acquired, helped his fellows to realize the right path by the most universal of all symbols—the woe of the world, the sorrow of mankind.

Like the Vedântist, he saw that the crux of the whole trouble was Ignorance (Avijjâ). Dispel this ignorance, and illumination would take its place, that insight into the real nature of things which, little by little, leads the aspirant out of the world of birth and death, the world of Samsâra, into that inscrutable Nibbâna where things in themselves cease to exist and with them the thoughts which go to build them up. Ignorance is the greatest of all fetters, and, "he who sins inadvertently," as Nâgâsena said, "has the greater demerit."

Enquiring into the particular nature of ignorance, Buddha discovered that the Tree of Knowledge of Good and Evil had three main branches, namely Lobha, Dosa and Moha—Craving, Passion and the Delusion of Self; and that these three forms of ignorance alone could be conquered by understanding the three great signs or characteristics of all existence, namely: change, sorrow and absence of an ego—Anikka, Dukkha, and Anatta, which were attained by meditating on the inmost meaning of the Four Noble Truths:

"The Truth about Suffering; the Truth about the cause of Suffering; the Truth about the Cessation of Suffering; and the Truth about the Path which leads to the Cessation of Suffering." These consist of the above Three Characteristics with the addition of the Noble Eightfold Path, which contains, as we shall presently see, the whole of Canonical Buddhism.

Up to this point, save for the denial of the ego, the whole of the above doctrine might have been extracted from almost any of the Upanishads, but there is a difference, and the difference is this. Though the Vedântist realized that ignorance (Avidyâ) was the foundation of all sorrows, and that all things, possessing the essence of change, were but illusion, or Mâyâ, a matter of name and form; Buddha now pointed out that the true path of deliverance was through the reason (Ruach) and not through the senses (Nephesh), as many of the Upanishads would give one to believe. Further, this was the path that Gotâma had trod, and, therefore, he besought others to tread it. The Vedântist attempted to attain unity with the Ātman (Kether) by means of his emotions (Nephesch) intermingled with his reason (Ruach), but the Buddha by means of his reason (Ruach) alone. Buddha attempted to cut off all joys from the world, substituting in its place an implacable rationalism, a stern and inflexible morality, little seeing that the sorrows of earth which his system substituted for the joys of heaven, though they might not ruffle his self-conquered self, must perturb the minds of his followers, and produce emotions of an almost equal intensity, though perhaps of an opposite character to those of his opponents. Yet, for a space, the unbending rationalism of his system prevailed and crushed down the emotions of his followers, those emotions which had found so rich and fertile a soil in the decaying philosophy of the old Vedânta. The statement in the Dhammapada that: "All that we are is the result of what we have thought: it is founded on our thoughts, it is made up of our thoughts," is equally true of the Vedânta as it is of Buddhism. But, in the former we get the great doctrine and practice of the Siddhis directly attributable to a mastering of the emotions and then to a use of the same, which is strictly forbidden to the Buddhist. Eventually, however, under the Mahâyâna Buddhism of China and Tibet, the power of the Siddhis is forced again into recognition' for even as early as the writing of "The Questions of King Milinda," unless the beautiful story of the courtesan Bindumati be a latter day interpolation, these powers were highly thought of under the name of the "Acts of Truth." Thus, though King Sivi gave his eyes to the man who begged them to him, he received others by an Act of Truth, by the gift of Siddhi, or Iddhi as the Buddhists call it. An act, which is explained by the fair courtesan Bindumati as follows. When King Asoka asked her by what power she had caused the waters of the Ganges to flow backwards, she answered:

> Whosoever, O King, gives me gold—be he a noble, or a brahmin, or a tradesman, or a servant—I regard them all alike. When I see he is a noble I make no distinction in his favour. If I know him to be a slave I despise him not. Free alike from fawning and from dislike do I do service to him who has bought me. This, your Majesty, is the basis of the Act of Truth by the force of which I turned the Ganges back.

In other words, by ignoring all accidents, all matters of chance, and setting to work, without favour or prejudice, to accomplish the one object in view, and so finally "to interpret every phenomenon as a particular dealing of God with the soul." In truth this is an Act of Truth, the power begot by concentration and nothing else.

We have seen in Chapter II how the Ātman (that Essence beyond Being and Not Being) allegorically fell by crying "It is I," and how the great hypocrisy arose by postulating an individual Ātman for each being which had to incarnate again and again before finally it was swallowed up in the One Ātman of the Beginning. This individualistic conception, Gotâma banned, he would have none of it; a soul, a spirit, a separate entity was anathema to him; but in overthrowing the corrupt Vedânta of the latter-day pundits, like Luther, who many centuries later tore the tawdry vanities from off the back of Papal Rome, Gotâma, the Enlightened One, the Buddha, now similarly went back to Vedic times and to the wisdom of the old Rishis. But, fearing the evil associations clinging to a name, he anathematized the Ātman, and in its place wrote Nibhâna, which according to Nâgâ-sena is cessation, a passing away in which nothing remains, in fact an end. Soon, however, under Mahâyâna-Buddhism, was the Ātman to be revived in all its old glory under the name of Amitâbha, or that Source of all Light, which so illuminates a man who is aspiring to the Bôdhi that he becomes a Buddha. "Amitâbha," so Paul Carus informs us, "is the final norm of wisdom and of morality, the standard of truth and of righteousness, the ultimate *raison d'être* of the Cosmic Order." This of course is nonsense. Amitâbha, as the Ātman, is "the light which shines there beyond the heaven behind all things, behind each in the highest worlds, the highest of all."

Once logically having set aside the idea of an individual soul, Buddha refused to discuss the idea of a first cause or beginning; for he well saw that this idea was the greatest of the dog-faced demons which seduced man from the path. "First and last causes are incomprehensible, therefore, why discuss them!" cries Buddha, "but there *is* sorrow and I intend to destroy it." If I can only get people to start on the upward journey they will very soon cease to care if there is a First Cause or if there is no First Cause; but, if I give them the slightest hope to expect any reward outside cessation of sorrow, it will set them all cackling over the future like hens over a china egg, and soon they will be back at the old game of counting their chickens before they are hatched. He also must have seen, that if he postulated a First Cause, every unfledged rationalist in Pâtaliputta would cry, "Oh, but what a God, what a wicked God yours must be to allow all this sorrow you talk of... now look at mine..." little seeing that sorrow was just the same with the idea of God as without it, and that all was indeed Moha or Mâyâ—both God and No-God, sorrow and joy.

But Buddha being a practical physician, though he knew sorrow to be but a form of thought, was most careful in keeping it as real a calamity as he could; for he well saw, that if he could only get people to concentrate upon sorrow and its causes, that the end could not be far off of both sorrow and joy; but, if they began to speculate on its illusiveness, this happy deliverance would always remain distant. His business upon earth was entirely a practical and exoteric one, in no way mystical; it was rational not emotional, catholic and not secret.

What then is the cause of sorrow? and the answer given by Gotâma is: Karma or action. Thus, a good action produces a good reaction, and a bad one a bad one. This presupposes a code of morals, furnished by what? We cannot call it Ātman, conscience, or soul—a selecting power, which is strenuously denied by the rigid law of cause and effect. However, the mental eyes of the vast majority of his followers were not so clear as to pierce far into the darkness of metaphysical philosophy, and so it happened that, where the idealism of the Vedânta had failed the realism of Buddhism succeeded.

This denial of a universal Ātman, and a personal Ātman, soon brought the ethical and philosophical arguments of Gotâma up against a brick wall (Kant's *"a priori")* As we have seen, he could not prop up a fictitious beginning by postulating an Ātman, and he dared not use Nibhâna as such, though in truth the beginning is just as incomprehensible with or without an Ātman. But, in spite of his having denied the latter, he had to account for causality and the transmission of his good and evil (Karma) by some means or another. Now, according to Nâgâsena, the Blessed One refused to answer any such questions as: "Is the universe everlasting?" "Is it not everlasting?" "Has it an end?" "Has it not an end?" "Is it both ending and unending?" "Is it neither the one nor the other?" And further all such questions as: Are the soul and the body the same thing?" "Is the soul distinct from the body?" "Does a Tathâgata exist after death?" "Does he not exist after death?" "Does he both exist and not exist after death?" "Does he neither exist nor exist after death? ... Because "the Blessed Buddhas lift not up their voice without a reason and without an object." But in spite of there being no *soul* "in the highest sense," Gotâma had to postulate some vehicle which would transmit the sorrow of one generation to another, of one instant of time to the next; and, not being able to use the familiar idea of Ātman, instead, he made that of Karma do a double duty. "He does not die until that evil Karma is exhausted," says Nâgâsena.

Now this brings us to an extraordinary complex question, namely the *practical* difference between the Karma minus Ātman of the Buddhists and the Karma plus Ātman of the later Vedântists?

The Brahmin's idea, at first, was of one complete whole; this, as the comment supplanted the text, got frayed into innumerable units, or Ātmans, which, on account of Karma, were born again and again until Karma was used up and the individual Ātman went back to the universal Ātman. Buddha erasing the Ātman, though he refused to discuss the beginning, postulates Nibhâna as the end, which fact conversely also postulates the beginning as Nibbâna. Therefore, we have all things originating from an *x* sign, Ātman, Nibhâna, God, Ain or First Cause, and eventually returning to this primordial Equilibrium. The difficulty which now remains is the bridging over of this divided middle. To Gotâma there is no unit, and existence *per se* is ignorance caused as it were by a bad dream in the head of the undefinable Nibbâna; which itself, however, is non-existent. Each man is, as it were, a thought in an universal brain, each thought jarring against the next and prolonging the dream. As each individual thought dies it enters Nibbâna and ceases to be, and eventually when all thoughts die the dream passes and Nibbâna wakes. This bad dream seems to be caused by a separateness of subject and object which means sorrow; when sleep vanishes this separateness vanishes with it, things assume their correct proportion and may be equated to a state of bliss or non-sorrow.

Thus, we find that Nirvâna and Nibbâna are the same in fact as in etymology, and that absorption into either the one or the other may be considered as re-entering that Equilibrium from which we originated.

The first and the last words have been written on this final absorption by both the Vedântist and the Buddha alike.

There no sun shines, no moon, nor glimmering star, nor yonder lightning, the fire of earth is quenched; from him, who alone shines, all else borrows its brightness, the whole world bursts into splendour at his shining.

And—

> There exists, O Brothers, a Realm wherein is neither Earth nor Water neither Flame nor Air; nor the vast Aether nor the Infinity of Thought, not Utter Void nor the co-existence of Cognition and Non-cognition is there: —not this World nor Another, neither Sun nor Moon. That, Brothers, I declare unto you as neither a Becoming nor yet a Passing-away: —not Life nor Death nor Birth; Unlocalised, Unchanging and Uncaused:—That is the end of Sorrow.

Gotâma had, therefore, to "hedge." Unquestionably the soul-idea must go, but in order to account for the universal law of causation

Karma must remain, and further, surreptitiously perform all the old duties the individual Ātman had carried out. He had abandoned the animism of a low civilization, it is true, but he could not, for a want of the exemption from morality itself, abandon the fetish of a slightly higher civilization, namely, ethics. He saw that though mankind was tired of being ruled by spirits, human beings were only too eager to be ruled by virtues, which gave those who maintained these fictitious qualifications a sure standpoint from which to rail at those who did not. He banned therefore reincarnation and soul and substituted in their place transmigration and Karma (doing), the Sankhârâ or tendencies that form the character (individuality) of the individual.

Ānanda Metteya in "Buddhism" explains transmigration in contradistinction to reincarnation as follows. Two men standing on the shore of a lake watch the waves rolling landwards. To the one who is unversed in science it appears that the wave travelling towards him retains its identity and shape, it is to him a mass of water that moves over the surface impelled by the wind. The other, who has a scientifically trained mind, knows that at each point upon the surface of the lake the particles of water are only rising and then falling in their place, that each particle in turn is passing on its motion to its neighbours. To the first there is a translation of matter, to the second one of force. "The Vedântist has seen Substance, an enduring Principle, an Ens; the Buddhist only Qualities, themselves in all their elements ever changing, but the sum-total of their doing passing steadily on, till the wave breaks upon Nibbâna's shore, and is no more a wave for ever."

I have not space to criticise this, all I ask is—What is the difference between force and matter, and if the annihilation of the one does not carry with it the annihilation of the other irrespective of which is first—if either?

Ānanda Metteya carries his illustration further still.

> John Smith, then, in a sense, is immortal; nay, every thought he thinks is deathless, and will persist, somewhere, in the depths of infinity .... But it is not this part of his energy that results in the formation of a new being when he dies ... We may then consider the moment of John Smith's death .... During his life he has not alone been setting in vibration the great ocean of the AEther, he has been affecting the structure of his own brain. So that at the moment of his death all his own life, and all his past lives are existing pictured in a definite and characteristic molecular structure, a tremendous

> complicated representation of all that we have meant by the term John Smith—the record of the thoughts and doings of unnumbered lives. Each cell of the millions of his brain may be likened to a charged leyden-jar, the nerve-paths radiating from it thrill betimes with its discharges, carrying its meaning through man's body, and, through the Æther, even to the infinitude of space. When it is functioning normally, its total discharge is prevented, so that never at any time can more than a fraction of its stored-up energy be dissipated.... And then death comes; and in the moment of its coming, all that locked-up energy flames on the universe like a new-born star.

Then Ānanda Metteya, in a lengthy and lucid explanation, demonstrates how the light of a flame giving off the yellow light of sodium may be absorbed by a layer of sodium vapour, so the Karma, released from the body of the dead man, will circle round until it finds the body of a new-born child tuned or synchronized to its particular waves.

Now we are not concerned here with stray children who, like the receivers of a wireless telegraph, pick up either good or evil messages; but it is an interesting fact to learn that at least certain orthodox Buddhists attribute so complex and considerable a power to the brain, that by leaving one body that body perishes, and by entering another that body revives. Can it be that we have got back to our old friend the Prāna which in its individual form so closely resembles the individual Karma, and in its entirety the totality of Nibbâna? Let us turn to Brihadâranyaka Upanishad. There in 1, 6, 3 we find a mystical formula which reads *Amritam satyena channam.* This means "The immortal (Brâhman) veiled by the (empirical) reality;" and immediately afterwards this is explained as follows: "The Prâna (*i.e.* the Ātman) to wit is the immortal, name and form are the reality; by these the Prâna is veiled." Once again we are back at our starting-point. To become one with the Prâna or Ātman is to enter Nibbâna, and as the means which lead to the former consisted of concentration exercises, such as Prânâyâma, etc.; so now do we find almost identical exercises used to hasten the aspirant into Nibbâna.

The student by now should be sufficiently well acquainted with the Yoga Philosophy, to feel that the crude Animism employed by many of its expounders scarcely tallies with his own attainments. The nearer he approaches the Ātman the less does it appear to him to resemble what he has been taught to expect. Indeed its translation into worldly comments is a matter of education, so it comes about that he discovers that the Great Attainment *per se* is identical in all systems irrespective of the symbol men seek it under. Thus, Yahweh, as a clay phallus in the ark, was as much a reality to the Jews of Genesis as Brâhman in Brâhmâ-loka was to the Aryas of Vedic India. Thus, the vision of Moses, when he beheld God as a burning bush, is similar to the vision of the fire-flashing Courser of the Chaldean Oracles. Thus, Nibbâna, the Non-existent, is little removed, if at all, from the Christian heaven with its angelic hosts. And the reason is, that the man who does attain to any of these states, on his return to consciousness, at once attributes his attainment to his conscious representation of God. He attempts to rationalize about the suprarational, and describe what is beyond description in the language of his country.

At first the student will find the outward simplicity of Buddhism most refreshing; but soon he discovers that, like all other religious systems, Buddhism is entangled in a veritable network of words. Realizing this, he must go a step further than Gotâma, and say: "Why bother about sorrow at all, or about transmigration? for these are not 'wrong viewness,' as Mr. Rhys Davids so 'poetically' puts it, but are matters of the Kindergarten and not of the Temple; matters for police regulation, and for underpaid curates, and matters that have nothing to do with true progress." He should then divide life into two compartments; into the first he must throw science, learning, philosophy and all things built of words—the toys of life; and into the second, The Invocations of Adonai—the work of attainment.

Thus it may come about that the study of Buddhism will cause the student to abandon the tinsel of the Vedânta as well as its own cherished baubles, and induce him, more than ever, to rely on work and work alone and not on philosophizing, moralizing and rationalizing. The more rational he becomes, the less will he reason outwardly; and the more he becomes endowed with the spirit of the Buddha, in place of the vapourings of Buddhism, the more will he see that personal endeavour and not the Scriptures is the key.

The Dharma is to be attained to by the wise, each one for himself. Salvation rests on work and not on faith; not in reforming the so-called fallen, but in conquering oneself. "If one man conquer in battle a thousand times a thousand men: and another conquer but himself;—he is the greatest of conquerors."

This is the whole of Buddhism, as it is of any and all systems of self-control.

Strenuousness is the Immortal Path— sloth is the way of death. The Strenuous live always,—the slothful are already as the dead.

Impermanent are the Tendencies—therefore do ye deliver yourselves by Strenuousness.

This last charge of the Buddha is the one supremely important thing he ever said.

6

Buddhism Persecuted

With the advent of the Śuṅgas Buddhism suffered a check. The Buddhist accounts are unanimous in representing Pushyamitra Śuṅga as a persecutor of Buddhism. His persecution started in Magadha where it is said he tried unsuccessfully to destroy the famous Kukkuṭārāma monastery in Pāṭaliputra. He went up to Śākala to execute his policy of persecution. There he offered a reward of 100 dīnāras for the head of every Buddhist monk. The Buddhist accounts further tell us that this policy involved him in a war with a Yaksha named Kṛimiśa and ultimately brought about his death at a place called Sthūlakoshṭha. This evidence cannot be completely discarded. The Buddhist accounts refer to the dissatisfaction felt by the ministers of Aśoka as well as by his grandson Samprati at the extravagance with which Aśoka was emptying the treasury on the Buddhist establishments. The state was impoverished and weakened and this led to the downfall of the Mauryas. Pushyamitra started with a reactionary policy, performed *aśvamedha* sacrifices and did his best to revive the Brahmanical religion. If his policy of persecution was followed with greater vigour from Śākala it was because the Greeks had become the protagonists of this religion and had declared war against him in its defence. Demetrius and Menander became the champions of the cause of Buddhism and overran the whole of Northern India. Pushyamitra disappeared and his successors ruled not from Magadha but from Vidiśā.

The temporary persecution of Buddhism at the hands of Pushyamitra was ineffective. The people had espoused the cause of Buddhism. It was probably this popular feeling that dissuaded Pushyamitra from destroying the Kukkuṭārāma at Pāṭaliputra. The same popular sentiment prepared the way for the great progress made by Buddhism during the Śuṅga-Kāṇva period. This is made amply clear by the very large number of private donations recorded on Buddhist monuments at this time. A number of famous Buddhist establishments like the Bhārhut Stūpa, the Kārle Caves, and the Sāñchī Stūpa belong to the Śuṅga-Kāṇva period and testify to the great prosperity which Buddhism was then enjoying Buddhism had developed from a monastic into a popular religion. It had become a theistic religion with Buddha and his relics as the objects of the cult. The *stūpas* contained the ashes of the Great Master. Mere circumambulation and worship of these *stūpas* came to be considered by the ordinary laity as an act of great piety. The sanctity of Buddha's person was still held in the highest estimation and it was a sacrilege to make an image of him for the purpose of worship. The Bodhi tree or the sacred wheel were considered to be sufficiently representative of the divine aspect of the Lord.

It was in this period that Buddhism was adopted by the Greeks in the North. King Menander was a great champion of the faith. The story of his conversion by Nāgasena is related in the *Milindapañha* and seems to have a historical basis. He was probably instrumental in inviting Demetrius to defend the cause of Buddhism against the persecution of Pushyamitra. After establishing his capital at Śākala he began to do many acts of piety. In these he seems to have emulated the example of Aśoka. He is said to have been charitable, attached to the Law and a builder of monasteries, gardens, *chaityas,* wells etc. Some of his coins bear the emblem of the wheel, and he calls himself a *trāta* and a *dhramia.* Buddhist tradition represents him as a saviour of Buddhism. The Greeks carried the story of his pious acts very far. Plutarch tells us that after his death, the large cities within his empire contended for the honour of preserving his ashes and ultimately divided them among themselves just as was done with the ashes of Buddha. Another Greek ruler, Agathocles, uses the emblems of the Buddhist *stūpa* and Bodhi tree on his coins, and he takes pride in calling himself a *Hinduja,* i.e. an Indian by birth.

From the time of Menander the Greeks in India adopted Buddhism as the religion of their faith. Henceforth they play the part of donors to Buddhist establishments. One Irila builds two cisterns for the monks at his own expense at Junnar, Chita builds a meeting-hall for the *saṅgha* at the same place. Indrāgnidata excavates a cave at

Nāsik, and Dhenukākaṭa builds a temple at Kārle. There were doubtless many other donations elsewhere, but the examples mentioned were made at the most important institutions of the period.

The Pāli texts represent the Greeks as taking part even in missionary activities. We are told that after the conversion of the Yavana (Greek) country to Buddhism, Moggaliputta Tissa went there and selected a Greek elder Dharmarakshita for missionary work. Dharmarakshita was then sent to Aparāntaka where he successfully preached the law of Buddha and converted thousands, including women and nobles. The Ceylonese chronicle further tells us that when Duṭṭhagāmaṇi founded the Great Stūpa (Mahāthūpa) in Ceylon in the middle of the second century B.C. Buddhist teachers came from various countries. The Greeks were represented by the Greek elder Mahādharmarakshita who came from the city of Alasando (Alexandria ad Caucasum).

The Greeks in India were also responsible for developing a new style of Buddhist art which is usually known as Indo-Greek and which flourished mostly in the Panjab and North-Western India. It also exercised a great influence on the Buddhist art flourishing in other parts of India and abroad, in later days. The Greeks were perhaps responsible for the first plastic representation of Buddha, and this indicated a great change in Buddhist ideology from purely ethical to theistic concepts.

The rapid extension of Buddhism after the time of Aśoka to various parts of India resulted in the rise of Buddhist sects of which the number is given as eighteen. These sects arose not from doctrinal differences except in certain cases, but from the geographical conditions. With the spread of Buddhism, communities were founded in various parts of the country and as there was no co-ordinating organisation many of them developed their own traditions respecting the ancient teachings. The differences between many of these schools were so small that a number of them died out or merged in a short time with others.

The first schism in the church, we have seen, took place at the time of the second council, and split the church in two, one section being called Mahāsāṅghika and the other Sthaviravāda (Pāli Theravāda). Various traditions both northern and southern would have us believe that from the time of the first schism for nearly one century the Sthaviravāda Church remained undivided, while the Mahāsāṅghika during the same period (the second century after Nirvāṇa) gave rise to eight different schools: Ekavyāvahārika, Lokottaravāda, Kaukkuṭika, Bahuśrutīya, Prajñaptivāda, Chaityaśaila, Aparaśaila and Uttaraśaila.

Divisions started in the Sthaviravāda camp a century later (third century after Nirvāṇa). The first gave rise to two schools: Sarvāstivāda and Mūla-Sthaviravāda (also called Haimavata). From the Sarvāstivāda arose the Vātsiputrīya which gave rise to four schools called Dharmottarīya, Bhadrayāniya, Sammatīya and Chhannagarika. Later on two other schools also arose from the Sarvāstivāda: Kāśyapīya and Mahīśāsaka, and the latter was parent of the Dharmaguptaka school. The last school to originate from the Sarvāstivāda came into existence a century later, and it was known as Saṁkrāntivāda (also called Sautrāntika).

The Mahāsāṅghika since its inception in Vaiśāli was mostly confined to the east from where it spread specially to the south. The followers of this school probably did not form a strong community in the north as they are mentioned only in two inscriptions: the Wardak vase inscription of the 51st year of Kanishka and the Mathurā Lion Pillar. The first refers to a *vihāra* being built by one Vagramarega for the Mahāsāṅghikas, but the reference in the second inscription is not very clear. It probably speaks of the interest that was being taken by one Buddhila, a Sarvāstivāda teacher, in the literature of the Mahāsāṅghika school. The Mahāsāṅghika and its sects had a larger following in the South. A Kārle cave inscription of the 24th year of the reign of Vāsishṭhīputra Pulumāyi records the gift of a nine-celled hall to the Mahāsāṅghikas. The gift was important and shows that the school was held in high esteem in that region. The Mahāsāṅghika and some of its branches also flourished in the region of Amarāvatī and Dhānyakaṭaka, but some of its earlier sects, such as the Ekavyāvahārika, Lokottaravāda and Kukkuṭika probably disappeared very early as they are not mentioned in any inscription.

The Mahāsāṅghika developed a literature of its own. In fact it claimed to have preserved the most authentic tradition of early Buddhism in so far as it traced its lineage from Mahākāśyapa who was responsible for convening the first Buddhist council in which, according to tradition the canon was recited for the first time. The Tibetan accounts say that the literature of the school was written in a Prākṛit language but no original text of the school having come down to us we do not know that sort of Prākṛit it was. The Vinayapiṭaka of this school has, however, survived in its entirety in a Chinese translation made by Fa-hien and Buddhabhadra in A.D. 424. Fa-hien discovered a manuscript of this text on his Indian travels in a Mahāyāna monastery in Magadha. The story as told by Fa-hien is interesting and throws some light on the antiquity of the Mahāsāṅghika-Vinaya: 'Fa-hien's original object had been to search for the Vinaya. In the various kingdoms of North India, however, he had found one master transmitting orally the rules to another but no written copies which he could transcribe. He had travelled far and come on to Central India. Here in the Mahāyāna monastery he found a copy of the Vinaya containing the Mahāsāṅghika rules—those which were observed in the first great council while Buddha was still in the world. The original copy was handed down in the Jetavanavihāra. Fa-hien's testimony proves that the Mahāsāṅghika-Vinaya was written down quite early at a time when manuscript copies of the Vinaya of other schools were not yet available. Fa-hien also refers to the Abhidharma of the Mahāsāṅghika school, a copy of which he got in Magadha, but it has not been preserved. We do not know if the school had a Sūtrapiṭaka of its own. No trace of any such collection has come down to us. Of the three early branches of the Mahāsāṅghika there are no vestiges except in the literature of one school, the Lokottaravāda. The *Mahāvastu* is declared to be a portion of the Vinayapiṭaka of this school. The *Mahāvastu* itself declares that it is 'the portion called Mahāvastu of the Vinayapiṭaka of the Lokottaravāda of Madhyadeśa of Madhyadeśa—a branch of the Mahāsāṅghika.'

The Mahāsāṅghika, along with its three branches—the Ekavyāvahārika, Lokottaravāda and Kaukkuṭika—believed in the supramundane *(lokottara)* character of Buddha. Buddha was thus considered to be infallible. Every word uttered by a Buddha has a deep religious significance. He is omniscient and not subject to human failings. The historical Buddha had no place in this theory. The Mahāsāṅghika also formulated the theory of *mūlavijñāna*, 'original consciousness', which was of great consequence. It is this subtle consciousness from which the five *skandhas* originate. Thus regarded, the *skandhas* do not transmigrate; it is the *mūlavijñāna* which is the real subject of transmigration.

The other branches of the Mahāsāṅghika, viz., the Bahuśrutīya, Prajñaptivāda, Chaityaśaila, Aparaśaila and Uttaraśaila, have also left definite traces in the history of the Buddhist Church. In addition to the last three schools, the Pāli sources mention a few others including them under the general heading Andhaka (Andhraka). The additional names are: Rājagiriya. Siddhatthika, Pubbaselia and Vājiriya. The schools are also generally known as Chetiya or Chaitya (ka). These schools flourished in the region of Dhānyakaṭaka near Amarāvatī and played an important part in the history of Buddhism during the first few centuries of the Christian era. Some of them continued to exist till the seventh century, when Hiuan Tsang visited the place.

The Chaityakas are already mentioned in a Nāsik cave inscription. A number of inscriptions discovered at Amarāvatī mention the Chetiya school and its chief place of worship—the Mahāchaitya at Dhānyakaṭaka. A number of inscriptions discovered at Nāgārjunakoṇḍa, a place near ancient Dhānyakaṭaka refer to the following Andhraka schools:

1. Chetiyavādaka
2. Rājagirinivāsika (the same as Rājagiriya mentioned by Pāli sources)
3. Puvasele (Purvaśaila)
4. Mahāvanseliya (this may be one of two other *seliya* schools: Apara—and Uttara—)
5. Siddhatthika.

The inscriptions also speak of the Airiya Hagha or Ārya-Saṅgha by which probably the Mahāsaṅgha is meant. The Nāgārjunakoṇḍa inscriptions mention another school of the Mahāsāṅghika, the Bahuśrutīya. The existence in the region of Dhānyakaṭaka of practically all the branches of the Mahāsāṅghika mentioned in literature shows that this area had become the most important stronghold of the Mahāsāṅghikas under the patronage of the Śātavāhanas and their successors in the Krishna valley. These schools continued to prosper till the third or fourth century, A.D. This place, as we know from one of the inscriptions, had attracted monks and nuns from various lands: Kāsmīra, Gandhāra, Chīna, Kirāta, Tosali, Aparānta, Vaṅga, Vanavāsi, Yavana, Ḍamila and Tāmbapāṇṇi (Ceylon).

The Andhraka schools had no literature of their own and seem not to have differed from the parent community, the Mahāsāṅghika, on any important doctrinal point. They evidently shared with other

Mahāsāṅghika sects the principal views of the school on Buddhalogy and transmigration.

The schools arising from the other camp, the Sthaviravāda, have also left their definite mark in literature and epigraphy, from the Śuṅga right up to the Kushān period, and may be said to have flourished from 200 B.C. to A.D. 200. The Sarvāstivāda and its branches flourished mostly in the north, being recorded in a number of inscriptions of the Kushān period e.g., the Zeda Inscription, the Kurram valley relic casket, the Mathurā Lion Pillar Inscription. One inscription records the gift to the Sarvāstivāda monks of the famous Kanishka-Vihāra of Purushapura. These inscriptions clearly show that the Sarvāstivāda school was esteemed in the entire region from Mathurā to Nagara (hāra) and from Taxila to Kāśmīra. The Haimavata school had its stronghold in Vidiśā. The Sonārī *stūpa* inscriptions of Bhilsa refer to this school and its apostle Dundubhisara. Other inscriptions of the same region record the names of two other teachers of the same school, Kāśyapagotra and Gauptiputra (Gotiputa). The Ceylonese chronicles as well as the *Samantapāsādikā* make special reference to Dundubhisara and Kassapagotta as the apostles of Buddhism in the Himalayan zone. The Haimavata school, as the name indicates, probably originated in the Himalayan region, perhaps in Kāśmīra.

A number of inscriptions of the Kaṇheri cave mention the Bhadrayānika school, and the Sārnāth Pillar Inscription refers to the Sammitīya and Vātsīputrika schools. We have seen that the Sammitīya was a branch of the Vātsīputrika, and hence they were intimately associated with each other. The Vātsīputrikas are also found in a Bhārhut inscription under the name Vacchiputra. The Kāśyapīya, another important branch of the Sarvāstivāda, is recorded in the inscriptions of the period. The oldest reference to them is in the Pabhosā Buddhist cave inscription which records the excavation of the cave for the use of the Kaśśapīya monks, by one Āshāḍhasena, the maternal uncle of king Bahasatimitra. The Bedali inscription (Hazara district) and the Taxila Copper Ladle inscription, both of which belong to the Kushān period refer to them as Kasavia or Kasyaviya. Inscriptions are silent about the Dharmaguptaka school but there are other evidences to show that this was a very important school of the period. Although the Mahīśāsaka was a branch of the Sarvāstivāda and an important school, it is not mentioned in any inscription of North India. It does, however, find a place along with the Andhraka schools in one of the inscriptions of Nāgārjunakoṇḍa.

Many of these branches of the Sthaviravāda have left their own literatures. The Pāli canon according to its own tradition is the sacred literature of the Theravāda (Sthaviravāda). The literature of the Sarvāstivāda has, however, been preserved only in Chinese and Tibetan translations. The complete Vinayapiṭaka of the school was translated into Chinese in A.D. 404 by Kumārajīva and Puṇyatrāta. Only the *Prātimoksha* of this school has been discovered in its original Sanskrit, from Central Asia. The Sūtrapiṭaka, consisting of four Āgamas, translated into Chinese between 397 and 427, in all likelihood belongs to the same school. Of the seven Abhidharma texts of the Sarvāstivādas, the *Jñānaprasthānaśāstra* is preserved in a Chinese translation of 383. The other six are in Chinese translations made by Hiuan Tsang between 651 and 660.

The Vinayapiṭakas of the Dharmaguptaka and Mahīśāsaka schools are also preserved in Chinese translations of the beginning of the fifth century. The literatures of the other schools, viz. Haimavata, Kāśyapīya and Sammitīya, have come down to us in the fragments preserved in Chinese translations. A small text called *Vinayamātrakā-śāstra,* which was translated into Chinese between 385 and 431, is a fragment of the Vinaya of the Haimavata school as stated by a colophon of the text itself. It has a close resemblance to the corresponding section of the Dharmaguptaka-vinaya. A fragment of the Vinaya of the Kāśyapīya school is the *Vimukti-śīla-sūtra* translated by Gautama Prajñāruchi at the beginning of the sixth century. A small section of the Vinaya of the Sammitīya school is the *Liu eul she eul ming leao lun* (22 explanations of the Vinaya) which was translated by Paramārtha in the middle of the sixth century. A Śāstra or Abhidharma of the same school entitled *Sammitīya-nikāya-śāstra* was translated into Chinese much earlier. It looks like an abridgement of a longer work giving the essential doctrines of the school. It is not impossible that some of these schools at least had more extensive literatures which have been lost. We know at least that Hiuan Tsang took 17 texts of the Sammitīya school from India to China, but translated none of them and the texts were ultimately lost.

This is not the place to enter into a discussion of the doctrines held by the various schools of the Sthaviravāda group. However, some of their important differences with the Mahāsāṅghika may be pointed out. The Sarvāstivādas, as the name indicates, were realists. They believed in the existence of both material and mental elements. They held Buddha, in opposition to the Mahāsāṅghikas, to be a historical figure who was not infallible. Not all that he said was the Law, and not all the *sūtras* that he delivered were perfect. The fundamental doctrines are embodied only in the eightfold Aryan path *(ārya-ashṭāṅgika-mārga).*

The Dharmaguptaka school, although a branch of the Sthaviravāda, had a near doctrinal affinity with the Mahāsāṅghika. It attached a sanctity to the person of Buddha and placed him higher than the Saṅgha. It also maintained that great merit could be acquired by worshipping the *stūpa.*

The Mahīśāsaka too differed on some important doctrinal matters from its parent body, the Sarvāstivāda. While the latter maintained that the things *(dharmas),* present, past and future exist, the Mahiśāsakas propounded the view that the past and the future do not exist. It is said, however, that the Mahīśāsakas later on modified this position.

We know something more definite on the special doctrines of the Sammitīya school. The Sammitīya was a branch of the Vātsīputrīya. The most important view held by them in common was a modification of the theory of transmigration. While most of the Buddhist sects believed that the *pudgala* (ego) was either identical with the *skandhas* or different from them, the Vātsīputrīya and the Sammitīya maintained that the ego was neither the *skandhas* nor different from them. This ego, they maintained, contrary to the views of others, could transmigrate. The conception of this ego was more or less like the Brahmanical conception of *ātman* and similar to the conception of *mūlavijñāna* of the Mahāsāṅghika. They were therefore accused of heresy by some schools. They also held another revolutionary view in common with the Sarvāstivāda that non-Buddhists also were capable of obtaining the supernormal powers *(ṛiddhi)* and attaining to the position of Arhatship.

The last of the eighteen schools, which is called Saṁkrāntivāda by some sources and Sautrāntika by others, and which originated in the fourth century after Nirvāṇa requires to be noted. They were called Saṁkrāṅtikā because they believed in the transmigration of the *skandhas.* But by these *skandhas* they mean something different from its ordinary conception. It is called *ekarasa-skandha,* an entity similar to the *pudgala* theory of the Sammitīyas and *mūlavijñāna* of the Mahāsāṅghikas. On this point the school seems to have been the precursor of the later Sautrāntikas, but on another point they maintained a doctrine quite contrary to that of the Sautrāntikas of later times. They shared with the Sarvāstivāda the view that the *sūtras* delivered by Buddha were not all authoritative. The later Sautrāntika school, however, considered the *sūtras* alone to be authoritative. The Saṁkrāntivāda therefore should be distinguished from the Sautrāntika school of later times, although in certain respects the former may be considered a precursor of the later.

It is thus clear that apart from some of the most important schools which developed their own literatures, the rest were local sects which as Fa-hien says 'agree in general meaning but they have small and trivial differences as when one opens and another shuts'.

Kanishka's reign is a landmark in the history of Buddhism. Tradition not only represents him as a great patron of the religion but also associates him with a galaxy of Buddhist masters who were responsible for shaping the Buddhism of later times. Only a few coins of Kanishka contain Buddhist emblems, but a very large number of inscriptions of his reign as well as of that of his successors clearly bear out that it was a period of great Buddhist activity. It was in this period that the Indo-Greek school of Buddhist art which originated earlier had its greatest development. Buddha for the first time began to be represented by images. Buddhist monks from India carried Buddhism to Central Asia and China. Buddhist philosophical schools came into existence and a new form of Buddhism, the Mahāyāna, of far-reaching consequence came to be evolved in this period. The Buddhist sects mentioned above assumed their definite position in the doctrinal and literary history of Buddhism.

Kanishka must have contributed a good deal to this progress of Buddhism. Buddhist legends tell us that he became the sovereign of all Jambudvipa 400 years after the death of Buddha. He at first treated Buddhism with contempt, but later on became a great champion of it. The story runs that while out hunting he met a cowherd-boy who inspired him with faith in Buddha by communicating to him a prophecy of the Lord that 400 years after him a king called Kanishka would build a great *stūpa* in his honour. This led to his conversion to Buddhism and the emperor in fulfilment of the prophecy built a great tope at Purushapura. This was the famous Kanishka-Mahavihāra of Peshawar which became an object of admiration to all foreign travellers for centuries. The Chinese sources give the name Tsiao-li to this *tihāra*. The Sanskrit name seems to have been something like Āścharya-vihāra.

We do not know how far the story of Kanishka's conversion to Buddhism is authentic. The date at least seems to be wrong for Kanishka did not flourish before the end of the first century, i.e.. about 500 years after Nirvāṇa, but the Mahāvihāra built by him is mentioned not only in literature but also in inscriptions. It was the abode of Pārśva, the venerable patriarch of the Sarvāstivāda school, who was a contemporary of the emperor and probably his preceptor. He presided over a general Buddhist council convoked by Kanishka. This is traditionally known as the Third Buddhist Council, evidently by the exclusion of the Council of Pāṭaliputra, which we have seen was only a party meeting. The Council was necessitated by the dissensions that had been raging in the Church. The Tibetan accounts tell us that the principal participants were Pārśva with 500 Arhats under him and Vasumitra with 500 Bodhisattvas under him. This really means that the points of view which we usually call Hīnayāna and Mahāyāna were both represented in the Council. According to one source, the Council acknowledged that all the eighteen schools preserved the genuine doctrine of Buddhism, it also put into writing the Vinaya as well as those parts of the Sūtra and Abhidharma that had not been written down before. The Chinese account as given by Hiuan Tsang tells us that the elders in this Council were concerned with the compilation of the commentaries *(Vibhāshā)* of the Sutra-Vinaya and the Abhidharma-piṭakas each containing 100,000 *ślokas*. These *Vibhāshās* were considered to be the authoritative interpretations of the canon, and by the order of Kanishka were engraved on copper-plates and enclosed in a *stūpa*. The venue of the Council, according to one source, was the Kuṇḍalavana-vihāra of Kāśmīra, according to the other, the Kuvana in Jālandhara.

Besides Pārśva, a number of other famous teachers was associated with Kanishka. Of these the foremost was Aśvaghosha. Aśvaghosha, originally a Brahmin, was converted to Buddhism by Pārśva. His activities were confined to Magadha, but his fame soon reached the frontiers. He was brought to Purushapura by Kanishka after his military expedition to the east. Aśvaghosha is famous for his literary works, *Buddhacharita, Sūtrālaṁkara, Śāriputraprakaraṇa*—a drama of which only fragments have been discovered from Central

Asia, *Saundarananda,* etc. His great literary genius has been recognised but in all probability he also originated a system of philosophy. This philosophy is sometimes called the Tathatā philosophy in which the ultimate reality is stated to be indefinable, attainable only by intuition. The phenomenal world is declared to be unreal. A systematic book of Mahāyāna philosophy called *Śraddhotpada-sastra,* which is found in Chinese and declared to be the translation of the Sanskrit original, is attributed to him. Some scholars, however, doubt the authenticity of this book. Other sources attribute to him a drama called *Rāshṭrapāla-nāṭaka* which is now lost and must have treated of philosophical topics. An account of this work as preserved in Chinese says: "In the city of Pāṭalīputra Aśvaghosha had been going about to preach his religion and to convert others to it. Inspired by the desire to save the residents of the city he composed a beautiful piece of song called *Rāshṭtrapāla.* Its tune was pure and elegant, and beauty and sadness perfectly harmonised in it. It dealt with sorrow, vacuity, essence of impersonality *(duḥkha, śūnyatā, anātmā)* that is to say all that constitute the illusory world. The three worlds or the *dhātus* are the prisons for imprisoning the people and it is impossible to be happy in any of these places ... all is impermanent... the body is empty and vain...". This is not quite a new philosophy; it is rather a fundamental thesis of Buddhism. It is therefore likely, as the tradition asserts, that Aśvaghosha was also an exponent of the Buddhist philosophy in some of his works.

Vasumitra, we have seen, was also a contemporary of Kanishka. There are different personages of this name, and some confusion about them in the Chinese and Tibetan accounts. We are told that there were three Vasumitras in the early period; one lived three hundred years after Nirvāṇa and was the author of the two Abhidharma works of the Sarvāstivāda, viz., *Prakaraṇapada* and *Dhātukāya;* the second Vasumitra lived four hundred years after Nirvāṇa and assisted Parśva in the compilation of the *Mahāvibhāshā;* the third was a Sautrāntika teacher. In spite of the tradition, it is possible to suppose that the first and the second were identical. There is no doubt that the Sarvāstivāda canon was rehearsed in the Third Council before the compilation of a comprehensive Vibhāshā could be undertaken. So Vaumitra may have been responsible for putting together the two Abhidharma texts mentioned before which pass under his name. He played that part of an editor, not of an author, in regard to the two texts. A few other works attributed to him such as the *History of Eighteen Schools, Saṅgīti-sūtra* etc. show that Vasumitra was interested in putting the traditional lore in order. This was also the main purpose of the Third Council—to take stock of the canonical books, to put them in order, to write them down, to fix the correct interpretation and to judge the value of the traditions as recorded by various schools. Vasumitra worked to that end.

Three more names are associated with him. Tāranāth says, 'Bhadanta Dharmatrāta, Ghoshaka, Vasumitra and Buddhadeva are the four great teachers of the Vaibhāshika school; Dharmatrāta was the maternal uncle of Vasumitra. He may have been one of the collaborators in the compilation of the *vibhāshā.* A great and important compilation, the *Udānavarga,* which is the Sanskrit version of the *Dhammapada,* is attributed to him. It contains many more verses than are found in the Pāli *Dhammapada,* and as a collection has greater importance than the Pāli text in the history of the Buddhist canon.

Ghoshaka was a Tukhāra and thus belonged to the same nationality as Kanishka. The tradition says that after the council and death of Kanishka, both Vasumitra and Ghoshaka were invited by the king of Aśmāparānta, a country to the west of Kāśmīra and near the country of Tukhāra. He is often quoted in the *Vibhāshā,* a fact which shows that he took part in the compilation of that great work. A separate work, the *Abhidharmāmṛita-śāstra,* is attributed to him. It is a very clear presentation of the fundamental doctrines of the Sarvāstivāda Abhidharma.

Buddhadeva is mentioned in the *Vibhāshā.* He is in all probability the person referred to in the Mathurā Lion Pillar Inscription along with another Sarvāstivāda teacher named Budhila. Both Buddhadeva and Dharmatrāta are said to have held the doctrine that 'everything exists.' Buddhadeva further maintained that the various conditions of the mind *(chaitta)* are only the various modes of thought *(vijñāna).* This was somewhat similar to the Sautrāntika view of the *ekarasakandha* and the Mahāsāṅghika doctrine of *mūlavijñāna.* Both Dharmatrāta and Buddhadeva seem to have been elder contemporaries of Kanishka.

The reign of Kanishka saw the rise of the two philosophical schools which originated from the Sarvāstivāda. The *Mahāvibhāshā* which was compiled in the Third Council with the object of supplying the most authoritative interpretation of the Sarvāstivāda Abhidharma was taken as the basis of the Vaibhāshika movement. The followers of this school explained the fundamental doctrines of Buddhism with the help of the Abhidharma of the Sarvāstivāda school. Hence they are also known as the Ābhidharmikas. The four teachers mentioned above, Vasumitra, Ghoshaka, Dharmatrāta and Buddhadeva, are considered to be the pioneers of the Vaibhāshika movement. This, however, is not literally true. The Vaibhāshika was not constituted as a full-fledged school until later, when their opponents, the Sautrāntikas, came to be organised as a school. We have seen that the Sautrāntika doctrine of an original consciousness of which the mental conditions are only expressions can be traced also to the works of the two Vaibhāshika teachers: Dharmatrāta and Buddhadeva. As a school Sautrāntika originated slightly later, and the Vaibhāshika then only assumed the form of an independent school.

The Sautrāntikas rejected the authority of the Abhidharma and the Vibhāshā and maintained that the *sūtras* were the only reliable source of the teachings of Buddha. We have seen that some old schools like the Mahāsāṅghika and the Saṅkrāntivāda considered the *sūtras* as the perfect utterances of Buddha, whereas the Sarvāstivāda maintained the contrary view that there are also imperfect *sūtras*. The Sautrāntika tendency at the beginning was known as Dārshṭāntika as it explained the doctrines by *dṛishṭānta* 'comparison'. The Dārshṭāntikas are mentioned in the *Mahāvibhashā*. The Sautrāntika, however, was constituted as a fully fledged school by Kumāralāta who seems to have flourished soon after Kanishka. Tradition speaks of him as one of the four luminaries along with Aśvaghosha, Nāgārjuna, and Āryadeva. He was thus either a yonger contemporary of Kanishka or lived in the time of his immediate successor. We hear of two disciples of Kumāralāta: Śrīlāta and Harivarman. A work of Harivarman, the *Tattvasiddhi-śāstra* has come down to us in the Chinese translation of Kumārajīva (end of the fourth century). The most fundamental view of the Sautrāntikas was that objects are nothing but images of a subtle consciousness.

The Kushāna period also witnessed the rise of a new way in Buddhism, called Mahāyāna which has two philosophical schools: Mādhyamaka and Yogāchāra. Mahāyāna was incipient even in the earlier Buddhism. We have seen that the Mahāsāṅghikas propounded the theory of *lokottaravāda,* and considered the historical Buddha to be nothing but an incarnation *(nirmāṇakāya)* of a supra-mundane Buddha *(saṁbhogakāya)*. This theory led to the formulation of the new Buddhalogy with *trikāya* or 'three bodies': Nirmāṇakāya, Saṁbhogakāya and Dharmakāya, in which Dharmakāya is identical with the ultimate reality. This *trikāya* theory is one of the most important doctrines of Mahāyāna.

We have also noted that Buddhism was slowly developing into a theistic religion with Buddha as the object of the cult. Aśoka, we have seen, does not speak of Nirvāṇa as the highest goal but of heaven *(svarga)*. His belief in the supernormal powers and in the possibility of leading others to the attainment of heavenly bliss through his own efforts is more a Mahāyāna than a Hīnayāna tendency, In fact, the new ideal which is extolled in Mahāyāna insists on active compassion for the weal of our fellow creatures and decries the egoistic ideal of the Arhats as advocated by the earlier schools which go under the general name of Hīnayāna. These new ways or ideals were being developed in an extensive literature which forms the canon of the Mahāyāna. Some of the works: *Prajñāpāramitāsūtra, Saddharmapuṇḍarīka, Laṅkāvatāra, Suvarṇaprabhāsa* and others seem to have come into existence at this period.

The Mahāyāna philosophy as a new school of interpretation of Buddha's original doctrines was developed in the two idealistic systems known as the Mādhyamaka and the Yogāchāra. There exponents of the Mādhyamaka were Nāgārjuna and his disciple Āryadeva. Nāgārjuna seems to have been a yonger contemporary of Kanishka and flourished in the second century A.D. Āryadeva belonged to a later generation. Both of them came from the South—Nāgārjuna from Southern Kośala, and Āryadeva from Ceylon. They appear to have worked in the South, probably at Dhānyakaṭaka. Tradition says that Nāgārjuna was born in a Brahmanical family, had at first a thorough Brahmanical training and became a Buddhist in consequence of a misadventure. He was a personal friend of the great Śātavāhana king Gautamīputra Śātakarṇi to whom he addressed an epistle (called *suhṛillekha)* that has been preserved in the Buddhist collections. Nāgārjuna, therefore, worked under the patronage of the Śātavāhana king. A Buddhist tradition credits the Śātavāhanas with the propagation of Mahāyāna. It is recorded in the form of a prediction of Buddha which says: 'There will be a king named Śātavāhana in South India. When the Law is on the point of extinction....he will appear and propagate the *Vaipulya-*

sūtra of the Mahāyāna and will save the Law from extinction.' In fact, we know from other sources that the Śātavāhanas were great patrons of Buddhism. Dhānyakaṭaka and its neighbourhood became the centre of the Mahāsāṅghika sects under this dynasty. A number of Buddhist cave temples, Kārle, Nāsik and the earlier caves of Ajaṇṭā belong to this period.

The Mahāsāṅghika sects with their theory of *lokottaravāda,* and the theory of *Kāya* and *mūlavijñāna,* supplied a propitious ground for the growth of Mahāyāna in the South. Although Mahāyāna was incipient in earlier Buddhism, and some of the texts which are admitted to be a part of the canon of the Mahāyāna originated earlier, Mahāyāna was recognised as a developed system only with the formulation of the Mādhyamaka philosophy by Nāgārjuna. Nāgārjuna, therefore, is legitimately considered to be its founder. A number of works is attributed to him, the most important being a stupendous commentary on the *Prajñāpāramitā.* He also composed an independent work—the *Māhyamaka-kārikā* in which he formulates the new philosophy. Āryadeva wrote a commentary on the work. Āryadeva expatiated on the new philosophy further in his *Chatuḥśataka, Śataśāstra* and a number of other works. The new philosophy is commonly characterised as Śūnyavāda—the philosophy of relativism. It is a logical outcome of the principles of ancient Buddhism, according to which the phenomenal world is a mere illusion from the point of view of ultimate truth. There are two kinds of truths: *Pāramārthika* (ultimate) and *Sāmvṛitika* (relative or conventional). Viewed from the ultimate standpoint, 'All is delusion, dreamlike. There is no existence there is no cessation of being, there is no birth, there is no Nirvāṇa, there is no difference between those who have attained Nirvāna and those who have not. All conditions, in fact, are like dreams.'

The other school, Yogāchāra, is of a slightly later origin. Two brothers Asaṅga and Vasubandhu, natives of Purushapura, are generally believed to have been the first exponents of this system. They lived, however, in the fourth century whereas Yogāchāra doctrines were already being formulated in the Kushāna period. It has been suggested by a number of scholars that the first exponent of this system was Bodhisattva Maitreya—or rather Maitreyanātha, who was the teacher of Asaṅga and lived in the third century. In fact, the story runs that Asaṅga while writing his books had often to go to Bodhisattva Maitreya in the Tushita heaven for the solution of his difficulties. If the supernatural element is eliminated from the story, Bodhisattva Maitreya would be only a human teacher. Whatever that may be, it is quite likely that Yogāchāra philosophy was formulated in some form or other before the time of Asaṅga and Vasubandhu. In fact, the fundamental doctrine of *ālayavijñāna*, which is considered to be the basis of phenomenality by this school, cannot be dissociated from the doctrine of *ekarasaskandha* of the Sautrāntika and the theory of *mūlavijñāna* of the Mahāsāṅghikas. Yogāchāra doctrines are also found in the *Laṅkāvatāra Sūtra*, which is quite old. The Yogāchāra like the Mādhyamaka is an idealist school and formulates two kinds of truths—the ultimate and the relative, and looks upon the phenomenal world as an illusion. It asserts, however, that this illusion, is a mental illusion and hence considers *vijñāna* or consciousness as real.

7

Theravāda Buddhism

As we have already seen, the centuries which saw the rise of Buddhism and Jainism in India were marked by continuing social change and profound intellectual ferment. What has been said above about the conditions in which the heterodox systems developed in the sixth and fifth centuries must be borne in mind in the study of Buddhism.

The founder of Buddhism was the son of a chief of the hill-tribe of the Shākyas, who gave up family life to become an ascetic when he was some twenty-nine years old, and, after some years, emerged as the leader of a band of followers who pursued the "Middle Way" between extreme asceticism and worldly life. The legends which were told about him in later times are mostly unreliable, though they may contain a grain of historical truth here and there. Moreover many of the sermons and other pronouncements attributed to the Buddha are not his, but the work of teachers in later times, and there is considerable doubt as to the exact nature of his original message. However, the historicity of the Buddha is certain, and we may believe as a minimum that he was originally a member of the Shākya tribe, that he gained enlightenment under a sacred pīpal tree at Gayā, in the modern Bihar, that he spent many years in teaching and organizing his band of followers, and that he died at about the age of eighty in Kusinārā, a small town in the hills. The Sinhalese Buddhists have preserved a tradition that he died in 544 B.C., but most modern authorities believe that this date is some sixty years too early.

The band of yellow-robed *bhikkhus* which the Buddha left behind him to continue his work probably remained for some two hundred years one small group among the many heterodox sects of India, perhaps fewer in numbers and less influential than the rival sects of

Jains and Ājīvikas. Though by Western standards its rule was rigid, involving continuous movement from place to place for eight months of the year and the consumption of only one meal a day, which was to be obtained by begging, it was light in comparison with the discipline of most other orders, the members of which were often compelled to take vows of total nudity, were not permitted to wash, and had to undergo painful penances. It is evident that between the death of the Buddha and the advent of Ashoka, the first great Buddhist emperor, over two hundred years later, there was considerable development of doctrine. Some sort of canon of sacred texts appeared, though it was probably not at this time written down, and the Buddhists acquired numerous lay followers. For the latter, and for the less spiritually advanced monks, the sect adapted popular cults to Buddhist purposes—notably the cult of stūpas, or funeral mounds, and that of the sacred pīpal tree. We have seen that these had probably been worshiped in the Ganges valley from time immemorial, and with such cults both Hinduism and Buddhism had to come to terms. Buddhist monks began to overlook the rule that they should travel from place to place except in the rainy season and took to settling permanently in monasteries, which were erected on land given by kings and other wealthy patrons, and were equipped with pīpal trees and stūpas, theoretically commemorating the Buddha's enlightenment and death respectively.

Quite early in the history of Buddhism sectarian differences appeared. The tradition tells of two great councils of the Buddhist order, the first soon after the Buddha's death, the second a hundred years later. At the latter a schism occurred, and the sect of *Mahāsaṅghikas* ("members of the Great Order") is said to have broken away, ostensibly on account of differences on points of monastic discipline, but probably on doctrinal grounds also. The main body, which claimed to maintain the true tradition transmitted from the days of the founder, took to calling their system *Theravāda* ("The Teaching of the Elders"). By little over a century after this schism the whole of India except the southern tip had been unified politically by Magadha, after a long and steady process of expansion, which culminated in the rise of the first great Indian imperial dynasty, that of the Mauryas. The third and greatest of the Mauryas, Ashoka, became a Buddhist. According to his own testimony he was so moved by remorse at the carnage caused by an aggressive war which he had waged that he experienced a complete change of heart and embraced Buddhism. His inscriptions, the earliest intelligible written records to have survived in India, testify to his earnestness and benevolence.

Buddhism seems to have received a great impetus from Ashoka's patronage. He erected many stūpas, endowed new monasteries, and enlarged existing Buddhist establishments. In his reign the message of Budhism was first carried over the whole of India by a number of missionaries, sent out, according to tradition, after a third council which met at Pātaliputra (the modern Patna) in order to purify the doctrine of heresy. It was in Ashoka's reign that Ceylon first became a Buddhist country, after the preaching of the apostle Mahinda, said to have been Ashoka's son, who had become a monk. From that day onwards Ceylon has remained a stronghold of the Buddhism of the Theravāda school; Mahāyāna and other Buddhist sects, though they have at times been influential, have never seriously shaken the hold of the form of Buddhism which Ceylon looks on as particularly its own.

It is probable that, by the end of the third century B.C., the doctrines of Theravāda Buddhism were in essentials much as they are now. The monks taught a dynamic phenomenalism, maintaining that everything in the universe, including the gods and the souls of living beings, was in a constant state of flux. Resistance to the cosmic flux of phenomena, and craving for permanence where permanence could not be found, led to inevitable sorrow. Salvation was to be obtained by the progressive abandonment of the sense of individuality, until it was lost completely in the indescribable state known as Nirvāna (Pāli, *Nibbāna,* "blowing out"). The Buddha himself had reached this state, and no longer existed as an individual; nevertheless he was still rather inconsistently revered by his followers, and the less-learned Buddhist layfolk tended to look on him as a sort of high God.

The fundamental truths on which Buddhism is founded are not metaphysical or theological, but rather psychological. Basic is the doctrine of the "Four Noble Truths": (1) that all life is inevitably sorrowful; (2) that sorrow is due to craving; (3) that it can only be stopped by the stopping of craving; and (4) that this can only be done by a course of carefully disciplined and moral conduct, culminating in the life of concentration and meditation led by the Buddhist monk. These four truths, which are the common property of all schools of Buddhist thought, are part of the true Doctrine (Pāli, *dhamma;* Skt. *dharma),* which reflects the fundamental moral law of the universe.

All things are composite, Buddhism would dispute the Hegelian theory that units may organize themselves into greater units which are more than the sum of their parts. As a corollary of the fact that all things are composite they are transient, for the composition of all aggregates is liable to change with time. Moreover, being essentially transient, they have no eternal Self or soul, no abiding individuality. And, as we have seen, they are inevitably liable to sorrow. This threefold characterization of the nature of the world and all that it contains—sorrowful, transient, and soulless—is frequently repeated in Buddhist literature, and without fully grasping its truth no being has any chance of salvation. For until he thoroughly understands the three characteristics of the world a man will inevitably crave for permanence in one form or another, and as this cannot, by the nature of things, be obtained, he will suffer, and probably make others suffer also.

All things in the universe may also be classified into five components, or are composed of a mixture of them: form and matter *(rūpa),* sensations *(vedanā),* perceptions *(saññā),* psychic dispositions or constructions *(saṃkhārā),* and consciousness or conscious thought *(viññāna).* The first consists of the objects of sense and various other elements of less importance. Sensations are the actual feelings arising as a result of the exercise of the six senses (mind being the sixth) upon sense-objects, and perceptions are the cognitions of such sensations. The psychic constructions include all the various psychological emotions, propensities, faculties, and conditions of the individual, while the fifth component, conscious thought, arises from the interplay of the other psychic constituents. The individual is made up of a combination of the five components, which are never the same from one moment to the next, and therefore his whole being is in a state of constant flux.

The process by which life continues and one thing leads to another is explained by the Chain of Causation (*Paṭicca-samuppāda,* lit. Dependent Origination). The root cause of the process of birth and death and rebirth is ignorance, the fundamental illusion that individuality and permanence exist, when in fact they do not. Hence there arise in the organism various psychic phenomena, including desire, followed by an attempt to appropriate things to itself—this is typified especially by sexual craving and sexual intercourse, which are the actual causes of the next links in the chain, which concludes with age and death, only to be repeated again and again indefinitely. Rebirth takes place, therefore, according to laws of karma which do not essentially differ from those of Hinduism, though they are explained rather differently.

As we have seen, no permanent entity transmigrates from body to body, and all things, including the individual, are in a state of constant flux. But each act, word, or thought leaves its traces on the collection of the five constituents which make up the phenomenal individual, and their character alters correspondingly. This process goes on throughout life, and, when the material and immaterial parts of the being are separated in death, the immaterial constituents, which make up what in other systems would be called the soul, carry over the consequential effects of the deeds of the past life, and obtain another body accordingly. Thus there is no permanent soul, but nevertheless room is found for the doctrine of transmigration. Though Buddhism rejects the existence of the soul, this makes little difference in practice, and the more popular literature of Buddhism, such as the *Birth Stories (Jātaka),* takes for granted the existence of a quasi-soul at least, which endures indefinitely. One sect of Buddhism, the *Sammitīya,* which admittedly made no great impression on the religious life of India, actually went so far as to admit the existence of an indescribable substratum of personality *(pudgala),* which was carried over from life to life until ultimately it was dissipated in Nirvāna, thus fundamentally agreeing with the pneumatology of most other Indian religions.

The process of rebirth can only be stopped by achieving Nirvāna, first by adopting right views about the nature of existence, then by a carefully controlled system of moral conduct, and finally by concentration and meditation. The state of Nirvāna cannot be described, but it can be hinted at or suggested metaphorically. The word literally means: blowing out," as of a lamp. In Nirvāna all idea of an individual personality or ego ceases to exist and there is nothing to be reborn—as far as the individual is concerned Nirvāna is annihilation. But it was certainly not generally thought of by the early Buddhists in such negative terms. It was rather conceived of as a transcendent state, beyond the possibility of full comprehension by the ordinary being enmeshed in the illusion of selfhood, but not fundamentally different from the state of supreme bliss as described in other non-theistic Indian systems.

These are the doctrines of the Theravāda school, and, with few variations, they would be assented to by all other schools of Buddhism.

But the Mahāyāna and quasi-Mahāyāna sects developed other doctrines, in favour of which they often gave comparatively little attention to these fundamental teachings.

Of the Lesser Vehicle only one sect survives, the Theravāda, now prevalent in Ceylon, Burma, Thailand, Cambodia, and Laos. There were several others in earlier times, some of which had distinctive metaphysical and psychological systems which approached more closely to those of the Greater Vehicle than did that of the Theravāda. The most important of these sects was perhaps that of the Sarvāstivādins, which stressed the absence of any real entity passing through time in transmigration, but on the other hand maintained the ultimate reality of the chain of events which made up the phenomenal being or object. A sub-sect of the Sarvāstivādins, the Sautrāntikas, emphasized the atomic nature of the component elements of the chain—every instant a composite object disappeared, to be replaced by a new one which came into being as a result of the last. This view of the universe, which appears in the systems of other Buddhist sects in a less emphatic form, is akin to the quantum theory of modern physics.

Another very interesting sect of the Lesser Vehicle was the Mahāsanghika, said to have been the first to break away from the main body of Buddhism. Subdivided into numerous schools, its chief characteristic was the doctrine that the things of the phenomenal world were not wholly real; thus it paved the way for the idealist world-view of Mahāyāna philosophy. Buddhas, on the other hand, according to the fully developed doctrine of the Mahāsanghikas, had full reality, as heavenly beings in a state of perpetual mystic trance, and earthly Buddhas such as the historical Gautama were mere docetic manifestations of the Buddhas in their true state. It is possible that gnostic doctrines from the Middle East influenced this form of Buddhism, which came very close to Mahāyānism, differing only in the doctrine of bodhisattvas.

Buddhism also taught an advanced and altruistic system of morality, which was a corollary to its metaphysics, since one of the first steps on the road to Nirvāna was to do good to others, and thereby weaken the illusion of egoity which was the main cause of human sorrow. Buddhism set itself strongly against animal sacrifice and encouraged vegetarianism, though it did not definitely impose it. It tended towards peace, even if Ashoka's successors did not heed his injunctions to avoid aggression. Its attitude to the system of class and caste is not always definite; while passages in the Buddhist scriptures can be found which attack all claims to superiority by right of birth, the four great classes seem to have been recognized as an almost inevitable aspect of Indian society; but the Buddhist classification of these classes varies significantly from that of the Hindus, for in Buddhist sources the warrior is usually mentioned before the brāhman.

The total literature of Buddhism is so large that it is quite impossible for a single individual to master it in his lifetime. Each of the numerous sects of Buddhism had its version of the sacred scriptures written either in a semi-vernacular Prākritic language or in a form of Sanskrit with peculiar syntax and vocabulary, generally known as "Buddhist Sanskrit." Besides these there was a great body of commentarial literature, and much philosophical and devotional writing of all kinds. Much of the literature of the sects other than the Theravāda has been lost, or only survives in Chinese or Tibetan translations, but the complete canon of Theravāda Buddhism has been fully preserved in Ceylon. It is therefore of fundamental importance in any study of Buddhism. It is written in Pāli, a language related to Sanskrit, and based on an ancient vernacular, probably spoken in the western part of India.

The canon is generally known as *Tripiṭaka* (the *Three Baskets)* after the three sections into which it is divided, namely *Conduct (Vinay), Discourses (Sutta),* and *Supplementary Doctrines (Abhidhamma).* The first *Piṭaka* contains the rules of conduct of the Buddhist order of monks and nuns, usually in connection with narratives which purport to tell the circumstances in which the Buddha laid down each rule. The second *Piṭaka* is the most important; it contains discourses, mostly attributed to the Buddha, divided into five sections: the *Long Group Digha Nikāya)* containing long discourses; the *Medium Group (Mujjhima Nikāya)* with discourses of shorter length; the *Connected Group (Saṃyutta Nikāya),* a collection of shorter pronouncements on connected topics; the *Progressive Group (Aṅguttara Nikāya),* short passages arranged in eleven sections according to the number of topics dealt with in each—thus the three types of sin, in act, word and thought, occur in section three, and so on; and finally the *Minor Group (Khuddaka Nikāya),* a number of works of varying type, including the beautiful and very ancient Buddhisht poems of the *Way of Righteousness (Dhammapada)* and a collection of verses which are filled out by a lengthy prose commentary to form the *Birth Stories (Jātaka)* relating the previous births of the Buddha.

The third *Piṭaka*, the *Supplementary Doctrines*, is a collection of seven works on Buddhist psychology and metaphysics, which are little more than a systematization of ideas contained in the *Discourses*, and are definitely later than the main body of the canon.

There is considerable disagreement about the date of the canon. Some earlier students of Buddhism believed that the *Conduct* and *Discourse Baskets* existed in much the sane form as they do now within a hundred years of the Buddha's death. Later authorities are inclined to believe that the growth of the canon was considerably slower. On the other hand many of the discourses may look back to the Buddha himself, though all have been more or less worked over, and none can be specified with certainty as being his own words. The orthodox tradition itself admits that the *Basket of Supplementary Doctrines (Abhidhamma Piṭaka)* is later than the other two, and was not completed until the time of Ashoka Sinhalese tradition records that the canon was not committed to writing until the reign of King Vattagāmani (89-77 B.C.), and it may not have finished growing until about this time. Thus it is possible that it is the product of as many as four centuries.

There are numerous other works in Pāli which are not generally considered canonical. Perhaps the most important of these works are the standard commentaries on the books of the canon, most of which, it is said, were compiled in Ceylon by the great doctor Buddhaghosa, of the fifth century A.D., from earlier commentaries. As well as passages of explanatory character, the commentaries contain much ancient Buddhist tradition not to be found elsewhere, and the elucidation of the *Jātaka* verses, in plain and vigorous prose, contains some of the finest narrative literature of the ancient world. Buddhaghosa is also the reputed author of a valuable compendium of Buddhist doctrine, *The Way of Purification (Visuddhimagga)*. Another very important Pāli work of early date is *The Questions of King Menander Milindapañha)*, from which several passages are translated here. The inscriptions of Emperor Ashoka (c. 273-232 B.C.) must also be included in any survey, since they are inspired by Buddhism and are at least in part intended to inculcate the morality of Buddhism.

Basic Doctrines of Theravāda Buddhism

The Four Noble Truths

According to Buddhist tradition this was the first sermon preached by the Buddha. After gaining enlightenment under the Tree of Wisdom at Gayā he proceeded to Vārānasī, where, in a park outside the city, he found five ascetics who had formerly been his associates, and who had left him in disgust when he gave up self-mortification and self-starvation as useless in his quest for supreme wisdom. In the presence of these five the Buddha "set in motion the Wheel of the Law" by preaching this sermon, which outlines the Four Noble Truths, the Noble Eightfold Path, and the Middle Way, three of the most important concepts of Buddhism.

[From *Saṃyutta Nikāya,* 5.421 ff.]

Thus I have heard. Once the Lord was at Vārānasī, at the deer park called Isipatana. There he addressed the five monks:

There are two ends not to be served by a wanderer. What are these two? The pursuit of desires and of the pleasure which springs from desire, which is base, common, leading to rebirth, ignoble, and unprofitable; and the pursuit of pain and hardship, which is grievous, ignoble, and unprofitable. The Middle Way of the Tathāghata avoids both these ends. It is enlightened, it brings clear vision, it makes for wisdom, and leads to peace, insight, enlightenment, and Nirvāna. What is the Middle Way? ... It is the Noble Eightfold Path—Right Views, Right Resolve, Right Speech, Right Conduct, Right Livelihood, Right Effort, Right Mindfulness, and Right Concentration. This is the Middle Way....

And this is the Noble Truth of Sorrow. Birth is sorrow, age is sorrow, disease is sorrow, death is sorrow; contact with the unpleasant is sorrow, separation from the pleasant is sorrow, every wish unfulfilled is sorrow—in short all the five components of individuality are sorrow.

And this is the Noble Truth of the Arising of Sorrow. It arises from craving, which leads to rebirth, which brings delight and passion, and seeks pleasure now here, now there—the craving for sensual pleasure, the craving the continued life, the craving for power.

And this is the Noble Truth of the Stopping of Sorrow. It is the complete stopping of that craving, so that no passion remains, leaving it, being emancipated from it, being released from it, giving no place to it.

And this is the Noble Truth of the Way which Leads to the Stopping of Sorrow. It is the Noble Eightfold Path—Right Views, Right Resolve, Right Speech, Right Conduct, Right Livelihood, Right Effort, Right Mindfulness, and Right Concentration.

The Nature of Consciousness and the Chain of Causation

The following *Discourse,* though it purports to be a single utterance of the Buddha, is evidently a conflation of separate passages, bearing on the character of consciousness. It contains a short statement of the contingent nature of consciousness or conscious thought, an appeal for an objective and clear realization that everything whatever is dependent on causes outside itself, an enumeration of the elements of the Chain of Causation, given first in reverse order, an exhortation to the monks not to bother unduly about the question of the survival of the personality and to realize the facts of the Doctrine for themselves, not taking them from the lips of the Teacher, and finally an impressive passage comparing the life of the ordinary man with that of the Buddha, which we have not space to give here.

[From *Majjhima Nikāya,* 1.256 ff.]

Once a certain monk named Sāti, the son of a fisherman, conceived the pernicious heresy that, as he understood the Lord's teaching, consciousness continued throughout transmigration. When they heard this several monks went and reasoned with him... but he would not give in, but held firm to his heresy .... So they went to the Lord and put the matter to him, and he sent a monk to fetch Sāti. When Sāti had come the Lord asked him if it was true that he held this heresy ... and Sāti replied that he did hold it.

"What, then," asked the Lord, "is the nature of consciousness?"

"Sir, it is that which speaks and feels, and experiences the consequences of good and evil deeds."

"Whom do you tell, you foolish fellow, that I have taught such a doctrine? Haven't I said, with many similes, that consciousness is not independent, but comes about through the Chain of Causation, and can never arise without a cause? You misunderstand and misrepresent me, and so you undermine your own position and produce much demerit. You bring upon yourself lasting harm and sorrow!"...

Then the Lord addressed the assembled monks:

> "Whatever form of consciousness arises from a condition is known by the name of that condition; thus if it arises from the eye and from forms it is known as visual consciousness... and so with the senses of hearing, smell, taste, touch, and mind, and their objects. It's just like a fire, which you call by the name of the fuel—a wood fire, a fire of sticks, a grass fire, a cowdung fire, a fire of husks, a rubbish fire, and so on."

"Do you agree, monks, that any given organism is a living being?" "Yes, sir."

"Do you agree that it is produced by food?" "Yes, sir."

"And that when the food is cut off the living being is cut off and dies?" "Yes, sir."

"And that doubt on any of these points will lead to perplexity?" "Yes, sir."

"And that Right Recognition is knowledge of the true facts as they really are?" "Yes, sir."

"Now if you cling to this pure and unvitiated view, if you cherish it, treasure it, and make it your own, will you be able to develop a state of consciousness with which you can cross the stream of transmigration as on a raft, which you use but do not keep?" "No, sir."

"But only if you maintain this pure views, but don't cling to it or cherish it... only if you use it but are ready to give it up?" "Yes, sir."

"There are four bases which support all organisms and beings, whether now existing or yet to be. They are: first, food coarse or fine, which builds up the body; second, contact; third, cogitation; and fourth, consciousness. All four derive and originate from craving. Craving arises from sensation, sensation from contact, contact from the six senses, the six senses from physical form, physical form from consciousness, consciousness from the psychic constructions, and the psychic constructions from ignorance.... To repeat: Ignorance is the cause of the psychic constructions, hence is caused consciousness, hence physical form, hence the six senses, hence contact, hence sensations, hence craving, hence attachment, hence becoming, hence birth, hence old age and death with all the distraction of grief and lamentation, sorrow and despair. This is the arising of the whole body of ill.... So we are agreed that by the complete cessation of ignorance the whole body of ill ceases.

"Now would you, knowing and seeing this, go back to your past, wondering whether you existed or didn't exist long ago, or how you existed, or what you were, or from what life you passed to another?" "No, sir."

"Or would you look forward to the future with the same thoughts?" "No, sir."

"Or would you, knowing and seeing this, trouble yourselves at the present time about whether or not you really exist, what and how you are, whence your being came, and whither it will go." "No, sir."

"Or would you, possessing this knowledge, say, 'We declare it because we revere our teacher'?" "No, sir."

"Or would you say, 'We don't declare it as from ourselves—we were told it by a teacher or ascetic'?" "No, sir."

"Or would you look for another teacher?" "No, sir."

"Ore would you support the rituals, shows, or festivals of other ascetics or brāhmans?" "No, sir."

"Do you only declare what you have known and seen?" "Yes, sir."

"Well done, brethren! I have taught you the doctrine which is immediately beneficial, eternal, open to all, leading them onwards, to be mastered for himself by every intelligent man."

False Doctrines About the Soul

The early Buddhists never ceased to impress upon their hearers the fact that the phenomenal personality was in a constant state of flux, and that there was no eternal soul in the individual in anything like the Hindu sense. On the other hand the perfected being had reached Nirvāna, and nothing could be meaningfully predicated about him. The following passage, attributed to the Buddha himself, criticizes the soul theories of other sects.

[From *Dīgha Nikāya,* 2.64 ff.]

It is possible to make four propositions concerning the nature of the soul— "My soul has form and is minute," "My soul has form and is boundless," "My soul is without form and is minute," and "My soul is without form and boundless." Such propositions may refer to this life or the next....

There are as many ways of not making propositions concerning the soul, and those with insight do not make them.

Again the soul may be thought of as sentient or insentient, or as neither one nor the other but having sentience as a property. If someone affirms that his soul is sentient you should ask, "Sentience is of three kinds, happy, sorrowful, and neutral. Which of these is your soul?" For when you feel one sensation you don't feel the others. Moreover these sensations are impermanent, dependent on conditions, resulting from a cause or causes, perishable, transitory, vanishing, ceasing. If one experiences a happy sensation and thinks "This is my soul," when the happy sensation ceases he will think "My soul has departed." One who thinks thus looks on his soul as something impermanent in this life, a blend of happiness and sorrow with a beginning and end, and so this proposition is not acceptable.

If someone affirms that the soul is not sentient, you should ask, "If you have no sensation, can you say that you exist?" He cannot, and so this proposition is not acceptable.

And if someone affirms that the soul has sentience as a property you should ask, "If all sensations of every kind were to cease absolutely there would be no feelings whatever. Could you then say 'I exist'?" He could not, and so this proposition is not acceptable.

When a monk does not look on the soul as coming under any of these three categories... he refrains from such views and clings to nothing in the world; and not clinging he does not tremble, and not trembling he attains Nirvāna. He knows that rebirth is at an end, that his goal is reached, that he has accomplished what he set out to do, and that after this present world there is no other for him. It would be absurd to say of such a monk, with his heart set free, that he believes that the perfected being survives after death—or indeed that he does not survive, or that he does and yet does not, or that he neither does nor does not. Because the monk is free his state transcends all expression, predication, communication, and knowledge.

The Simile of the Chariot

This passage from the *Questions of King Menander* is among the best known arguments in favour of the composite nature of the individual. The Greek king Milinda, or Menander, ruled in northwestern India about the middle of the second century B.C. According to the text he was converted to Buddhism by Nāgasena, and the wheel which appears on some of his numerous coins would suggest that he was in fact influenced by the Indian religion. The style of the *Questions* is in some measure reminiscent of the Upanishads, but some authorities have thought to find traces of the influence of Plato and have suggested that the author or authors knew Greek. Though in its present form the work may be some centuries later, its kernel may go back to before the Christian era.

[From *Milindapañha* (Trenckner ed.) pp. 25 f.]

Then King Menander went up to the Venerable Nāgasena, greeted him respectfully, and sat down. Nārgasena replied to the greeting, and the King was pleased at heart. Then King Menander asked: "How is your reverence known, and what is your name?"

"I'm known as Nāgasena, you Majesty, that's what my fellow monks call me. But though my parents may have given me such a name... it's only a generally understood term, a practical designation. There is no question of a permanent individual implied in the use of the word."

"Listen, you five hundred Greeks and eighty thousand monks!" said King Menander. "This Nāgasena has just declared that there's no permanent individuality implied in his name!" Then, turning to Nāgasena, "If, Reverend Nāgasena, there is no permanent individuality, who gives you monks your robes and food, lodging and medicines? And who makes use of them? Who lives a lift of righteousness, meditates, and reaches Nirvāna? Who destroys living beings, steals, fornicates, tells lies, or drinks spirits? ... If what you say is true there's neither merit nor demerit, and no fruit or result of good or evil deeds If someone were to kill you there would be no question of murder And there would be no masters or teachers in the [Buddhist] Order and no ordinations. If your fellow monks call you Nāgasena, what then is Nāgasena? Would you say that your hair is Nāgasena?" "No, your Majesty."

"Or your nails, teeth, skin, or other parts of your body, or the outward form, or sensation, or perception, or the psychic constructions, or consciousness? Are any of these Nāgasena?" "No, you Majesty."

"Then are all these taken together Nāgasena?" "No, your Majesty."

"Or anything other than they?" "No, your Majesty."

"Then for all my asking I find no Nāgasena. Nāgasena is a mere sound! Surely what your Reverence has said is false!"

Then the Venerable Nāgasena addressed the King.

"Your Majesty, how did you come here—on foot, or in a vehicle?"

"In a chariot."

"Then tell me what is the chariot? Is the pole the chariot?" "No, your Reverence."

"Or the axle, wheels, frame, reins, yoke, spokes, or goad?" "None of these things is the chariot."

"Then all these separate parts taken together are the chariot?" "No, your Reverence."

"Then is the chariot something other than the separate parts?" "No, your Reverence."

"Then for all my asking, your Majesty, I can find no chariot. The chariot is a mere sound. What then is the chariot? Surely what your Majesty has said is false! There is no chariot!..."

When he had spoken the five hundred Greeks cried "Well done!" and said to the King, "Now, your Majesty, get out of that dilemma if you can!"

"What I said was not false," replied the King. "It's on account of all these various components the pole, axle, wheels, and so on, that the vehicle is called a chariot. It's just a generally understood term, a practical designation."

"Well said, your Majesty! You know that the word 'chariot' means! And it's just the same with me. It's on account of the various components of my being that I'm known by the generally understood term, the practical designation Nāgasena."

Change and Identity

After convincing Menander of the composite nature of the personality by the simile of the chariot, Nāgasena shows him by another simile how it is continually changing with the passage of time, but possesses a specious unity through the continuity of the body.

[From *Milindapañha* (Trenckner ed.), p. 40]

"Reverend Nāgasena," said the King, "when a man is born does he remain the same [being] or become another?"

"He neither remains the same nor becomes another."

"Give me an example!"

"What do you think, your Majesty? You were once a baby lying on your back, tender and small and weak. Was that baby you, who are now grown up?"

"No, your Reverence, the baby was one being and I am another."

"If that's the case, your Majesty, you had no mother or father, and no teachers in learning, manners, or wisdom.... Is the boy who goes to school one [being] and the young man who has finished his education another? Does one person commit a crime and another suffer mutilation for it?"

"Of course not, your Reverence! But what do your say on the question?"

"I am the being I was when I was a baby," said the Elder... "for through the continuity of the body all stages of life are included in a pragmatic unity."

"Give me an illustration."

"Suppose a man were to light a lamp, would it burn all through the night?" "Yes, it might."

"Now is the flame which burns in the middle watch the same as that which burned in the first?" "No, your Reverence."

"Or is that which burns in the last watch the same as that which burned in the middle?" "No, your Reverence."

"So is there one lamp in the first watch, another in the middle, and yet another in the last?"

"No. The same lamp gives light all through the night."

"Similarly, your Majesty, the continuity of phenomena is kept up. One person comes into existence, another passes away, and the sequence runs continuously without self-conscious existence, neither the same nor yet another."

"Well said, Reverend Nāgasena!"

The Process of Rebirth

In this little passage Nāgasena presses the analogy of the lamp further, and shows Menander how rebirth is possible without any soul, substratum of personality, or other hypothetical entity which passes from the one body to the other.

[From *Milindapañha* (Trenckner ed.), p. 71]

"Reverend Nāgasena," said the King, "is it true that nothing transmigrates, and yet there is rebirth?"

"Yes, your Majesty."

"How can this be?... Give me an illustration."

"Suppose, your Majesty, a man lights one lamp from another—does the one lamp transmigrate to the other?"

"No, your Reverence."

"So there is rebirth without anything transmigrating!"

Karma

Buddhism accepted the prevailing doctrine of karma, though it had an original explanation of the process whereby karma operated. In this passage from the *Questions of King Menander* karma is adduced as the reason for the manifest inequalities of human fate and fortune. Had Nāgasena been disputing with an Indian king instead of with a Greek one the question would not have been asked, for the answer would have been taken for granted.

[From *Milindapañha* (Trenckner ed.), p. 65]

"Venerable Nāgasena," asked the King, "why are men not all alike, but some short-lived and some long, some sickly and some healthy, some ugly and some handsome, some weak and some strong, some poor and some rich, some base and some noble, some stupid and some clever?"

"Why, your Majesty," replied the Elder, "are not all plants alike, but some astringent, some salty, some pungent, some sour, and some sweet?"

"I suppose, your Reverence, because they come from different seeds."

"And so it is with men! They are not alike because of different karmas. As the Lord said... 'Beings each have their own karma. They are... born through karma, they become members of tribes and families through karma, each is ruled by karma, it is karma that divides them into high and low.'"

"Very good, your Reverence!"

Right Mindfulness

The following passage is of interest as showing the means which the monk should take in order thoroughly to realize the transience and otherness of all things, and thus draw near to Nirvāna. The *bhāvanās,* or states of mind, are practiced by Buddhist monks to this day, and are part of "Right Mindfulness," the seventh stage of the Noble Eightfold Path. The translation is considerably abridged.

[From *Majjhima Nikāya,* 1.420 ff.]

The Lord was staying at Sāvatthī at the monastery of Anāthapindaka in the Grove of Jeta. One morning he dressed, took his robe and bowl, and went into Sāvatthī for alms, with the Reverend Rāhula following close behind him. As they walked the Lord,... without looking round, spoke to him thus:

"All material forms, past, present, or future, within or without, gross or subtle, base or fine, far or near, all should be viewed with full understanding—with the thought 'This is not mine, this is not I, this is not my soul.' "

"Only material forms, Lord?"

"No, not only material forms, Rāhula, but also sensation, perception, the psychic constructions, and consciousness."

"Who would go to the village to collect alms today, when he has been exhorted by the Lord himself?" said Rāhula. And he turned back and sat cross-legged, with body erect, collected in thought.

Then the Venerable Sāriputta, seeing him thus, said to him: "Develop concentration on inhalation and exhalation, for when this is developed and increased it is very productive and helpful."

Towards evening Rāhula rose and went to the Lord, and asked him how he could develop concentration on inhalation and exhalation. And the Lord said:

"Rāhula, whatever is hard and solid in an individual, such as hair, nails, teeth, skin, flesh, and so on, is called the personal element of earth. The personal element of water is composed of bile, phlegm, pus, blood, sweat, and so on. The personal element of fire is that which warms and consumes or burns up, and produces metabolism of food and drink in digestion. The personal element of air is the wind in the body which moves upwards or downwards, the winds in the abdomen and stomach, winds which move from member to member, and the inhalation and exhalation of the breath. And finally the personal element of space comprises the orifices of ears and nose, the door of the mouth, and the channels whereby food and drink enter, remain in, and pass out of the body. These five personal elements, together with the five external elements, make up the total of the five universal elements. They should all be regarded objectively, with right understanding, thinking 'This is not mine, this is not me, this is not my soul.' With this understanding attitude a man turns from the five elements and his mind takes no delight in them.

"Develop a state of mind like the earth, Rāhula. For on the earth men throw clean and unclean things, dung and urine, spittle, pus and blood, and the earth is not troubled or repelled or disgusted. And as you grow like the earth no contacts with pleasant or unpleasant will lay hold of your mind or stick to it.

"Similarly you should develop a state of mind like water, for men throw all manner of clean and unclean things into water and it is not troubled or repelled or disgusted. And similarly with fire, which burns all things, clean and unclean, and with air, which blows upon them all, and with space, which is nowhere established.

"Develop the state of mind of friendliness, Rāhula, for, as you do so, ill-will will grow less; and of compassion, for thus vexation will grow less; and of joy, for thus aversion will grow less; and of equanimity, for thus repugnance will grow less.

"Develop the state of mind of consciousness of the corruption of the body, for thus passion will grow less; and of the consciousness of the fleeting nature of all things, for thus the pride of selfhood will grow less.

"Develop the state of mind of ordering the breath,... in which the monk goes to the forest, or to the root of a tree or to an empty house, and sits cross-legged with body erect, collected in thought. Fully mindful he inhales and exhales. When he inhales or exhales a long breath he knows precisely that he is doing so, and similarly when inhaling or exhaling a short breath. While inhaling or exhaling he trains himself to be conscious of the whole of his body,... to be fully conscious of the components of his mind,... to realize the impermanence of all things,... or to dwell on passionlessness.... or renunciation. Thus the state of ordered breathing, when developed and increased, is very productive and helpful. And when the mind is thus developed a man breathes his last breath in full consciousness, and not unconsciously."

The Last Instructions of the Buddha

The following passage occurs in the *Discourse of the Great Passing-away (Mahāparinibbāna Sutta)* which describes the last days and death of the Buddha. The Master, an old and ailing man, is on the way to the hills where he was born, and where soon he is to die. These are among his last recorded instructions to his disciples. Unfortunately we cannot be sure of their authenticity; the fine phrases concerning "the closed fist of the teacher" are particularly suspect, for they are just the sort of interpolation which an earnest Theravāda monk would be likely to make, in order to discredit the doctrines of schismatics of a Mahāyānist type, who claimed to possess the esoteric teachings of the Master. But, whether authentically the Buddha's words or not, the following passage perhaps gives the quintessence of Theravāda Buddhism, with its call for self-reliant striving against all that seems base and evil.

[From *Dīgha Nikāya*, 2.99 f., 155-56]

Soon after this the Lord began to recover, and when he was quite free from sickness he came out of his lodging and sat in its shadow on a seat spread out for him. The Venerable Ānanda went up to him, paid his respects, sat down to one side, and spoke to the Lord thus:

> "I have seen the Lord in health, and I have seen the Lord in sickness; and when I saw that the Lord was sick my body became as weak as a creeper, my sight dimmed, and all my faculties weakened. But yet I was a little comforted by the thought that the Lord would not pass away until he had left his instructions concerning the Order."

"What, Ānanda! Does the Order expect that of me? I have taught the truth without making any distinction between exoteric and esoteric doctrines; for...with the Tathāgata there is no such thing as the closed fist of the teacher who keeps some things back. If anyone thinks 'It is I who will lead the Order,' or 'The Order depends on me,' he is the one who should lay down instructions concerning the Order. But the Tathāgata has no such thought, so why should he leave instructions? I am old now, Ānanda, and full of years; my journey nears its end, and I have reached my sum of days, for I am nearly eighty years old. Just as a worn out cart can only be kept going if it is tied up with thongs, so the body of the Tathāgata can only be kept going by bandaging it. Only when the Tathāgata no longer attends to any outward object, when all separate sensation stops and he is deep in inner concentration, is his body at ease.

"So, Ānanda, you must be your own lamps, be your own refuges. Take refuge in nothing outside yourselves. Hold firm to the truth as a lamp and a refuge, and do not look for refuge to anything besides yourselves. A monk becomes his own lamp and refuge by continually looking on his body, feelings, perceptions, moods, and ideas in such a manner that he conquers the cravings and depressions of ordinary men and is always strenuous, self-possessed, and collected in mind. Whoever among my monks does this, either now or when I am dead, if he is anxious to learn, will reach the summit." [p. 99 f.]

"All composite things must pass away. Strive onward vigilantly." [pp. 155-56]

The Buddha in Nirvāna

This brief passage from the *Questions of King Menander* illustrates the Theravāda conception of Nirvāna. It is not total annihilation, but at the same time it involves the complete disintegration of the phenomenal personality—a paradox which cannot be explained in words.

[From *Milindpañha* (Trenckner, ed.), p. 73]

"Reverend Nāgasena," said the King, "does the Buddha still exist?"

"Yes, your Majesty, he does,"

"Then is it possible to point out the Buddha as being here or there?"

"The Lord has passed completely away in Nirvāna, so that nothing is left which could lead to the formation of another being. And so he cannot be pointed out as being here or there."

"Give me an illustration."

"What would your Majesty say—if a great fire were blazing, would it be possible to point to a flame which had gone to and say that it was here or there?"

"No, your Reverence, the flame is extinguished, it can't be detected."

"In just the same way, your Majesty, the Lord has passed away in Nirvāna.... He can only be pointed out in the body of his doctrine, for it was he who taught it."

"Very good, Reverend Nāgasena!"

The City of Righteousness

This fine passage, from the latter part of the *Questions of King Menander*, is probably the work of a hand different from that which composed the dialogues which we have already quoted. In it the Buddha almost takes on the character of a saviour God, who, like Amitābha in the developed Mahāyāna mythology, built a heaven for his followers. Nirvāna is not described in negative terms, but in very positive ones, and the metaphor of the busy, populous, and prosperous city hardly suggests the rarified Nirvāna of the previous passage, but a heaven in which personality is by no means lost. It suggests in fact to the Western reader the New Jerusalem of the Book of Revelation. Clearly this passage is the work of a writer whose attitude approached closely to that of Mahāyāna, but it must be remembered that Theravāda Buddhists look on the text from which it is taken as semi-canonical.

[From *Milindapañha* (Trenckner ed.), pp. 330 ff.]

The builder of a city... first chooses a pleasant and suitable site; he makes it smooth, and then sets to work to build his city fair and well proportioned, divided into quarters, with ramparts round about it.... And when the city is built, and stands complete and perfect, he goes away to another land. And in time the city becomes rich and prosperous, peaceful and happy, free from plague and calamity, and filled with people of all classes and professions and of all lands.... even with Scythians, Greeks, and Chinese..... All these folk coming to live in the new city and finding it so well planned, faultless, perfect, and beautiful exclaim: "Skilled indeed must be the builder who built this city!"

So the Lord... in his infinite goodness... when he had achieved the highest powers of Buddhahood and had conquered Māra and his hosts, tearing the net of false doctrine, casting aside ignorance, and producing wisdom,... built the City of Righteousness.

The Lord's City of Righteousness has virtue for its ramparts, fear of sin for its moat, knowledge for its gates, zeal for its turrets, faith for its pillars, concentration for its watchman, wisdom for its palaces. The *Basket of Discourses* is its marketplace, the *Supplementary Doctrines* its roads, the *Conduct* its court of justice, and earnest self-control is its main street.....

The Lord laid down the following subjects for meditation: the ideas of impermanence, of the non-existence of an enduring self, of the impurity and of the wretchedness of life, of ridding oneself of evil tendencies, of passionlessness, of stopping the influx of evil tendencies, of dissatisfaction with all things in the world, of the impermanence of all conditioned things, of mindful control of breath, of the corpse in disintegration, of the execution of criminals with all its horrors; the ideas of friendliness, of compassion, of joy, of equanimity, the thought of death, and mindfulness of the body.... Whoever wishes to be free from age and death takes one of these as a subject for meditation, and thus he is set free from passion, hatred, and dullness, from pride and from false views; he crosses the ocean of rebirth, dams the torrent of his cravings, is washed clean of the threefold stain [of passion, hatred, and dullness], and destroys all evil within him. So he enters the glorious city of Nirvāna, stainless and undefiled, pure and white, unaging, deathless, secure and calm and happy, and his mind is emancipated as a perfected being.

The Ethics of Theravāda Buddhism

In the sphere of personal relations Buddhism inculcated a morality gentler and more humanitarian than the stern early Hindu ethic, based chiefly on duty rather than fellowship. The four cardinal virtues of Buddhism—friendliness, compassion, joy, and equanimity—are extolled in many passages of the scriptures. The *Birth Stories* teach friendly relations between man and man and between man and animal, and encourage the warm virtues of family love, brotherhood, and honesty (not to speak of shrewdness) in one's dealings with others. Though the surviving Buddhist religious literature is chiefly intended for the monastic community Buddhism certainly had, and still has a message going far beyond the monastery to the millions of ordinary believers who have no hope of Nirvāna until after many lives, but who may yet rise in the scale of being by faith in the teaching of the Buddha, by service to the Buddhist Order, and by fair dealing with their fellows.

In this connection we would draw attention to the most important passage on lay morality in the Pāli scriptures—the *Discourse of Admonition to Siṅgāla (Siṅgālovāda Sutta).* It is a solid bourgeois morality tha: thix text encourages. Like many older writings of Protestant Christianity it stresses the virtue of thrift—expensive ceremonies and domestic rituals are wasteful as well as useless; fairs and festivals lead men to squander precious time and wealth; from the layman's point of view drink and gambling are evil chiefly for the same reasons; to increase the family estates is a meritorious act. But there is more in the *Discourse* than this. In modern terms the ideal it sets forth is of a society in which each individual respects the other's personality, an intricate network of warm and happy human relaitonships, where parents and children, teachers and pupils, husbands and wives, masters and servants, and friends and friends look on one another as ends in themselves, and dwell together in mutual respect and affection, each helping the other upward in the scale of being through a cosmos which, though theoretically a vale of tears, yet contains pleasant places and gives many opportunities for real if transient happiness if fellowship with friends and kin. And the inevitable sorrow of all who are born only to grow old and pass away, the lonely anguish of the individual being who finds himself at odds with an unfiendly universe, can only be lessened, at least for the ordinary layman, by brotherhood.

The Morals of the Monk

The following extract is part of a long panegyric of the Buddha, leading up to a description of his perfect wisdom. The moral virtues attributed to him in the earlier part of the passage, which is quoted here, are those after which every monk should strive; and, allowing for their different circumstances, the monk's example should be followed as far as possible by the layman.

[From *Dīgha Nikāya,* 1.4 ff.]

The monk Gautama has given up injury to life, he has lost all inclination to it; he has laid aside the cudgel and the sword, and he lives modestly, full of mercy, desiring in compassion the welfare of all things living.

He has given up taking what is not given, he has lost all inclination to it. He accepts what is given to him and waits for it to be given; and he lives in honesty and purity of heart....

He has given up unchastity, he has lost all inclination to it. He is celibate and aloof, and has lost all desire for sexual intercourse, which is vulgar....

He has given up false speech, he has lost all inclination to it. He speaks the truth, he keeps faith, he is faithful and trustworthy, he does not break his word to the world....

He has given up slander, he has lost all inclination to it. When he hears something in one place he will not repeat it in another in order to cause strife,... but he unites those who are divided by strife, and encourages those who are friends. His pleasure is in peace, he loves peace and delights in it, and when he speaks he speaks words which make for peace....

He has given up harsh speech, he has lost all inclination to it. He speaks only words that are blameless, pleasing to the ear, touching the heart, cultured, pleasing the people, loved by the people....

He has given up frivolous talk, he has lost all inclination to it. He speaks at the right time, in accordance with the facts, with words full of meaning. His speech is memorable, timely, well illustrated, measured, and to the point.

He does no harm to seeds or plants. He takes only one meal a day, not eating at night, or at the wrong time. He will not watch shows, or attend fairs with song, dance, and music. He will not wear ornaments, or adorn himself with garlands, scents, or cosmetics. He will not use a high or large bed. He will not accept gold or silver, raw grain or raw meat. He will not accept women or girls, bondmen or bondwomen, sheep or goats, fowls or pigs, elephants or cattle, horses or mares, fields or houses. He will not act as go-between or messenger. He will not buy or sell, or falsify with scales, weights, or measures. He is never crooked, will never bribe, or cheat, or defraud. He will not injure, kill, or put in bonds, or steal, or do acts of violence.

Care of the Body

The Buddhist Order was very solicitous for the bodily health of its members, and the Buddha is reported to have said, on one occasion: "He who would care for me should care for the sick." Buddhist monasteries often served as dispensaries, and it has been suggested that one of the reasons for the spread of Buddhism in Southeast Asia and elsewhere was the medical lore of the Buddhist monks, which. though of course primitive by modern standards, was superior to anything known to the local inhabitants, and thus added to the reputation of the new religion.

The *Questions of King Menander* explains the apparent anomaly that a system which stressed to strongly the evils of the things of the flesh should also value physical wellbeing so highly.

[From *Milindapañha* (Trenckner ed.), pp. 73-74]

The King said: "Reverend Nāgasena, is the body dear to you wanderers?"

"No, your Majesty."

"Then why do you feed it and care for it so well?"

"Have you ever gone to battle, and been wounded by an arrow?"

"Yes, your Reverence, I have."

"And in such a case isn't the wound smeared with ointment, anointed with oil, and bound with a bandage?"

"Yes, that's what is done."

"And is the wound dear to you, your Majesty, that you care for it so well?"

"Certainly not! All those things are done to make the flesh grow together again."

"So, you see, wanderers do not hold the body dear, your Majesty! Without clinging to it they bear the body in continence, for the Lord declared that the body was like a wound....

'Covered with clammy skin, with nine openings, a great wound,

The body oozes from every pore, unclean and stinking.' "

"Well spoken, Reverend Nāgasena!"

"Lay Not Up for Yourselves Treasures upon Earth...."

In theory "right views" about the nature of the world are the first step along the Eightfold Path. But the Buddhist literature meant chiefly for laymen tends to emphasize right actions rather than right views. Whatever the beliefs of a man may be, his good deeds and self-discipline are an unfailing source of merit, and lead to a happier rebirth, which may give him the opportunity for further spiritual progress. We quote the following little passage partly because it recalls a famous verse of the Sermon on the Mount. Notice that the treasure "cannot be given to others." This is the doctrine of the Theravāda sect. The Mahāyāna teaches that the merit accruing from good deeds can be transferred by a voluntary act of will, and men are encouraged, by the example of the compassionate bodhisattvas (See Chapter VII), to make such transfers of merit.

[From *Khuddaka Pāṭha,* 8]

A man buries a treasure in a deep pit, thinking: "It will be useful in time of need, or if the king is displeased with me, or if I am robbed or fall into debt, or if food is scarce, or bad luck befalls me."

But all this treasure may not profit the owner at all, for he may forget where he has hidden it, or goblins may steal it, or his enemies or even his kinsmen may take it when he is careless.

But by charity, goodness, restraint, and self-control man and woman alike can store up a well-hidden treasure—a treasure which cannot be given to others and which robbers cannot steal. A wise man should do good—that is the treasure which will not leave him.

The Virtue of Friendliness

The following poem is evidently a conflation from two sources, for in the middle of the third verse its whole tone changes, and in place of a rather pedestrian enumeration of the Buddhist virtues we have an impassioned rhapsody on the theme of friendliness *(mettā),* the first of the four cardinal virtues. "Mindfulness of friendliness" is among the daily exercises of the monk, and can also be practised by the layman; he detaches himself in imagination from his own body, and, as though looking down on himself, pervades himself with friendliness directed towards himself, for it is impossible to feel true friendliness or love for others unless, in the best sense of the term, one feels it for oneself; then he proceeds in imagination to send waves of friendliness in every direction, to reach every being in every corner of the world. After pervading the world with love he may repeat the process with the three other cardinal virtues—compassion, joy, and equanimity. These forms of the practice of "right mindfulness" are known as *Brahma-vihāras,* freely translated, "sublime moods." They are still practised by Buddhists throughout the world, and it is believed, especially among the Mahāyānist sects, that the waves of friendliness constantly poured out by many thousands of meditating monks have a very positive effect on the welfare of the world.

[From *Sutta Nipāta,* p. 143 ff.]

This a man should do who knows what is good for him,
Who understands the meaning of the Place of Peace [i.e., Nirvāna]—
He should be able, upright, truly straight,
Kindly of speech, mild, and without conceit.

He should be well content, soon satisfied,
Having few wants and simple tastes,
With composed senses, discreet,
Not arrogant or grasping....

In his deeds there should be no meanness
For which the wise might blame him.

May all be happy and safe!
May all beings gain inner joy—
All living beings whatever
Without exception, weak or strong,
Whether long or high
Middling or small, subtle or gross,
Seen or unseen,
Dwelling afar or near,
Born or yet unborn—
May all beings gain inner joy.

May no being deceive another,
Nor in any way scorn another,
Nor, in anger or ill-will,
Desire another's sorrow.

As a mother cares for her son,
Her only son, all her days,
So towards all things living
A man's mind should be all-embracing.
Friendliness for the whole world,
All-embracing, he should raise in his mind,
Above, below, and across,
Unhindered, free from hate and ill-will.

Standing, walking or sitting,
Or lying down, till he falls asleep,
He should remain firm in this mindfulness,
For this is the sublime mood.
Avoiding all false views,
Virtuous, filled with insight,
Let him conquer the lust of the passions,
And he shall never again be born of the womb.

Hatred and Love

The idea of "turning the other cheek" in one's personal relations is frequently to be found in Buddhist literature. Nevertheless there are few condemnations of warfare, as distinct from acts of violence on the part of individuals, and the Theravāda scriptures contain no passages on this latter topic as forthright as Ashoka's Thirteenth Rock-Edict (quoted later). The following verses from the *Way of Righteousness* exemplify these points.

[From *Dhammapada,* 3-5, 201]

"He insulted me, he struck me,
He defeated me, he robbed me!"
Those who harbour such thoughts
Are never appeased in their hatred....
But whose who do not harbour them
Are quickly appeased.

Never in this world is hate
Appeased by hatred;
It is only appeased by love—
This is an eternal law *(sanantana-dhamma).*

Victory breeds hatred
For the defeated lie down in sorrow.
Above victory or defeat
The calm man dwells in peace.

Buddhism and Everyday Life

The *Admonition to Siṅgāla* is the longest single massage in the Pali scriptures devoted to lay morality. Though put in the mouth of the Buddha, it is probably not authentically his; parts of it, however, may be based on a few transmitted recollections of his teaching. Like many other *Discourses* it seems to emanate from more than one source, for the earlier part, enumerating the many sins and faults to which the layman is liable, and describing the true friend, is divided by a series of verses from the later and finer passage, defining the duties of the layman in his sixfold relationship with his fellows.

The reader should notice the solid, frugal, mercantile virtues which are inculcated, especially in the first part. This sermon is evidently not directed chiefly at the very poor or the very rich, but at the prosperous middle class. Also noteworthy are the paragraphs on the duties of husbands and wives and masters and servants in the second part of the sermon—if read in terms of rights rather than of duties they seem to imply the wife's right to full control of household affairs and to an adequate dress allowance, and the employee's right to fair wages and conditions, regular holidays, and free medical attention.

[From *Dīgha Nikāya,* 3.180 ff.]

Once when the Lord was staying in the Bamboo Grove at Rajagaha, Singāla, a householder's son, got up early, went out from Rājagaha, and, with his clothes and hair still wet from his morning ablutions, joined his hands in reverence and worshiped the several quarters of earth and sky—east, south, west, north, above, and below. Now early that same morning the Lord dressed himself, and with bowl and robe went into Rājagaha to beg his food. He saw Singāla worshiping the quarters, and asked him why he did so.

"When my father lay dying," Singāla replied, "he told me to worship the quarters thus. I honour my father's words, and respect and revere them, and so I always get up early and worship the quarters in this way."

"But to worship the six quarters thus is not in accordance with noble conduct."

"How then, Sir, should they be worshipped in accordance with noble conduct? Will the Lord be so good as to tell me?"

"Listen then" said the Lord, "and I'll tell you. Mark well what I say!"

"I will, Sir," Singāla replied. And the Lord spoke as follows:

> "If the noble lay-disciple has given up the four vices of action, if he does not evil deed from any of the four motives, if he doesn't follow the six ways of squandering his wealth, if he avoids all these fourteen evils—then he embraces the six quarters, he is ready for the conquest of both worlds, he is fortunate both in this world and the next, and when his body breaks up on his death he is reborn to bliss in heaven.

"What are the four vices of action that he gives up? They are injury to life, taking what is not given, base conduct in sexual matters, and false speech....

"What are the four motives of evil deeds which he avoids? Evil deeds are committed from partiality, enmity, stupidity, and fear.

"And what are the six ways of squandering wealth? They are addiction to drink, the case of carelessness; roaming the streets at improper times; frequenting fairs; gambling; keeping bad company; and idleness.

"There are six dangers in addiction to drink: actual loss of wealth; increased liability to quarrels; liability to illness; loss of reputation; indecent exposure; and weakened intelligence.

"There are six dangers in roaming the streets at improper times: the man who does so is unprotected and unguarded; so are his wife and children; and likewise his property; he incurs suspicion of having committed crime; he is the subject of false rumours; in fact he goes out to meet all kinds of trouble.

"There are six dangers in frequenting fairs: the man who does so becomes an insatiable addict of dancing; singing; music; story-telling; jugglers; or acrobats.

"There are six dangers in gambling: the winner incurs hatred; the loser regrets his lost money; there is obvious loss of wealth; a gambler's word is not respected in the law courts; he is scorned by his friends and counselors; and he is not cultivated by people who want to marry their daughters, for the rogue who's always dicing isn't fit to keep a wife.

"There are six dangers in keeping bad company: a man who does so has as his friends and companions rogues; libertines; drunkards; confidence men; swindlers; and toughs.

"And there are six dangers in idleness; A man says, 'it's too cold' and doesn't word; or he says, 'it's too hot'; or 'it's too early'; or 'it's too late'; or 'I' am too hungry'; or 'I' m too full.' And so all the while he won't do what he ought to do, and he earns no new wealth, but fritters away what he has already earned.

"There are four types who should be looked on as enemies in the guise of friends: a grasping man; a smooth-spoken man; a man who only says what you want to hear; and a man who helps you waste your money.

"The grasping man is an enemy on four grounds: he is grasping; when he gives a little he expects a lot in return; what duty he performs he does out of fear; and he only serves his own interests.

"The smooth-spoken man is an enemy on four grounds: he speaks you fair about the past; he speaks you fair about the future; he tries to win you over by empty promises; but when there's something to be done he shows his shortcomings.

"The man who only says what you want to hear is an enemy on four grounds: he consents to an evil deed; he doesn't consent to a good one; he praises you to your face; but he runs you down behind your back.

"The wastrel is an enemy on four grounds: he is your companion when you drink; when you roam the streets at improper times; when you go to fairs; and when you gamble.

"But there are four types who should be looked on as friends true of heart: a man who seeks to help you; a man who is the same in weal and woe; a man who gives good advice; and a man who is sympathetic....

The friend who is a helper,
The friend in weal and woe,
The friend who gives good counsel,
The friend who sympathizes—
These the wise man should know
As his four true friends,
And should devote himself to them
As a mother to the child of her body.

The wise and moral man
Shines like a fire on a hilltop,
Making money like the bee,

Who does not hurt the flower.
Such a man makes his pile
As an anthill, gradually.
The man grown wealthy thus
Can help his family
And firmly bind his friends
To himself. He should divide
His money in four parts;
On one part he should live,
With two expand his trade,
And the fourth he should save
Against a rainy day.

"And how does the noble lay-disciple embrace the six quarters? He should recognize these as the six quarters: mother and father as the east; teachers as the south; wife and children as the west; friends and counsellors as the north; slaves and servants as below; and ascetics and brāhmans as above.

"A son should serve his mother and father as the eastern quarter in five ways: having been maintained by them in his childhood he should maintain them in their old age; he should perform the duties which formerly devolved on them; he should maintain the honour and the traditions of his family and lineage; he should make himself worthy of his heritage; and he should make offerings to the spirits of the departed. And thus served by their son as the eastern quarter his mother and father should care for him in five ways: they should restrain him from evil; encourage him to do good; have him taught a profession; arrange for his marriage to a suitable wife; and transfer his inheritance to him in due time. Thus he embraces the eastern quarter and makes it safe and propitious.

"A pupil should serve his teacher as the southern quarter in five ways: by rising [to greet him when he enters]; by waiting upon him; by willingness to learn; by attentive service; and by diligently learning his trade. And thus served by his pupil as the southern quarter a teacher should care for him in five ways: he should train him in good conduct; teach him in such a way that he remembers what he has been taught; thoroughly instruct him in the lore of every art [of his trade]; speak well of him to his friends and counsellors; and protect him in every quarter. Thus he embraces the southern quarter and makes it safe and propitious.

"A husband should serve his wife as the western quarter in five ways: by honouring her; by respecting her; by remaining faithful to her; by giving her charge of the home; and by duly giving her adornments. And thus served by her husband as the western quarter a wife should care for him in five ways: she should be efficient in her household tasks; she should manage her servants well; she should be chaste; she should take care of the goods which he brings home; and she should be skillful and untiring in all her duties. Thus he embraces the western quarter and makes it safe and propitious.

"A gentleman should serve his friends and counsellors as the northern quarter in five ways: by generosity; by courtesy; by helping them; by treating them as he would treat himself; and by keeping his word to them. And thus served by a gentleman as the northern quarter his friends and counsellors should care for him in five ways: they should protect him when he is careless; they should guard his property on such occasions; they should be a refuge for him in trouble; in misfortune they should not leave him; and they should respect other members of his family. Thus he embraces the western quarter and makes it safe and propitious.

"A master should serve his slaves and servants as the lower quarter in five ways: he should assign them work in proportion to their strength; he should give them due food and wages; he should care for them in sickness; he should share especially tasty luxuries with them; and he should give them holidays at due intervals. Thus served by their master as the lower quarter they should care for him in five ways: they should get up before him; they should go to bed after him; they should be content with what he gives them; they should do their work well; and they should spread abroad his praise and good name. Thus he embraces the lower quarter and makes it safe and propitious.

"In five ways a gentleman should serve ascetics and brāhmans as the upper quarter: by affectionate acts; by affectionate words; by affectionate thoughts; by not closing his doors to them; and by duly supplying them with food. Thus served by a gentleman as the upper quarter they should care for him in six ways: they should restrain him from evil; they should encourage him to do good; they should feel for him with a friendly mind; they should teach him what he has not heard before; they should encourage him to follow what he has already learned; and they should show him the way to heaven. Thus he embraces the upper quarter and makes it safe and propitious."

Society and the State in Theravāda Buddhism

Few pages in the massive literature of Buddhism lay down definite instructions on social or political life, and the amount of speculation by Buddhist authors on the problems of state and society is not large. Indeed Buddhism has sometimes been stigmatized as not a true religion at all, but a mere system of self-discipline for monks, with no significant message for the ordinary man except that he should if possible leave the world and take the yellow robe. In fact Buddhists have always realized that not every layman was morally or intellectually capable of becoming a monk, and the scriptures, as we have seen above, do contain here and there instructions especially intended for layfolk, together with occasional passages with a social or political message. Nevertheless it may be that one of the reasons for the disappearance of Buddhism in the land of its birth was that it left the laymen too dependent on the ministrations of the brāhmans, and, instead of giving a lead in political and social matters, was too often willing to compromise with the existing ways of everyday life.

Though in practice Buddhism seems to have accepted the existence of a society with sharp class divisions and to have made no frontal attack on it, there are many passages in Buddhist literature in which the four classes of Hindu society are declared to be fundamentally equal, and in which men are said to be worthy of respect not through birth, but only through spiritual or moral merit. Though we cannot show that Buddhism had any definite effect on the Indian system of class and caste, its teachings obviously tended against the extremer manifestations of social inequality. In those lands where Buddhism was implanted upon societies little influenced by Hindu ideas the caste system in its Indian form is not to be found.

In politics Buddhism definitely discouraged the pretensions of kings to divine or semidivine status. While Hindu teachers often declared that kings were partial incarnations of the gods and encouraged an attitude of passive obedience to them, the Buddhist scriptures categorically state that the first king was merely the chosen leader of the people, appointed by them to restrain crime and protect property, and that his right to levy taxation depended not on birth or succession but on the efficient fulfillment of his duty. The *Birth Stories*, among the most influential of the Buddhist scriptures, contain several tales of wicked kings overthrown as a result of popular rebellion. Thus Buddhism had a rational attitude to the state. The constitution of the Buddhist order, in which each monastery was virtually a law unto itself, deciding major issues after free discussion among the assembled monks, tended toward democracy, and it has been suggested that it was based on the practices of the tribal republics of the Buddha's day. Though Buddhism never formulated a distinctive system of political ethics it generally tended to mitigate the autocracy of the Indian king.

On the question of war Buddhism said little, though a few passages in the Buddhist scriptures oppose it. Like the historical Ashoka, the ideal emperor of Buddhism gains his victories by moral suasion. This did not prevent many Buddhist kings of India and Ceylon from becoming great conquerors and pursuing their political aims with much the same ruthlessness as their Hindu neighbours. Two of pre-Muslim India's greatest conquerors, Harsha of Kanauj (666-647) and Dharmapāla of Bihār and Bengal (c. 770-810), were Buddhists. In fact Buddhism had little direct effect on the political order, except in the case of Ashoka, and its leaders seem often to have been rather submissive to the temporal power. An Erastian relationship between church and state is indicated in the inscriptions of Ashoka, and in Buddhist Ceylon the same relationship usually existed.

Early travellers have left a number of valuable accounts of conditions in ancient India. Two of these, that of the Greek Megasthenes (c. 300 B.C.) and that of the Chinese pilgrim Fa-hsien (A.D. c. 400), are of special interest for our purposes, for the first was written before Buddhism had become an important factor in Indian life, and the second when it had already passed its most flourishing period and had entered on a state of slow decline. Megasthenes found a very severe judicial system, with many crimes punished by execution or mutilation. The existence of such a harsh system of punishment is confirmed by the famous Hindu text on polity, the *Arthaśāstra,* the kernel of which dates from about the same time. Under Chandragupta Maurya, the grandfather of Ashoka, the state was highly organized and all branches of human activity were hemmed in by many troublesome regulations enforced by a large corps of government officials. Fa-hsien, on the other hand, found a land where the death penalty was not imposed, and mutilation was inflicted only for very serious crime; and he was especially impressed by the fact that human freedom was respected and people were able to move freely from one part of the land to the other without passports or other forms of interference from the government. In Megasthenes' day all classes freely ate meat, while in the time of Fa-hsien only the outcastes did so. It seems certain that Buddhism had something to do with the great change in the direction of mildness and nonviolence which had taken place in the seven hundred years between the two travellers. Certainly Buddhism was not the only factor in the change, for sentiments in favour of tolerance, mildness, and non-violence are to be found also in Hindu and Jain writings, but it is very probable that Buddhism was the greatest single factor, for it was the most active and vigorous religion in the period in question.

Though Ashoka was practically forgotten by India his message calling for good relations between rulers and ruled was not, and echoes of it may be heard in many non-Buddhist sources of later date. On the other hand his fond hope that aggressive wars would cease forever as a result of his propaganda was unfulfilled, and the successors of Ashoka seem to have been if anything more militant than his predecessors. It would seem that Buddhism had little effect in encouraging peace within the borders of India.

How the World Evolved

Buddhism, like all Indian religious systems, believed that the world goes through periods of evolution and decline. While it did not reject the existence of the gods, it denied that they had any significant effect upon the cosmic process. Brahmā, at the time of the Buddha a much more important figure than he became in later Hinduism, imagines that he is the creator, when in fact the world came into being through the operation of natural laws. In Brahmā's case the primal ignorance, which affects gods and men alike, has led to the wish fathering the thought. The following passage is attributed to the Buddha himself.

[From *Dīgha Nikāya,* 3.28 ff.]

There are some monks and brāhmans who declare as a doctrine received from their teachers that the beginning of all things was the work of the god Brahmā. I have gone and asked them whether it was true that they maintained such a doctrine, and they have replied that it was; but when I have asked them to explain just how the beginning of things was the work of the god Brahmā they have not been able to answer, and have returned the question to me. Then I have explained it to them thus:

There comes a time, my friends, sooner or later,... when the world is dissolved and beings are mostly reborn in the World of

Radiance. There they dwell, made of the stuff of mind, feeding on joy, shining in their own light, flying through middle space, firm in their bliss for a long, long time.

Now there comes a time when this world begins to evolve, and then the World of Brahmā appears, but it is empty. And some being, whether because his allotted span is past or because his merit is exhausted, quits his body in the World of Radiance and is born in the empty World of Brahmā, where he dwells for a long, long time. Now because he has been so long alone he begins to feel dissatisfaction and longing, and wishes that other beings might come and live with him. And indeed soon other beings quit their bodies in the World of Radiance and come to keep him company in the World of Brahmā.

Then the being who was first born there thinks: "I am Brahmā, the mighty Brahmā, the Conqueror, the Unconquered, the All-seeing, the Lord, the Maker, the Creator, the Supreme Chief, the Disposer, the Controller, the Father of all that is or is to be. I have created all these beings, for I merely wished that they might be and they have come here!" And the other beings... think the same, because he was born first and they later. And the being who was born first lived longer and was more handsome and powerful than the others.

And it might well be that some being would quit his body there and be reborn in this world. He might then give up his home for the homeless life [of an ascetic]; and in his ardor, striving, intentness, earnestness, and keenness of thought, he might attain such a stage of meditation that with collected mind he might recall his former birth, but not what went before. Thus he might think: "We were created by Brahmā, eternal, firm, everlasting, and unchanging, who will remain so for ever and ever, while we who were created by the Lord Brahmā... are transient, unstable, short-lived, and destined to pass away."

That is how your traditional doctrine comes about that the beginning of things was the work of the god Brahmā.

The Origin of Society and the State

This most important and interesting legend should be read as a sequel to the former passage, since it describes a further stage in the process of cosmic evolution. It tells of the gradual progress of humanity, on account of its own greed, from the blissful golden age when there was no need of food or clothing to a fully evolved society with a king and class system. It should be noted especially that neither the state nor the class system has any ultimate sanction other than human expediency. The first king holds office by virtue of a contract with his subjects, and this is probably one of the world's oldest versions of the contractual theory of the state. The passage concludes by emphasizing the fundamental equality of all the four classes. Again the words are attributed to the Buddha.

[From *Dīgha Nikāya,* 3.80 ff.]

Sooner or later, after a long, long time... there comes a time when this world passes away. Then most living beings pass to the World of Radiance, and there they dwell, made of the stuff of mind, feeding on joy, shining in their own light, flying through middle space, firm in their bliss for a long, long time. Sooner or later there comes a time when this world begins to evolve once more. Then those being who pass away from the World of Radiance are usually born here on earth; but they are still made of the stuff of mind... and are firm in their bliss for a long, long time.

At that time the world is wholly covered in water, dark with a blinding darkness. No moon or sun, no constellations are to be seen, nor the forms of stars; there are no nights or days, no phases of the moon or months, no seasons or years. And there are no men or women then, for the beings living on earth are simply reckoned as beings. And for those beings, after a long, long time, a sweet earth is spread out on the waters, just as the skin forms on the surface of hot milk as it cools. And it had colour, fragrance and flavour, for it was the colour of fine ghee or butter, and sweet as the choicest honey.

Then a certain being, greedy from a former birth, said, "What can this be?" and tasted the sweet earth with his finger. He was delighted with the flavour, and craving overcame him. Then others followed his example, and tasted the earth,... until they were all feasting on it, breaking off pieces with their hands. And as they did so their radiance faded; and as it faded the moon and sun appeared, with the constellations and the forms of stars, nights and days, phases of the moon and months, seasons and years....

Beings continued thus, feeding on the sweet earth, for a long, long time. And the more they ate the more solid their bodies became, some beautiful and some ugly. And the beautiful scorned the ugly, boasting of their greater beauty. And as they became vain and conceited because of their beauty the sweet earth disappeared....

Then growths appeared on the soil, coming up like mushrooms, with colour, scent and flavour like those of the sweet earth. The beings began to eat those growths, and so they continued for a long, long time... until the growths too disappeared.

Then creeping plants arose, growing like rattans; and the beings lived on them until the creepers too disappeared....

Then, when the creepers had vanished, rice appeared, already ripe in the untilled soil, without dust or husk, fragrant and clean-grained. If they gathered it in the evening and took it away for supper it would grow and be ripe again by the next morning. If they gathered it in the morning for breakfast it would grow and be ripe again by the evening. It grew without a pause. And those beings continued to live on the rice... for a long, long time, and their bodies became more and more solid, and their differences in beauty, even more pronounced. In women female characteristics appeared, and in men male. The women looked at the men too intently, and the men at the women, and so passion arose, and a raging fire entered their bodies. In consequence they took to coupling together. When people saw them doing so some threw dust at them, others ashes, others cowdung, and shouted, "Perish, you foul one! Perish, you foul one!! How could one person treat another like that?" And even now people in certain districts, when a bride is led away after a wedding, throw dust or ashes or cowdung, and repeat the custom of long ago, but do not understand its significance.

What was considered immoral in those days is now considered moral. For in those days the people who took to coupling together were not allowed to enter a village or town for a month afterward or even for two. So, as they incurred so much blame for their immorality, they took to building huts in order to conceal it.

Then someone of a lazy disposition thought to himself, "Why do I go to the trouble of fetching rice night and morning? I'll fetch enough for supper and breakfast in one journey!" Then another man saw him and said, "Come on, my friend, let's go and fetch our rice!" "I've got enough," the first man replied, "I've fetched enough in one journey for both supper and breakfast." So the second man followed the first man's example, and fetched enough rice for two days at once. [Thus gradually people took to storing enough rice for as much as eight days at a time].... And from the time that people took to feeding on stored rice and grain became covered with dust, and husks enveloped it; the reaped stems did not grow again, and there were pauses in its growth, when the stubble stood in clumps.

Then the people gathered together and lamented, saying: "Evil customs have appeared among men. Once we were made of the stuff of mind ... and were firm in our bliss for a long, long time.... But now, through our evil and immoral ways, we have degenerated until our grain has become covered with dust.... and the stubble stands in clumps. So let us divide the rice fields, and set up boundary marks."

Then someone of a greedy disposition, while watching his own plot, appropriated another plot that had not been given to him, and made use of it. The people seized him and said: "You've done an evil deed in taking and using a plot which was not given to you. Don't let it happen again!" "Very well," he replied. But he did the same thing again and yet a third time. Once more the people seized him and admonished him in the same terms, but this time some of them struck him with their hands, some with clods, and some with sticks. From such beginnings arose theft, censure, false speech, and punishment.

Then the people gathered together and lamented, saying: "Evil ways are rife among the people—theft, censure, false speech, and punishment have appeared among us. Let us choose one man from among us, to dispense wrath, censure, and banishment when they are right and proper, and give him a share of our rice in return. So they chose the most handsome,... attractive, and capable among them and invited him to dispense anger, censure, and banishment. He consented and did so, and they gave him a share of their rice.

Mahāsammata means approved *(sammata)* by the whole people *(mahājana)*, and hence Mahāsammata was the first name of be given to a ruler. He was lord of the fields *(khettānam)* and hence *khattiya* [Skt. *kṣatriya*] was his second name. He pleases *(rañjeti)* others by his righteousness—hence his third name, *rājā*. This was the origin of the class of kshatriyas, according to the tale of long ago. They originated from those same folk and no others, people like themselves, in no way different; and their origin was quite natural and not otherwise.

Then it happened that some men thought, "Evil ways are rife among the people... Now let us put away such evil and unwholesome ways." The word *brāhman* implies that they put away *(būhenti)* such evil and unwholesome ways, and so brāhman became their earliest name. They built themselves huts of leaves in the woodland, and there they sat and meditated. They had no more use for charcoal or the smoke of cooking, or for the pestle and mortar, but they went out to villages, towns, or cities, seeking their food, in the evening their supper, in the morning their breakfast. When they had enough to eat they came back and meditated in their huts, and so they were given the second name of mystics *(jhāyaka)* because they meditated *(jhāyanti)*.

Now some of them grew tired of meditating in their huts, and so they went away, settled on the outskirts of villages and towns, and made books. When they saw this the people said, "These good folk can't meditate!", and so they were called teachers *(ajjhāyaka)*, and this became their third name. In those days these teachers were looked on as the lowest of brāhmans, but now they are thought the best. This was the origin of the class of brāhmans.... They originated quite naturally and not otherwise.

There were other people who married and took to all kinds of crafts and trades; and because they took to all kinds *(vissa)* of crafts and trades they were called *vessa* [Skt. *vaiśya*]. This was the origin of the class of vaishyas.... They originated quite naturally and not otherwise.

Those who remained were hunters. Those who live by hunting *(ludda)* have a man *(khudda)* trade, and thus they were called *sudda* (Skt. *śūdra)*. This was the origin of the class of shūdras.... They originated quite naturally and not otherwise.

Then there came a time when a kshatriya, scorning his own way of life, went out from his home and took up the homeless life, thinking to become an ascetic—[and then a brāhman, a vaishya, and a shūdra did the same]. From these four classes arose the class of ascetics.... And they too originated quite naturally and not otherwise.

A kshatriya who has led a bad life, whether in deed, word, or thought, and who has had wrong views about the world, because of his outlook and his deeds will be reborn after parting with his body in the waste and woeful pit of purgatory. And a brāhman, a vaishya, and a shūdra will fare likewise. If on the other hand they lead good lives in thought, word, and deed, and have right views about the world, they will be reborn in the happy world of heaven. If their lives and their views are mixed they will be reborn in a state where they feel both happiness and sorrow. But if they are self-restrained in body, speech and mind... they may find Nirvāna, even in this present life.

For whoever from among the members of these four classes becomes a monk and later a perfected being, with all his stains destroyed, has done what he had to do; he has laid down his burden, gained salvation, destroyed the bonds of becoming; he is free in his perfect wisdom. And he is declared to be to the chief of them all, by the law of Righteousness and not otherwise; for the Law is the best thing men can have, both in this life and the next.

The Ideal of Government and the Decay and Growth of Civilization

The following *Discourse,* again attributed to the Buddha, attempts, like the preceding one, to account for the origin of crime and evil, but it gives a different answer. According to a former passage crime began in the state of nature, and kingship was introduced to suppress it. Here government precedes crime. The golden age has its governments and indeed its conquests, but they are not conquests by the sword. It seems more than likely that this account of the Universal Emperor's peaceful victories over his neighbours is in some way linked with Ashoka's "Conquest by Righteousness," and we are inclined to believe that the present passage is post-Ashokan. Note that sin and crime, and the consequent lowering of the standards of civilization and of human conditions generally, are said to be due to the shortcomings of the ruler, and especially to his failure to continue the policy of his predecessors in caring for the poor. Hence crime appears, morality declines, and with it the standards of life deteriorate, until, after a brief period of complete anarchy, human love and fellowship again prevail, and gradually restore the golden age. Interesting is the reference to Metteya (Sanskrit, *Maitreya*), the future Buddha. This indicates that the *Discourse* is a comparatively late one. Our version is considerably abridged.

[From *Dīgha Nikāya,* 3.58 ff.]

In the past... there was a king called Dalhanemi. He was a Universal Emperor... a king of Righteousness, a conqueror of the four quarters, a protector of his people, a possessor of the Seven Jewels—the Wheel, the Elephant, and Horse, the Gem, the Woman, the Householder, and the General. He had over a thousand sons, all heroes brave of body, crushers of enemy armies. He conquered the earth from ocean to ocean and ruled it not by the rod or by the sword, but by the Law of Righteousness.

Now after many thousands of years King Dalhanemi ordered one of his men thus: "When you see that the Divine Wheel has sunk or slipped from its place, come and tell me." ... And after many thousand years more the man saw that the Divine Wheel had sunk .... and went and told the King. So King Dalhanemi sent for his eldest son, and said: "Dear boy, the Divine Wheel has sunk, and I've been told that when the Wheel of a Universal Emperor sinks he has not long to live. I have had my fill of human pleasure—now the time has come for me to look for divine joys. Come, dear boy, you must take charge of the earth..." So King Dalhanemi duly established his eldest son on the throne, shaved his hair and beard, put on yellow robes, and left his home for the state of homelessness. And when the royal sage had left his home seven days the Divine Wheel completely vanished.

Then a certain man went to the King, the anointed warrior, and told him that it has vanished. He was beside himself with sorrow. So he went to the royal sage his father and told him about it. "Don't grieve that the Divine Wheel has disappeared," he said, "The Divine Wheel isn't an heirloom, my dear boy! You must follow the noble way of the Universal Emperors. If you do this and keep the fast of the full moon on the upper terrace of your palace the Divine Wheel will be seen again, complete with its thousand spokes, it tire, its nave, and all its other parts."

"But what, your Majesty, is the noble way of the Universal Emperors?"

"It is this, dear boy, that you should rely on the Law of Righteousness, honour, revere, respect, and worship it. You should be yourself the banner of Righteousness, the emblem of Righteousness, with Righteousness as your master. According to Righteousness you should guard, protect, and watch over your own family and people, your armed forces, your warriors, your officers, priests and householders, townsmen and country folk, ascetics and brāhmans, beasts and birds. There should be no evil-doing throughout your domains, and whoever is poor in your land should be given wealth.... Avoid evil and follow good. That is the noble way of the Universal Emperors."

"Very good, your Majesty," the King replied, and he followed the way of the Universal Emperors, until one day the Divine Wheel revealed itself... complete and whole. And he thought: "A king to whom the Divine Wheel reveals itself thus becomes a Universal Emperor—so may I now become such a Universal Emperor." He uncovered one shoulder, took a pitcher of water in his left hand, and sprinkled the Divine Wheel with his right, saying: "Roll on, precious Wheel! Go forth and conquer, lordly and precious Wheel!"

Then the precious Wheel rolled on towards the east, and the King followed it with his fourfold army. Wherever the Wheel stopped the Universal Emperor encamped with his army, and all the kings of the east came to him and said, "Come, your Majesty! Welcome, your Majesty! All this is yours, Your Majesty! Command, us, your Majesty!" And the Universal Emperor said, "Do not take life; do not take what is not yours; do not act basely in sexual matters; do not tell falsehoods; do not drink spirits. Now enjoy your kingdoms as you have done in the past." And all the kings of the east submitted to him.

Then the Divine Wheel plunged into the eastern ocean, and rose again and rolled towards the south. And so the Wheel conquered the south, west, and north, until it had covered the whole earth from sea to sea. Then it returned to the capital, and stood at the door of the Universal Emperor's private apartments, facing the council hall, as though fixed to the place, adorning the inner palace.

With the passage of many thousands of years other kings did as this one had done, and became Universal Emperors—and it all happened as it had done before. But one day a Universal Emperor left his palace to become an ascetic, and his son, who succeeded him, heard that the Divine Wheel had vanished, but, though grieved at its disappearance, did not go to his father, the royal sage, to ask about the noble way of the Universal Emperors. He ruled the land according to his own ideas, and the people were not governed as they had been in the past; so they did not prosper as they had done under former kings who had followed the noble way of the Universal Emperors.

Then the ministers and counsellors, the officers of the treasury, the captains of the guard, the ushers, and the magicians, came to the King in a body and said: "The people do not prosper, your Majesty, because you govern them according to your own ideas. Now, we maintain the noble way of the Universal Emperors. Ask us about it and we will tell you." The King asked them about it and they explained it to him. When he had heard them he provided for the care and protection of the land, but he did not give wealth to the poor, and so poverty became widespread. Soon a certain man took what had not been given to him, and this was called stealing. They caught him and accused him before the King.

"Is it true that you have taken what was not given to you?" asked the King.

"It is, your Majesty," replied the man.

"But why did you do it?"

"Because I'd nothing to live on, your Majesty."

Then the King gave him wealth, saying, "With this keep yourself alive, care for your father and mother, children and wife, follow a trade, and give alms to ascetics and brāhmans, to help yourself along the way to heaven."

"I will, your Majesty," he replied.

And another man stole and was accused before the King, and the King rewarded him in just the same way. People heard of this and thought that they would do the same in order to receive wealth from the King. But when a third man was brought before the King and accused of theft the King thought: "If I give wealth to everyone who takes another man's property theft will increase. I'll put a stop to this! I'll sentence him to execution and have him beheaded!"

So he ordered his men to tie the culprit's arms tightly behind him with a strong rope, to shave his head with a razor, to lead him from street to street and from square to square to the strident sound of the drum, and to take him out of the southern gate of the city, and there to cut off his head. And they did as the King commanded.

But when people heard that thieves were to be put to death they thought: "We'll have sharp swords made, and when we steal we'll cut off the heads of those we rob." And they did so, and looted in village and town and city, besides committing highway robbery.

Thus, where formerly wealth had been given to the poor, poverty became widespread. Hence came theft, hence the sword, hence murder ... and hence the span of life was shortened and men lost their comeliness, until where the fathers had lived for eighty thousand years the sons lived for only forty thousand.

Then it happened that a certain man stole and was accused, and when the King asked him whether it was true that he had stolen he replied, "No." Thus lying became widespread, and where the fathers had lived for forty thousand years the sons lived for only twenty thousand.

And again, when a certain man took what was not given him, another man came to the King and said: "So and so has taken what was not given him, he has committed ... theft." Thus he spoke evil of the thief. So speaking evil of others became widespread, until where the fathers had lived for twenty thousand years the sons lived for only ten thousand.

Now some people were handsome and some ugly. And the ugly were jealous of the handsome, and took to committing adultery with other men's wives. So base conduct in sexual matters became widespread, and men's life-span and comeliness diminished until where the fathers had lived for ten thousand years the sons lived for only five thousand.

Next abusive speech and foolish gossip increased, and so where the fathers had lived for five thousand years the sons lived some for two thousand five hundred and some for two thousand years. Then cupidity and ill-will increased, and the life-span became only one thousand years. With the growth of false doctrines it fell to five hundred, and then incest, inordinate greed, and unnatural lust spread, and hence the span of life dropped to two hundred and fifty or two hundred years. Finally three further sins—disrespect for father and mother, disrespect for ascetics and brāhmans, and refusal to heed the head of the family—reduced man's life to one hundred years.

A time will come when the descendants of these people will live for only ten years, and when girls will reach puberty at the age of five. Then there will not be even the taste of ghee, butter, sesamum oil, sugar, or salt, and the finest food of the men of that time will be mere millet, where now it is rice and curry. Among those men... good deeds will entirely disappear, and evil deeds will flourish exceedingly—there will not even be a word for good, much less anyone who does good deeds. Those who do not honour mother and father, ascetic and brāhman, and those who do not heed the head of the family will be respected and praised, just as today those who do these things are respected and praised.

Among those people there will be no distinction of mother or aunt or aunt-by-marriage or teacher's wife—society will be just as promiscuous as goats and sheep, fowls and pigs, dogs and jackals. There will be bitter enmity one with another, bitter ill-will, bitter animosity, bitter thoughts of murder, and parents will feel toward their children, children toward their parents, brothers toward their brothers... as a hunter feels toward a deer.

Then there will be a transitional period of the Seven Days of the Sword, during which men will look upon one another as wild beasts, and with sharp swords in their hands will take one another's lives.... But a few will think: "We don't want anyone to kill us and we don't want to kill anyone. Let us hide in grassland, in jungle, in hollow trees, in rivermarshes, or in the rough places of the mountains, and live on the roots and fruits of the forest."

And thus they will survive. And after the Seven Days of the Sword are passed they will come out and embrace one another, and with one accord comfort one another, saying, "How good it is, my friend, to see you still alive!" Then they will say: "We have lost so many of our kinsfolk because we took to evil ways—now we must do good! But what good deed can we do? We must stop taking life—that is a good custom to adopt and maintain!"

They will do this, and increase in both age and comeliness. And their virtues will increase until once more they live to the age of eighty thousand years and girls reach puberty at the age of five hundred.... India will be rich and prosperous, with villages and towns and cities so close together that a cock could fly from one to the next. India will be as crowded then as purgatory is now, as full of people as a thicket is of canes or reeds. Vārānasī... will be a rich and prosperous capital, full of people, crowded, and flourishing, and there will be born Sankha, a Universal Emperor, who will... like Dalhanemi... conquer the earth from ocean to ocean and rule it... by the Law of Righteousness.

And among those people will be born the Lord Metteya, the perfected being, the fully enlightened, endowed with wisdom and virtue, the blessed, the knower of all the worlds, the supreme guide of willing men, the teacher of gods and men, a Lord Buddha, even as I am now. Like me, with his own insight, he will know the world and see it clearly, with its spirits, with Māra, with Brahmā, with its ascetics and brāhmans, with its gods and men. He will teach the Law of Righteousness in spirit and in letter, lovely in its beginning, lovely in its middle, lovely in its end, and he will live the pure life of celibacy in all its completeness, just as I do now. But he will have thousands of monks as his followers, where I have only hundreds.

Conditions of the Welfare of Societies

The following passage occurs in the *Discourse of the Great Passing-away,* which describes the last days and death of the Buddha. Though the words are put into his own mouth, it is quite likely that the passage is based on a series of popular aphorisms current among the Vajjian tribesmen themselves. It is followed by a longer passage in which the Buddha is purported to have adapted the list of the seven conditions of the welfare of republics to the circumstances of the Buddhist Order. According to a tradition preserved by the commentator Buddhaghosa, King Ajātasattu's wily minister Vassakāra, hearing the Buddha's words, set to work by "fifth column" methods to sow dissension among the leaders of the Vajjis, with the result that Magadha was able to annex their lands within a few years.

Notice especially the third condition. No early Indian sect took kindly to innovation, and according to orthodox Hindu thought the purpose of government was not to legislate, but only to administer the eternal law *(Sanātanadharma)*. Though the Buddhists had a somewhat different conception of dharma they shared the conservatism of the Hindus in this respect. Nevertheless new legislation was enacted from time to time, as will be seen later in the edicts of Ashoka.

[From *Dīgha Nikīya,* 2.72 ff.]

Once the Lord was staying at Rājagaha on the hill called Vulture's Peak... and the Venerable Ānanda was standing behind him and fanning him. And the Lord said: "Have you heard, Ānanda, that the Vajjis call frequent public assemblies of the tribe?" "Yes, Lord," he replied.

"As long as they do so," said the Lord, "they may be expected not to decline, but to flourish."

"As long as they meet in concord, conclude their meetings in concord, and carry out their policies in concord;... as long as they make no laws not already promulgated, and set aside nothing enacted in the past, acting in accordance with the ancient institutions of the Vajjis established in olden days;... as long as they respect, esteem, reverence, and support the elders of the Vajjis, and look on it as a duty to heed their words;... as long as no women or girls of their tribes are held by force or abducted;... as long as they respect, esteem, reverence, and support the shrines of the Vajjis, whether in town or country, and do not neglect the proper offerings and rites laid down and practised in the past;... as long as they give due protection, deference, and support to the perfected beings among them so that such perfected beings may come to the land from afar and live comfortably among them, so long may they be expected not to decline, but to flourish.

Birth is No Criterion of Worth

Though in practice it would seem that Indian Buddhists maintained the system of class and caste, the theoretical attitude of Buddhism was equalitarian. We have seen that the division of the four classes was believed to be a functional one, with no divine sanction. The Buddhist view is summed up in the verse of the *Discourse Section* (*Sutta Nipāta,* verse 136):

> No Brāhman is such by birth.
> No outcaste is such by birth.
> An outcaste is such by his deeds.
> A brāhman is such by his deeds.

In the following passage the Buddha puts forward numerous arguments in favour of this view, though many other passages show that lay Buddhists were encouraged to treat worthy brāhmans with respect.

[From *Majjhima Nikāya,* 2.147 ff.]

Once when the Lord was staying at Sāvatthī there were five hundred brāhmans from various countries in the city... and they thought: "This ascetic Gautama preaches that all four classes are pure. Who can refute him?"

At that time there was a young Brāhman named Assalāyana in the city,... a youth of sixteen, thoroughly versed in the Vedas... and in all brāhmanic learning. "He can do it!", thought the brāhmans, and so they asked him to try; but he answered, "The ascetic Gautama teaches a doctrine of his own, and such teachers are hard to refute. I can't do it!" They asked him a second time... and again he refused; and they asked him a third time, pointing out that he ought not to admit defeat without giving battle. This time he agreed, and so, surrounded by a crowd of Brāhmans, he went to the Lord, and, after greeting him, sat down and said:

"Brāhmans maintain that only they are the highest class, and the others are below them. They are white, the others black; only they are pure, and not the others. Only they are the true sons of Brahmā, born from his mouth, born of Brahmā, creations of Brahmā, heirs of Brahmā. Now what does the worthy Gautama say to that?"

"Do the brāhmans really maintain this, Asslāyana, when they're born of women just like anyone else, of brāhman women who have their periods and conceive, give birth and nurse their children, just like any other women?"

"For all you say, this is what they think...."

"Have you ever heard that in the lands of the Greeks and Kambojas and other peoples on the borders there are only two classes, masters and slaves, and a master can become a slave and vice versa?"

"Yes, I've heard so."

"And what strength or support does that fact give to the brāhmans claim?"

"Nevertheless, that is what they think."

"Again if a man is a murderer, a thief, or an adulterer, or commits other grave sins, when his body breaks up on death does he pass on to purgatory is he's a kshatriya, vaishya, or shūdra, but not if he's a brāhman?"

"No, Gautama. In such a case the same fate is in store for all men, whatever their class."

"And if he avoids grave sin, will he go to heaven if he's a brāhman but not if he's a man of the lower classes?"

"No, Gautama. In such a case the same reward awaits all men, whatever their class."

"And is a brāhman capable of developing a mind of love without hate or ill-will, but not a man of the other classes?"

"No, Gautama. All four classes are capable of doing so."

"Can only a brāhman go down to a river and wash away dust and dirt, and not men of the other classes?"

"No, Gautama, all four classes can."

"Now suppose a king were to gather together a hundred men of different classes and to order to the brāhmans and kshatriyas to take kindling wood of sāl, pine, lotus or sandal, and light fires, while the low class folk did the same with common wood. What do you think would happen? Would the fires of the high-born men blaze up brightly... and those of the humble fail?"

"No, Gautama. It would be alike with high and lowly... Every fire would blaze with the same bright flame."...

"Suppose there are two young brāhman brothers, one a scholar and the other uneducated. Which of them would be served first at memorial feasts, festivals, and sacrifices, or when entertained as guests?"

"The scholar, of course; for what great benefit would accrue from entertaining the uneducated one?"

"But suppose the scholar is ill-behaved and wicked, while the uneducated one is well-behaved and virtuous?"

"Then the uneducated one would be served first, for what great benefit would accrue from entertaining an ill-behaved and wicked man?"

"First, Assalāyana, you based your claim on birth, then you gave up birth for learning, and finally you have come round to my way of thinking, that all four classes are equally pure!"

At this Assalāyana sat silent... his shoulders hunched, his eyes cast down, thoughtful in mind, and with no answer at hand.

Ashoka: The Buddhist Emperor

The great emperor Ashoka (c. 268-233 B.C.), third of the line of the Mauryas, became a Buddhist and attempted to govern India according to the precepts of Buddhism as he understood them. His new policy was promulgated in a senses of edicts, which are still to be found, engraved on rocks and pillars in many parts of India. Written in a form of Prākrit, or ancient vernacular, with several local variations, they can claim little literary merit, for their style is crabbed and often ambiguous. In one of these edicts he describes his conversion, and its effects:

[From the Thirteenth Rock Edict]

When the king, Beloved of the Gods and of Gracious Mien, had been consecrated eight years Kalinga was conquered, 150,000 people were deported, 100,000 were killed, and many times that number died. But after the conquest of Kalinga, the Beloved of the Gods began to follow Righteousness (Dharma), to love Righteousness, and to give instruction in Righteousness. Now the Beloved of the Gods regrets the conquest of Kalinga, for when an independent country is conquered people are killed, they die, or are deported, and that the Beloved of the Gods finds very painful and grievous. And this he finds even more grievous—that all the inhabitants—brāhmans, ascetics, and other sectarians, and householders who are obedient to superiors, parents, and elders, who treat friends, acquaintances, companions, relatives, slaves, and servants with respect, and are firm in their faith—all suffer violence, murder, and separation from their loved ones. Even those who are fortunate enough not to have lost those near and dear to them are afflicted at the misfortunes of friends, acquaintances, companions, and relatives. The participation of all men in common suffering is grievous to the Beloved of the Gods. Moreover there is no land, except that of the Greeks, where groups of brāhmans and ascetics are not found, or where men are not members of one sect or another. So now, even if the number of those killed and captured in the conquest of Kalinga had been a hundred or a thousand times less, it would be grievous to the Beloved of the Gods. The Beloved of the Gods will forgive as far as he can, and he even conciliates the forest tribes of his dominions; but he warns them that there is power even in the remorse of the Beloved of the Gods, and he tells them to reform, lest they be killed.

For all beings the Beloved of the Gods desires security, self-control, calm of mind, and gentleness. The Beloved of the Gods considers that the greatest victory is the victory of Righteousness; and this he has won here (in India) and even five hundred leagues beyond his frontiers in the realm of the Greek king Antiochus, and beyond Antiochus among the four kings Ptolemy, Antigonus, Magas, and Alexander. Even where the envoys of the Beloved of the Gods have not been sent men hear of the way in which he follows and teaches Righteousness, and they too follow it and will follow it. Thus he achieves a universal conquest, and conquest always gives a feeling of pleasure; yet it is but a slight pleasure, for the Beloved of the Gods only looks on that which concerns the next life as of great importance.

I have had this inscription of Righteousness engraved that all my sons and grandsons may not seek to gain new victories, that in whatever victories they may gain they may prefer forgiveness and light punishment, that they may consider the only [valid] victory the victory of Righteousness, which is of value both in this world and the next, and that all their pleasure may be in Righteousness....

Ashoka's Buddhism, as his title shows, did not lessen his belief in the gods. Here he expresses his faith in Buddhism, and declares that the gods have appeared on earth as a result of his reforms:

[From a minor Rock Edict (Maski Version)]

Thus speaks Ashoka, the Beloved of the Gods. For two and a half years I have been an open follower of the Buddha, though at first I did not make much progress. But for more than a year now I have drawn closer to the [Buddhist] Order, and have made much progress. In India the gods who formerly did not mix with men now do so. This is the result of effort, and may be obtained not only by the great, but even by the small, through effort—thus they may even easily win heaven.

Father and mother should be obeyed, teachers should be obeyed; pity... should be felt for all creatures. These virtues of Righteousness should be practised.... This is an ancient rule, conducive to long life.

[From the Ninth Rock Edict]

It is good to give, but there is no gift, no service, like the fit of Righteousness. So friends, relatives, and companions should preach it on all occasions. This is duty; this is right; by this heaven may be gained—and what is more important than to gain heaven?

The emphasis on morality is if anything intensified in the series of the seven Pillar Edicts, issued some thirteen years after the Rock Edicts, when the king had been consecrated twenty-six years:

[From the First Pillar Edict]

This world and the other are hard to gain without great love of Righteousness, great self-examination, great obedience, great circumspection, great effort. Through my instruction respect and love of Righteousness daily increase and will increase.... For this is my rule—to govern by Righteousness, to administer by Righteousness, to please my subjects by Righteousness, and to protect them by Righteousness.

Ashoka's solicitude extended to the animal life of his empire, which in ancient India was generally thought to be subject to the king, just as was human life. He banned animal sacrifices at least in his capital, introduced virtual vegetarianism in the royal household, and limited the slaughter of certain animals; his policy in this respect is made clear in his very first Rock Edict:

[From the First Rock Edict]

Here no animal is to be killed for sacrifice, and no festivals are to be held, for the king finds much evil in festivals, except for certain festivals which he considers good.

Formerly in the Beloved of the God's kitchen several hundred thousand animals were killed daily for food; but now at the time of writing only three are killed—two peacocks and a deer, though the deer not regularly. Even these three animals will not be killed in future.

[From the Second Pillar Edict]

I have in many ways given the fit of clear vision. On men and animals, birds and fish I have conferred many boons, even to saving their lives; and I have done many other good deeds.

In accordance with the precepts of Buddhism Ashoka, for all his apparent other-worldliness, did not neglect the material welfare of his subjects, and was specially interested in giving them medical aid:

[From the Second Rock Edict]

Everywhere in the empire of the Beloved of the Gods, and even beyond his frontiers in the lands of the Cholas, Pāndyas, Satyaputras, Keralaputras, and as far as Ceylon, and in the kingdoms of Antiochus the Greek king and the kings who are his neighbours, the Beloved of the Gods has provided medicines for man and beast. Wherever medicinal plants have not been found they have been sent there and planted. Roots and fruits have also been sent where they did not grow, and have been planted. Wells have been dug along the roads for the use of man and beast.

Ashoka felt a moral responsibility not only for his own subjects, but for all men, and he realized that they could not lead moral lives, and gain merit in order to find a place in heaven, unless they were happy and materially well cared for:

[From the Sixth Rock Edict]

I am not satisfied simply with hard work or carrying out the affairs of state, for I consider my work to be the welfare of the whole world, of which hard work and the carrying out of affairs are merely the basis. There is no better deed than to work for the welfare of the whole world, and all my efforts are made that I may clear my debt to all beings. I make them happy here and now that they may attain heaven in the life to come.... But it is difficult without great effort.

He speaks in peremptory tones to the officers of state who are slow in putting the new policy into effect:

[From the First Separate Kalinga Edict]

By order of the Beloved of the Gods. Addressed to the officers in charge of Tosali.... Let us win the affection of all men. All men are my children, and as I wish all welfare and happiness in this world and the next for my own children, so do I wish it for all men. But you do not realize what this entails—here and there an officer may understand in part, but not entirely.

Often a man is imprisoned and tortured unjustly, and then he is liberated for no [apparent] reason. Many other people suffer also [as a result of this injustice]. Therefore it is desirable that you should practice impartiality, but it cannot be attained if you are inclined to habits of jealousy, irritability, harshness, hastiness, obstinacy, laziness, or lassitude. I desire you not to have these habits. The basis of all this is the constant advoidance of irritability and hastiness in your business.....

This inscription has been engraved in order that the officials of the city should always see to it that no one is ever imprisoned or tortured without good cause. To ensure this I shall send out every five years on a tour of inspection officers who are not fierce or harsh.... The prince at Ujjain shall do the same not more than every three years, and likewise at Taxila.

Later, in his Pillar Edicts, Ashoka seems more satisfied that his officers are carrying out the new policy:

[From the Fourth Pillar Edict]

My governors are placed in charge of hundreds of thousands of people. Under my authority they have power to judge and to punish, that they calmly and fearlessly carry out their duties, and that they may bring welfare and happiness to the people of the provinces and be of help to them. they will know what brings joy and what brings sorrow, and, conformably to Righteousness, they will instruct the people of the provinces that they may be happy in this world and the next.... And as when one entrusts a child to a skilled nurse one is confident that... she will care for it well, so have I appointed my governors for the welfare and happiness of the people. That they may fearlessly carry out their duties I have given them power to judge and to inflict punishment on their own initiative. I wish that there should be uniformity of justice and punishment.

In numerous passages Ashoka stresses the hard work which the new policy demands of him. He has given up many of the pleasures of the traditional Indian king in order to further it, including, of course, hunting:

[From the Eighth Rock Edict]

In the past kings went out on pleasure trips and indulged in hunting and similar amusements. But the Beloved of the Gods... ten years after his consecration set out on the journey to Enlightenment. Now when he goes on tour... he interviews and gives gifts to brāhmans and ascetics; he interviews and gives money to the aged; he interviews the people of the provinces, and instructs and questions them on Righteousness; and the pleasure which the Beloved of the Gods derives therefrom is as good as a second revenue.

As we have seen, Ashoka, though a Buddhist, respects brāhmans and the members of all sects, and he calls on his subjects to follow his example:

[From the Twelfth Rock Edict]

The Beloved of the Gods... honours members of all sects, whether ascetics or householders, by gifts and various honours. But he does not consider gifts and honours as important as the furtherance of the essential message of all sects. This essential message varies from sect to sect, but it has one common basis, that one should so control one's tongue as not to honour one's own sect or disparage another's one the wrong occasions' for on certain occasions one should do so only mildly, and indeed on other occasions one should honour other men's sects. By doing this one strengthens one's own sect and helps the others, while by doing otherwise one harms one's own sect and does a disservice to the others. Whoever honours his own sect and disparages another man's, whether from blind loyalty or with the intention of showing his own sect in a favorable light, does his own sect the greatest possible harm. Concord is best, with each hearing and respecting the other's teachings. It is the wish of the Beloved of the Gods that members of all sects should be learned and should teach virtue... Many officials are busied in this matter...and the result is the progress of my own sect and the illumination of Righteousness.

Though he was by no means a rationalist, it appears that Ashoka thought little of the many rituals and ceremonies of Indian domestic life:

[From the Ninth Rock Edict]

People perform various ceremonies, at the marriage of sons and daughters, at the birth of children, when going on a journey...or on other occasions.... On such occasions women especially perform many ceremonies which are various, futile, and useless. Even when they have to be done [to conform to custom and keep up appearances] such ceremonies are of little use. But the ceremonies of Righteousness are of great profit—these are the good treatment of slaves and servants, respect for elders, self-mastery in one's relations with living beings, gifts to brāhmans and ascetics, and so on. But for their success everyone—fathers, mothers, brothers, masters, friends, acquaintances, and neighbours—must agree—"These are good! These are the ceremonies that we should perform for success in our undertakings...and when we have succeeded we will perform them again!" Other ceremonies are of doubtful utility—one may achieve one's end through them or one may not. Moreover they are only of value in this world, while the value of the ceremonies of Righteousness is eternal, for even if one does not achieve one's end in this world one stores up boundless merit in the other, while if one achieves one's end in this world the gain is double.

We conclude this selection of the edicts of Ashoka with his last important inscription, in which the emperor, eighteen years after his conversion, reviews his reign:

[From the Seventh Pillar Edict]

In the past kings sought to make the people progress in Righteousness, but they did not progress.... And I asked myself how I might uplift them through progress in Righteousness.... Thus I decided to have them instructed in Righteousness, and to issue ordinances of Righteousness, so that by hearing them the people might conform, advance in the progress of Righteousness, and themselves make great progress.... For that purpose many officials are employed among the people to instruct them in Righteousness and to explain it to them....

Moreover I have had banyan trees planted on the roads to give shade to man and beast; I have planted mango groves, and I have had ponds dug and shelters erected along the roads at every eight kos. Everywhere I have had wells dug for the benefit of man and beast. But this benefit is but small, for in many ways the kings of olden time have worked for the welfare of the world; but what I have done has been done that men may conform to Righteousness.

All the good deeds that I have done have been accepted and followed by the people. And so obedience to mother and father, obedience to teachers, respect for the aged, kindliness to brāhmans and ascetics, to the poor and weak, and to slaves and servants, have increased and will continue to increase.... And this progress of Righteousness among men has taken place in two manners, by enforcing conformity to Righteousness, and by exhortation. I have enforced the law against killing certain animals and many others, but the greatest progress of Righteousness among men comes from exhortation in favour of non-injury to life and abstention from killing living beings.

I have done this that it may endure...as long as the moon and sun, and that my sons and my great-grandsons may support it; for by supporting it they will gain both this world and the next.

—*A.L. Basham*

8

The Buddhist Doctrine of Karma and Development of Indian Civilization

I. The Buddhist Doctrine of *Karma* and Religious Thought

The origin of suffering and of the inequalities in life is a mystery which is even more baffling than the mystery of life and death.

The phenomena of the origin, growth and decay of living beings can be explained as being inherent in their constitution by the Buddhist doctrine of *pratītyasamutpāda,* 'dependent origination.' But this is no scientific explanation for the inequalities and sufferings of individuals. The Vedic *ṛta* also was no answer to the problem.

The Buddha and the Theravāda Buddhism, for the first time, provided comparatively a most plausible explanation for this problem: individual suffering and inequality have their origin in a person's *karma* in this and previous lives. *Majjhima Nikāya*[1] iii, 204 observes that "it is their (human beings') deeds which divide people into high and low." Again, the *Milindapañha*[2] (1st century A.D.) 65.12 says "..... it is through a difference in the *karma* that men are not all alike, but some long lived and some short lived, some healthy and some sickly, some handsome and some ugly, some powerful and some weak, some rich and some poor, some of high degree and some of low degree, some wise and some foolish... ... *karma* allots beings to meanness and greatness."

The essential features of the classical form of this doctrine are indicated below:

Each *karma* or deed or action produces its reaction or effect. *Karma* is a causative factor in creation. It is *vipākahetu* or moral causation, as distinct from causation in the inanimate and organic world. It operates automatically.

It is the actions born of attachment, of passion, *tṛṣṇā* which are productive of consequences, whereas detached, passionless actions, when desire has been suppressed, are sterile or barren. Thus *Aṅguttaranikāya* i, III. 33 is explicit: the *karmas* or deeds born of lust, malice, and delusion (infatuation) ripen and come to fruition whereas deeds free from these are barren. The same text in iii, VI. 63 emphasises: *cetanā ahaṁ bhikave kamman vadāmi; cetayitā kamman karoti, kāyena,. vācayā, manasā;* determinate thought or will or intention is action; it is will that acts through body, speech and mind. *Milindapañha*[3] 221 is unambiguous: "Evil done by one who is unhinged....... is not of great blame here and no, nor is it so in respect of its ripening in a future state." A mad man who has committed murder is to be exonerated and only to be ejected. Buddhaghoṣa in *Visuddhimagga*[4] XX. 28 defines *karma* as *kammam nāma kusalākusalacetanā: Karma* is the name of awareness of good and bad.

It is the intention of the doer that determines the quality of each productive, fruit-producing action, good or bad, and consequently of the quality of the results or fruits of that act. Good deeds produce good results and happiness, and evil deeds produce bad results and suffering. In short, evil and inequalities are products of man's *karmas.*

A *karma* may or may not produce its effect immediately. In fact, *karmas* take time to ripen and to bear fruit. This often happens in subsequent lives or incarnations of a soul, The *gatis* or future incarnations are determined by the quality of a person's *karma.* Herein lies the mystery of *karma* inasmuch as it is not possible to relate specific present day suffering or inequality in a person's life as the consequence of a particular *karma* or *karmas* done previously. That is why *karma* is also called *apūrva* or *adṛṣṭa.*

The theory of *karma,* for its operation, presupposes the survival of the soul, *ātmā, pudgala,* after physical death and a belief in *punarjanma,* transmigration to a new physical frame, the precise *gati* or form of life being determined by the accumulated *karma.*

While *karma* is the causal factor in determining the *gati* or future incarnation after physical death, the total destruction of 'effect-oriented' *karma,* through suppression of *tṛṣṇā,* will make the *karmas* barren and "the last consciousness becomes like a fire without fuel, and passes into *nirvāṇa......*" *Visuddhimagga*[4a] XXII. As *Milindapañha*[5] 32.12 says "......if there shall be in me any attachment, I shall be born into another existence; if there shall be in me no attachment, I shall not be born into another existence."

The Theravāda Buddhists emphasised two features of this doctrine of *karma*. Firstly, the law of *karma* is automatic and inexorable in its operation. There is no escape from it under any circumstances. The *Dhammapada*[6] 128 states: "not in the sky, not in the midst of the sea, nor anywhere else on earth is there a spot where a man may be freed from (the consequences) of an evil deed." Aśvaghoṣa in the *Buddha-Carita* XX. 32 stresses that "the result of action is unalterable" (*syāt karmaṇastu phalaṁ dhruvam*).

Secondly, each individual is responsible for bearing the consequences of his own action. In the *Sāmañña-phala-sutta*[7] of the *Dīghanikāya* ii, 54 it is stated that while the wise thinks that by doing virtue, duty or penance or righteousness, he can make unripe *karmas* to mature, and the fool thinks that by the same means he can get rid of *karmas* that have matured, "neither of them can do it, 'ease and pain.... ... cannot be altered in the course of transmigration, there can be neither increase nor decrease thereof, neither excess nor deficiency.... both fools and wise alike, wandering in transmigration exactly for the allotted term, shall then and only then, make an end of pain." The *Saṁyutta-nikāya*[8] III. 1.4. states:

> His good deeds and his wickedness,
> Whatever a mortal does here,
> 'This his that he can call his own,
> This with him take as he goes hence.
> This is what follows after him,
> And like a shadow never departs."

Again, *Saṁyutta-nikāya*[9] III, 2.10 reiterates

> "But every deed a man performs
> This is that he can call his own....."

Majjhimanikāya I. 390 states: *yaṁ karoti tena upapajjati*. Again the *Majjhimanikāya*[10] III. 204 emphasises "Their (human beings') deeds are their possessions and heritage, their parent, their kindred and their refuge." The *Aṅguttaranikāya*[11] V. 288-291 states: "Beings are responsible for their deeds, kinsmen of their deeds, to them their deeds come back again. Whatsoever deed they do... ... of that thing they are the heirs."

The *Dhammapada*[12] 165 makes the categorical statement "By oneself evil is done, by oneself one suffers. By oneself evil is undone, by oneself one is purified."

In the *Aṅguttaranikāya*[13] iii, 35 Yama tells the deceased person awaiting decision on his further *gati* "O man! Through thoughtlessness you failed to act nobly with body, voice and mind. Verily, it shall be done unto you. O man, in accordance with your thoughtlessness. And it was not your mother who did this wickedness, nor was it your father, nor your brother, nor your sister, nor your friends and companions, nor your relatives and kinsfolk, nor the deities, nor the monks and Brahmans; but it was you yourself who did this wickedness, and you alone shall feel its consequences."

The *Suttanipāta*[14] 653 asserts "The past decides how men shall fare..." and further (*ibid.* 666) avers "For no man's deeds are blotted out, each deed comes home, the doer finds it waiting for him, in the worlds to come......"

In the *Nāgasenabhikṣusūtra,* the Chinese version of *Milindapañha,*[15] Na-hsien (Nāgasena) asked "If a man infringes the law and is punished, can the non-guilty replace him?" The king replied: "This cannot be....'. Again Na-hsien tells the king: "The performance of good and bad actions follows the doer, just like the shadow that follows the body. When a man dies, only his body is destroyed but his performance is not destroyed...". *Milindanañha*[16] II, 2. 6, keeping in view the Buddhist doctrine of *anattā,* explains that although the name and form which is born in the next existence is different from the name and form which is "to end at death", nevertheless it springs from it, and is therefore not freed from its evil deeds". Aśvaghoṣa in the *Buddha-Carita* XX. 32 proclaims: *yaḥ kartā so hi bhoktā,* 'the doer indeed bears the fruit of his action.'

The *Mahāvastu*[17] is equally explicit. In the *Śyāmaka Jātaka* of the *Mahāvastu* ii, 224 it is stated that it was not possible "to evade the results of deeds committed by oneself", and that (*ibid.* ii, 204) six years life of austerity in the forest by Gautama had failed "to secure the fading away of *karma*", that (*ibid.* ii, 215) "Neither weeping nor mourning for him (Śyāma) can ensure his escape from the results of the deeds he has himself committed."

Dhonasakha Jātaka[18] No. 353 states: "Each one shall fare according to his deed. And reap the harvest as he sows the seed (*yādisaṁ vapeta bījam, tādisaṁ harate phalam*), whether of goodly herb or may be noxious weed."

Again in *Sirikalakanni-Jātaka*[19] No. 382 the goddess Siri states: "Each man's fortune and misfortune are his own work, not another's. Neither fortune nor misfortune can a man make for his brothers".

The relentless and inflexible law of *karma* necessarily led to a search for expedients to get round this law, to moderate or neutralise its operation. These expedients were *bhakti* or devotion, and the cult of *avatāras* (divine incarnations), pilgrimages to sacred places *(tīrthas), dāna* (charity) and *Prāyaścitta* or expiation through bodily mortifications.

The Mahāyāna Buddhism evolved the concept of *bodhisattva mahāsattva* who not only foregoes his personal *nirvāṇa* for redemption of mankind from transmigration and the suffering inherent therein, but also has the powers to free his devotees from the consequences of their evil actions. In the *Amitāyurdhyāna sūtra*[20] § 19 it is said that those who meditate on Avalokiteśvara and Mahāsthāmprāpta "will utterly remove the obstacle that is raised by *karma* and expiate the sins which will involve them in births and deaths for numberless *kalpas.*" In § 32 of the same *sūtra* it is said that the *sūtra* can be called "the *sūtra* on the entire removal of *karma.*" In the *Suvarṇaprabhāsa-sūtra,*[21] the devotee prays to the compassionate Buddha to take away his transgressions and to bear away the fruit of his depraved deeds. In the *Śikṣāsamuccaya*[22] the *bodhisattva* resolves to take upon himself "all the mass of pain and all evil *karma"* from which mankind suffers. In the *Vajradhvaja sūtra* of *Śikṣāsamuccaya* 280-281, the *bodhisattva* resolves, *inter alia,* to redeem the mankind from Yama, Again Śāntideva in the *Bodhicaryāvatāra*[23] worships the Buddhas and the *bodhisattvas* so that he can meet the greatest of all dangers which is identified as his sins. Likewise, hearing the names and the sight of *bodhisattvas*[24] Bhaiṣajya-rāja and Bhaiṣajyasamudgata and of Maitreya obliterate the *karmas* of their devotees and give them remission from their sins. Again paying homage to Kṣitigarbha[25] relieves a person from the three states of suffering, and by the chanting of his name, the devotees "will be exonerated from the sins they have committed even thirty *kalpas* ago," and escape punishment in hell. In short, the *bodhisattva mahāsattvas* nullified the evil deeds of their devotees by *puṇya-parināmnā,* transference of merit.

The medieval Brahmanical texts accept this doctrine of *karma,* of sin and retribution therefor. The *Purāṇas* accept that 'one has to bear the consequences of one's action whether good or ill'[26], that "a man cannot fly from the effects of his prior deeds"[27], that "no man in the world is able to annual the effects of actions done in previous existences"[28], and acts done in a former birth determine the *gati* or form of the present birth.[29] The *Adhyātma Rāmāyaṇa*[30] emphasises "all beings are bound by the chains of their *karman*" and that the accumulated *karman* is alone cause of fortune and misfortune. The *Śivañāṇabodham*[31] of Meykaṇḍadeva reiterates that Lord Śiva "causes transmigration for human beings in conformity with their deeds." Consistently with this trend of thinking, *Carakasaṁhitā* I. 116 recognises actions of past life as a causative factor in producing diseases and I. 117 avers that "Diseases arising out of such action *(karma-rogaḥ)* are not amenable to any therapaeutic measures. They are cured only after the results of past actions are exhausted."

But the Hindu psyche is dominated, nay obsessed, by the thought of escape from the overpowering *karmas.*

The doctrines of *bhakti,* devotion in Vaiṣṇavism and of *śakti,* divine power in Śaivism, were attempts at by-passing *karma* through divine grace, or annuling *karma* by acquiring divine power through *tapas.*

It is significant that Viṣṇnu is called *gopā,* the protector, in the *Vedas.*[32] Another name of Viṣṇu is *Hari* which is derived from the root[33] *hri* meaning 'take away or remove evil or sin'. Śiva[34] is the 'auspicious one' who is benign, kind, benevolent. So the good offices of these gods are invoked to modify the consequences of an individual's *karma.*

In the *Mahābhārata* Sāvitrī vanquishes Yama and wins back to life her dead husband, Satyavān, by virtue of her chastity and devotion. In the *Devīmāhātmya* of the *Mārkaṇḍeya Purāṇa,*[35] Caṇḍikā is supplicated:

> "Thou destroyest all sickness, when gratified
> No calamity befalls men who sought unto thee."

Again:

(XCI. 27)

> 'O Goddess be gracious! Protect us wholly from
> fear of our foes....
>
> And bring thou quickly to rest the sins of all the worlds
> And the great calamities which have sprang from the maturing of portents.'

(XCI. 32)

The *Padma Purāṇa*[36] (1000-1400 A.D.) narrates how Mārkaṇḍeya defeats Yama through Śiva Bhakti.

The force of devotion as a means to overcome *karma,* therefore, finds widespread expression in Hindu *bhakti* literature. The very first poem of Tirunāvukkaraśu[37] (7th century A.D.) breathes of repentance. He asks for forgiveness for the sins committed by him. *Tirujñānasambandhar*[38] (7th century A.D.) sings "Oh, ye who ever think in terms of *karma*.....Let us devote ourselves to worship of His Feet in humble ways. By his Blue Throat (then you can be sure) no deed can have the power to bend us". Nammālvār[39] preaches surrender *(prapatti)* to the Lord: "He will protect and save you."

Tulsi Das[40] (16th-17th century A.D.) in his *stutis* or laudatory songs in honour of Rāma, Śiva, Devī, Gaṅgā etc. sings of the supreme benefits of the repetition of their names, of devotion to them as they remove all obstacles, redeem the sinners or destroy the sins and save men from taking rebirths as a result of *karma.*

Tukārāma (17th century A.D.) sings:

> "I am a mass of sin,
> Thou art all purity;
> Yet thou must take me as I am,
> and bear my load from me.
> Ah! do not, do not cast on me
> The guilt of mine iniquity."[41]

Again, he wrote:

> "My countless sins, I, Tukā, say,
> upon Thy loving heart I lay."[42]

The Hindus also accepted the doctrine of *puṇya parināmnā.* In the *Mārkaṇḍeya Purāṇa*[43] XV. 75-76 King Vipaśeit speaks thus: "How shall men attain their desire in things connected with me, if in my presence, these people gain no prosperity. Hence, whatever good deeds I possess, O lord of the thirty gods! by means thereof let the sinners who are undergoing torment be delivered from hell!"

To sum up, the doctrine of intense devotion and surrender to God, as a means of salvation from sins, was at the root of the cult of *avatāras,* God taking earthly form to free mankind from evil and not merely an individual from the sin committed by him. That explains the teaching of the *Gītā* IV. 7-8 that whenever there is decline of religion *(dharma)* and advance of irreligion *(adharma),*Kṛṣṇa takes birth in this world to protect the good and to destroy the wicked.

II. The Doctrine of *Karma* and Indian Society

Karma, as already stated, also provided the most rational explanation of the inequalities of life, of affluence and poverty, of happiness and suffering in the lives of individuals. According to the doctrine, a man is not the creature of his environment and circumstances on which he may have no control or for which he may not be responsible. The economic and social inequalities and inequities which individuals suffer are not the products or results of the acquisitive activities of selfish classes who exploit weaker sections of society. On the other hand, these are the products of each man's *karma* in this and in his previous lives. In the *Bodhicaryāvatāra*[44] VI, Śāntideva observes "Since the forest of sword-leaves and the bird of hell are engendered by my own *karma,* why then be angry?" (VI. 46). "Those who injure me have been prompted by the impulse of my *karma*... ..." (VI. 47).

In *ibid.* VI. 68, he says "Why did you previously act in such a way that you are oppressed in the same way by others? All are dependent upon *karma.* Who am I to alter this?" Spence Hardy[45] has summed up: "It is firmly held by the Buddhists and Brahmins that the present position of all men is the result of the merit or demerit of former births," and in consequence an outcaste is "in reality a condemned criminal, undergoing the sentence that has been pronounced against him by a tribunal that cannot err in its decrees." It made the individual believe that he is himself responsible for his status and suffering and that he could obtain salvation and improvement in his economic condition and social well-being by following an ethical discipline.

It also assured that while a person suffers for his own sins, the victimizer, in his turn, would not escape the inexorable consequences of his own *karma.* So the victim had no motive or incentive to take revenge, to obtain compensation for any alleged wrong done to him or to harbour ill-will against the victimizer.

Such a philosophy was the most powerful factor in the Indian people accepting without protest any system ol tyranny and oppression. It made for the perpetuation of the *status quo,* for economic and social stability and absence of any urge for change and redress.

It should be clearly understood that it did not make for passivity or indifference[46] on the part of an individual to his lot because his salvation lay in an intetnse observance of ethical behaviour. In fact, ethical discipline was his only hope of redemption. *Karma* doctrine made his work for his personal salvation through acts of piety but not for a social reconstruction or better comic order. It promoted an attitude not of demoralised fatalism but of philosophic complacency.

Karma and ahiṁsā or non-violenee

The Jainas and Buddhists had made *ahiṁsā,* non-destruction of life and non-violence, physical and mental, an essential feature of their doctrines; it is one of the five *śīlas* or principles of moral conduct which must be observed both by laymen and monks. Any violation of or deviation from the *śīlas* was regarded as sin. Thus the practice of *śīlas* including *ahiṁsā* got linked with the doctrine of *karma.* As such, the triumph of the doctrine of *karma* also made for the total acceptance of the doctrine of *ahiṁsā* by the followers of Indian faiths including Hindusim and led to the total displacement of the Vedic Cult of animal sacrifices.

Karma and the Caste System

The doctrine of *karma* found a powerful *raison d'etre* for the caste system practised in India. Thought the original division into castes had originated in the practice of various professions, the caste system, as it eventually developed, determined the status of an individual in the caste hierarchy on the basis of birth and not on the basis of profession.

The severance of the relationship between profession and caste and the essential features of the caste system viz. rigidity, its hereditary character and absence of any mobility from one caste to another, were the consequences of he *karma* doctrine.

Both the *Upaniṣads* and Buddhism had emphasised a man's past acts as determinants of his present status in life. The *Śatapatha Brāhmaṇa*[17] VI. 2, 2, 27 had emphasised that 'man is born in the world made by himself (that is, man receives, in further existence, the reward or punishment for the deeds during this life). The *Upaniṣads* elaborated this dictum. The *Bṛhadāraṇyaka*[48] III 2.13 says "Verily one becomes good by good actions, bad by bad actions" after death. Thus the *Kaṭhakopaniṣad*[49] II. 2.7 maintains "Some souls enter into the womb for embodiment, others enter stationary objects according to their deeds and according to their thoughts."

The *chāndogya*[50] V. 10.7 makes the unambiguous statement: "Those whose conduct here has been good, will quickly attain a good birth (literally womb). the birth of a Brahmin, the birth of a Kṣatriya or the birth of a Vaiśya. But those whose conduct has been evil, will quickly attain an evil birth, the birth of a dog, the birth of a hog, the birth of a *Cāṇḍāla*."

In the same sense the *Śvetāśvatara Upaniṣad*[51] V. 11 reiterates "According to his deeds, the embodied self assumes successively various forms in various conditions." The *Kauṣītaki Brāhmaṇa Upaniṣad*[52] 1.2 states "Either as a worm, or as an insect, or as a fish, or as a bird, or as a lion, or as a boar, or as a snake, or as a tiger, or as a person or as some other in this or that condition he is born again according to his deeds, according to his knowledge..."

Buddhism only reinforced the support which the law of *karma*, as enunciated in *Upaniṣads*, gave to the caste system. No doubt the Buddha had condemned and repudiated a caste system based on birth, on heredity. In the *Vasalasutta* (7.21) of the *Suttanipāta*[53] the Buddha had observed with great prescience: "Not by birth does one become an outcaste, not by birth does one become a Brāhmaṇa; by deeds one becomes an outcaste, by deeds alone one becomes Brāhmaṇa." But there is little doubt that the Buddha accepted that the caste distinctions were not man made but were a product of one's past *karmas*. In the *Cula-Kamma-Vibhaṅga-Sutta* of the *Majjhimanikāya*[54] iii, 204 the Buddha emphasised that "It is their deeds which divide people into high and low" and explain the disparities in life, length of life, health, wealth and looks. "Such deeds, if persisted in of deliberate choice, either bring that person *at the body's dissolution* after death, to misery or woe or to purgatory...". In other words, the consequences of these acts are manifest in another life. The *Assalāyanasutta* of *Majjhimanikāy*[55] ii, 149-150 is more explicit: the Buddha emphasises that a person belonging to any caste, including the superior castes of the Brahmin and Kṣatriya, who commits murder, theft, indulges in sexual pleasures, is covetous or malevolent etc., will "after death, at the body's dissolution pass to a state of misery and woe...". Likewise those who observe the *pañcaśīla,* would "after death at the body's dissolution," attain heaven irrespective of whether he be a *brahmin,* a *kṣatriya,* a *vaiśya* or a peasant, In the *Milindapañha* 127, 128, it is stated that beings, who have roots of good *karmas,* are reborn according to their wish, in a family of rich warrior, nobles, rich *brāhmaṇas* or rich householders. In *Divyāvadāna*[56] 616, Prakṛti, the *Cāṇḍāla* girl, is freed from her previously accumulated sins which had brought about her low birth *(pūrva saṁcita pāpam durgati).* In the *Śārdūla Karṇāvadāna* of *Divya* it is said that men are architects of their own fortunes, that they are of the same class with differences arising out of their *karmas.*

The *Bhagavadgītā* IV. 13 and XVIII. 41 put its imprimatur on the caste structure when it postulated that the *karmas,* along with the *guṇas,* are responsible for the division of the society into four castes. According to *Manu* xii. 9, as a result of the mental sins, a person becomes a low caste *(antya-jāti)* in the next birth. In the story of Kauśika and Vyādha (fowler or a butcher) in the *Mbh (Vanaparva* XXXIV) the Brahmin Kauśika states that it was some *karma* that had made Vyādha to take birth as a *śūdra* (low caste) and the latter confirmed that he had been previously a Brahmin but was degraded as a butcher due to an inadvertent fault of his own in the earlier birth.

Similarly, according to the Jainas, there are eight kinds of *karma.*[57] The sixth kind called *nāma-karma* determines the *gati* of a soul i.e. whether it is embodied as a human being, goat, insect or a denizen of hell. The seventh viz. *gotra-karma* determines the caste, occupation and other personal factors like marriage, food, etc. But the *gotra-karma* has a decisive bearing on the fact whether a person is born in a high caste or low caste.

Śrīmad Bhāgavatam XXXI maintains that "the result of the acts done in former birth owes its form to the Divine agency. As such, the body of the being in further birth is due to the results of the acts done in former birth."

Thus, the theory of *karma* found an apparently scientific justification for the caste system. The triumph of the theory of *karma,* when it received powerful support from horoscopic astrology in the 4th century A.D., helped to establish caste system as a divinely ordained institution.

At the caste status came to be based on birth and was therefore divorced from wealth and economic power—there could be rich and very poor people in the same caste group—economic changes and consequent redistribution of wealth, or the economic affluence of an individual or family did not affect the social structure. In that sense the caste system based on birth made for social stability and social stagnation.

III. The Doctrine of *Karma* and Hindu Mythology

The transformations in the role and character of Yama in Hindu mythology is the result of the development of the doctrine of *karma* in Hinduism. This would be evident from a comparison of the character of Yama in Vedic and epic mythology.

In the Vedic texts,[58] Yama is the chief of the blessed dead. In the *Rgveda* he is *Yamarāja,* the king who rules the dead and is the chief of the souls of the departed. In the *Atharvaveda,* he comes to be the god of death. He has, however, nothing to do with the punishment of the wicked.

In the epic mythology,[59] Yama also becomes a judge of the dead. That is why he acquires the title of Dharmarāja or Dharmendra. In the postepic period he is assisted by Citragupta[60] who keeps a record of the good and evil acts of all men and helps Yama is dispensing justice with reference to those acts. It is significant that one of the titles of Yama is *daṇḍī* or *daṇḍadhara.*[61]

This change in the character of Yama is reflected in *Vasiṣṭha-dharma-Sūtra*[62] XX. 3, which states "The spiritual teacher corrects the learned, the king corrects the evil minded, but Yama, the son of Vivasvat, forsooth, punishes those who offend secretly." Evidently the king punishes the offenders against positive law by operating *daṇḍa* or the coercive apparatus and powers of the State, and Yama punishes those who are guilty of unexpiated sins by operating the law of *karma.*

The concept of Yama in Buddhism[63] and Jainism[64] is essentially similar. He is the king who punishes the wicked with the help of his messengers or *dūtas.*

IV. The Law of *Karma* and Hindu Jurisprudence

The compulsive need to find an escape from the inexorable operation of the law of *karma* led to the development of the doctrine of *prāyaścitta* or penance or expiation.

In the *Śruti* or the *Vedas,* the term *prāyaścitta* has a technical significance: the measures to be adopted or action to be taken to rectify any errors[65] in the performance of sacrificial rituals, such as use of defective materials, incorrect procedure or defilement of sacrifices by animals etc.

In the post-Vedic *Smṛti* literature, however, the term *prāyaścitta* acquires a radically different connotation. While, according to the *Śruti* leterature, *prāyaścitta* has to be performed for correcting ritual errors or lapses. the *Smṛtis* prescribe *prāyaścitta* for *karmic* lapses-*mahāpātakas*[66] and the *upapātakas.*[67] These lapses are offences against positive laws, *vyavahāra,* and against accepted moral code, *ācāra.*

The evidence from the *Dharma-sūtra* texts (600-300 B.C.) and the *Smṛtis* (100 B.C.-400 A.D.) clearly establishes that this change in the meaning of *prāyaścitta* was the result of the doctrine of *karma.*

Gautama[68] XIX. 3-6 and *Vasiṣṭha*[69] XII. 2-5 point out that some persons doubted the utility of performing penances for a vile or reprovable action inasmuch as "the deed does not perish," i.e. the actions must bear fruits and the consequences of the actions are inescapable. But they emphasised that the authortitative view is that penances should be performed. *Gautama* XIX. 11 and *Vasiṣṭha* XXII. 8 add, "Reciting the *Veda,* austerity, sacrifice, fasting, giving gifts are the means for expiating... a blamable act." Āpastamba[70] 1.9, 24,25 and 26 and *Baudhāyana*[71] II. 1.1 and 1.2 describe the penances to be performed for various offences, murder, theft, drinking liquor or adultery etc.

The *Manusmṛti*[72] (200 B.C. to 100 A.D.) XI. 44-48 reiterates unambiguously the importance of *prāyaścitta* or penance: "A man who omits a prescribed act or performs a blamable act, or cleaves to sensual enjoyments, must perform a penance" and emphasises, "A sin unintentionally committed is expiated by the recitation of Vedic texts but that which (men) in their folly commit intentionally, by various (special) penances."

The *Viṣṇu Smṛti*[73] likewise prescribes certain penances in the form of rites, recitation of *mantras* and breathing practices to expiate for all sins including mortal sins.

These texts not only show the change in the meaning of the term *prāyaścitta,* they also establish clearly the link between penances and the doctrine of *karma*. The clearest exposition is to be found in *Manu*[74] which maintains: "Thus in consequence of a remnant of (the guilt of former) crimes, are born idiots, dumb, blind, deaf and deformed men" (XI. 54); and "Penances, therefore, must always be performed for the sake of purification, because those whose sins have not been expiated, are born (again) with disgraceful marks" (XI. 54). This relationship between penances and the law of *karma* is also seen in *Vasiṣṭha*[75] XX. 3 where he says" "The spiritual teacher corrects the learned, the king corrects the evil minded, but Yama, the son of Vivasvat, forsooth, punishes those who offend secretly." The meaning of *Vasiṣṭha* is quite clear: the king punishes the evil doer through *daṇḍa* or coercive power of the State and Yama, the God of justice who operates the law of *karma,* punishes those guilty of violating *ācāra* and heinous offences committed in secret.

The relationship between the doctrines of *karma* and *prāyaścitta* is conclusively proved by the doctrines of *sarva-prāyaścitta* (all expiating penance) and *karma-vipāka.* According to the medieval digests[76] *Antyeṣṭipaddhati* or Nārāyaṇa-bhaṭṭa (16th century A.D.) and *Antyakarmadīpaka* of Nityānanda (16th century A.D.), the *sarvaprāyaścitta* is to be performed by a dying person or his son or relative by making gifts of a cow or of gold. Likewise, the doctrine of *karma-vipāka,* the maturing of *karmas,* in the *Smṛtis*[77] emphasises that those sinners who have not expiated their sins through *prāyaścitta* have torments in hell and are reborn as insects or lowly animals, trees or as diseased or deformed human beings. Thus *Śātātapa*[78] declares that men guilty of grave sins who have not undergone *prāyaścitta* are, after undergoing torments of hell, born with signs or marks indicative of their sins. *Yājñavalkya Smṛti*[79] III. 133 states "The ripening results of the deeds done is after death, and of certain ones arises in this (world) alone.....". Again *Yājñavalkya* III. 221 states "Men who are steeped in sins and who do not perform penances and repent (for their evil deeds) go to painful and dreadful hells."

The *Purāṇas* clearly stress the significance of *karma-vipāka.* Thus *Viṣṇudharmottara*[80] (400-500 A.D.) II. 73. 3-4 declares that those sinners who do not undergo penances nor are punished by the king, fall into hell and are born as lower animals and with bodily defects. Many other *Purāṇas*[81] also reiterate the same.

The *Mahārṇava Karma-vipāka*[82] of Māndhātṛ states that the consequences of *karma* are destroyed or reversed either by *Kṛcchra* (penances) or by diseases (i.e. suffering). Thus the doctrines of *prāyaścitta, sarvaprāyaścitta* and *karma-vipāka* in the *Smṛtis, Purāṇas* and medieval legal digests establish that by performing *prāyaścitta,* one could neutralise or abate the consequences of *karma* or deeds. In fact, *prāyaścitta* enables a person to control and regulate the operation of the law of *karma* in a planned and self-determined manner.[83] The rationale of *prāyaścitta* therefore was that it enable a person to wipe off the potential effects of any evil *karma* or deed.

Tapas is essentially a form of *prāyaścitta. Manu*[84] XII. 239-241 states that those who are guilty of evil deeds, are freed from sins by *tapas.* The Jainas shared the same view as the *Uttarādhyayana-sūtra*[85] XXIV. 27 teaches that "by austerities he cut off *karman.*" These austerities were of two types—external and internal; the external austerities involved *kāya-kilesas,* tormening of the body (*Uttarādhyayana* XXX. 7, 8) and internal austerities or *prāyaścitta (Uttarādhyayana* XXX. 30, 31).

V. Other expedients to overcome the law of *karma*

Prāyaścittas were not always an easy expedient against the consequences of *karma.* Another means to free a person from his sins was *tīrtha-yātrā* or pilgrimage and bathing in holy rivers. In the *Mahābhārata* and the *Purāṇas* the pilgrimages[86] are considered superior to the sacrifice offered to gods. According to the *Viṣṇudharmasūtra* XXXV. 6, Devala and Parāśara XII. 58, a *mahāpātaka* becomes pure, *inter alia,* by visiting the sacred places. According to *Vāyupurāṇa*[87] (300-600 A.D.) 77, 125 and 127, a steadfasts man visiting the *tīrthas* "would be purified even if he has been guilty of sins". The *Viṣṇudharmottara-purāṇa*[88] (III. 273.7 and 9) avers that pilgrimage "removes the sins of the sinful... ...".

Another important expedient for counteracting the consequences of sins was charity or *dāna. Dāna* is supposed to be a good deed and therefore produces merit. As such it was a means of diluting and thereby making the potentiality of sins ineffective. Aśoka's Pillar[89] Edict No. IV (Delhi Topra text) records the belief that gifts and fasts secure happiness in the next world. *Vasiṣṭhadharmasūtra*[90] 29.16 says that the gift of even a small piece of land purifies a man from the sin, committed in distress. *Viṣṇudharmasūtra*[91] (92.4) states that the gift of gold, cows and land destroys the sins committed in another life.

The above survey clearly indicates that the Buddhist doctrine of *karma* has exercised a profound and abiding influence on Indian religion and society. Contemporaneously it justified the caste system and the maintenance of *status quo* in society. Prospectively it has exercised a most beneficent formative influence on the ethics of Indians as ethical discipline came to be accepted as an essential prerequisite for attaining a happier and superior existence. It promoted the cult of *ahiṁsā*. Retrospectively, so far as actions already committed in moments of weakness known or unknown, in this life or previous existences, are concerned, this doctrine has led to the adoption of various expedients such as *bhakti* (devotion), *prāyaścitta* (purificatory penances), *tapas* (austerities), *Tīrthayātrās* (pilgrimages), *dāna* (charities) and above all the cult of *avatāras* (divine incarnations), to neutralise or to moderate the operation of the law of *karma* in respect of their consequences.

—*Y. Krishan*

References

1. Chalmers: *Further Dialogues of the Buddha*, Vol. II.
2. H.C. Warren: *Buddhism in Translations* (New York, Antheneum 1963), p. 215
3. I.B. Horner: *Milinda-Questions*, London, 1964, Vol. II.
4. See also *Ibid.* XIX. 14.

4a. Warren: *Ibid.* § 86.

5. Warren: *Ibid.* § 45, p. 233.
6. Max Müller: tr. The *Dhammapada. The Sacred Books of the East (S.B.E.)* Vol. X (Delhi, Reprint, 1965).

   Dharmatrāta in his *Udānavarga* (75 B.C. to 200 A.D.) IX. 4 states "If thou hast done evil deeds, or if thou wouldst do them; thou mayest arise and run where'er thou wilt, but thou canst not free thyself of thy suffering". Rockhill (tr.) *Udānavarga* Amsterdam 1975 Reprint.
7. T.W. Rhys Davids: *Dialogues of the Buddha*, Pt. I, London, 1956.
8. Warren: *Ibid.* p. 214.
9. Warren: *Ibid.* p. 228.
10. Chalmers: *Ibid.*
11. Woodward: (tr.) *The Book of Gradual Savings.*
12. Max Müller: *Ibid.*

13. Warren: *Ibid,* § 51, p. 256.
14. Dharmatrāta in his *Udānavarga* XXVIII. 36 states:

    "He who has done what is evil is made to suffer; though he has done it long ago, though he has done it afar off, he is made to suffer; though he has done it in solitude, he is made to suffer; and when it has ripened it brings him suffering,' Rockhill (tr) *Ibid.*
15. Thich Minh Chau: *Miliandapañha and Nāngasena-bhikṣu-sūtra, A Comparative Study,* Patna, 1964, pp. 60-61.
16. Rhys David: *S. B. E.* Vol. XXXV Delhi, 1965.
17. J. Jones (tr.) The *Mahāvastu,* London, 1949.
18. Francis & Neil (tr.) *Jātakas,* Vol. III. London, 1957.
19. Francis & Neil (tr.) *Ibid.*
20. *S.B.E.* Vol. XLIX, p. 183 and 195.
21. E.J. Thomas: *The Perfection of Wisdom* (New York, 1952), p. 62.
22. de Bary: ed. *Sources of Indian Tradition* (New York, 1958) p. 164.
23. *Encyclopaedia of Religion & Ethics* (Edinbourgh, 1964), Vol. II, p. 749 (a).
24. Soper: 'Literary Evidence for Early Buddhist Art in China' *Artibus Asiae* (Switzer land, 1959), pp. 203, 205, 206 and 215.
25. *Kṣitigarbha's Fundamental Vows:* Bilingual *Sūtra* on the original Vows and the attainment of Merits of Kṣitigarbha Bodhisattva. Tr, from Chinese into English by Men Pitt Chin Hui, Singapore Regional Centre of the World Fellowship of Buddhists, pp. 12, 17, 18, 19. As pointed out by A Csoma Korosi *(The Life and Teachings of the Buddha),* Calcutta, 1957, reprint, p. 126, the repetition of the invocation '*Om Maṇi padme hum*' is to coerce Chenraisi's spirit, incarnated in the Dalai Lama, to favour the repeater.
26. *Nārada-purāṇa* I. 29.18. The *Mahābhārata (Vana & Śānti parvans)* shows a contradictory attitude towards the doctrine of *karma.* It maintains that each man is squarely responsible for his actions and that consequences of *karma* can never be destroyed. At the same time it ascribes the results of actions of God, man, luck and *karma,* and invokes the doctrine of pre-determinism.
27. *Garuḍa-purāṇa:* quoted in Robert O Bellon ed. *The World Pocket Bible* (London, 1964).
28. *Padmapurāṇa* II, 81, 48 and II. 94. 17, 18.
29. *Śrīmad Bhāgavatam* 3 XXXI.
30. Louis Renou, ed. *Hinduism* (New York, 1963), p. 172.
31. Louis Renou: (ed) *Ibid.,* p. 180.
32. *Rgveda* X, 61, 70; Monier Williams - *Sanskrit English Dictionary.*

33. Monier Williams: *Ibid.*
34. Monier Williams:*Ibid.*
35. Pargiter (tr) *Mārkaṇḍeya Purāṇa,* (Varanasi 1969).
36. V.K. Aiyer: *Stories from Indian Classics,* Tr. into English by P. Sankaranarayan. (Bharatiya Vidya Bhavan, Bombay 1966), pp. 135-139.
37. T.M.P. Mahadevan: *Ten Saints of India,* Bharatiya Vidya Bhavan, Bombay, 1965), p. 37.
38. Mahadevan: *Ibid.* p. 27.
39. Mahadevan: *Ibid.* p. 80.
40. Tulsidas: *Vinaya Patrikā* in Hindi, (Gorakhpur, 1975).
41. Renou: *Ibid.* p. 187.
42. Renou: *Ibid.* p. 188.
43. Pargiter (tr.) *Mārkaṇḍeya Purāṇa,* (Varanasi, 1969).
44. Marion L. Matics: *Entering the Path of Englightenment.* (The *Bodhicaryāvatāra*) (George Allen & Unwin, London, 1970), pp. 177, 179. In the 14th century the Sikh Guru Nänak said the same thing: "Why blameth thou others, blame thy deeds. For thou receiveth the fruit of what thou sowest."

    V. Raghavan (ed.) *Devotional Poets and Mystics,* Government of India, New Delhi 1978.
45. Spence Hardy: *A Manual of Buddhism* (Indian Edition, 1967, Varanasi), p. 79.
46. Macdonell: *Lectures on Comparative Religion* 1925, p. 67 observes: "A result of the combined doctrine of transmigration and *karma* is ......to reconcile men to their fate as the just retribution for deeds done in a previous life, but on the other hand, it paralyses action, drives to asceticism, and makes action self-regarding, since it becomes the aim of every man to win salvation for himself individually, by acquiring the right knowledge. There is consequently scope for the development of other—regarding virtues, as each individual is intent on gaining his own salvation."
47. Julius Eggeling (tr) *S.B.E.* Vol. XLI, pp. 180-181 and footnote I.
48. Radhakrishnan: *The Principal Upaniṣad.*
49. Radhakrishnan: *Ibid.*
50. Radhakrishnan: *Ibid.*
51. Radhakrishnan: *Ibid.*
52. Radhakrishnan: *Ibid.*
53. Fausböll: (tr) *S.B.E.* Vol. X. Pt. II, p. 23.
54. Chalmers: *The Further Dialogues of the Buddha,* Vol. II.

55. Chalmers: *Ibid.* Vol. II.

56. Nilakantha Sastri: *Aspects of India's History & Literature,* pp. 61-62.

57. S. Stevenson: *The Heart of Jainism,* pp. 177-183. See also B.C. Law: *Karma in the Cultural Heritage of India,* Vol. I, p. 543. M.L. Mehta: *Jaina Psychology,* p. 16 and 21.

58. A.A. Macdonell: *The Vedic Mythology,* Varanasi, 1971, § 77. See also Dowson: *A Classical Dictionary of Hindu Mythology,* 9th Edn. London 1950.

59. E.W. Hopkins: *Epic Mythology,* (Delhi, Reprint 1974), § 58 and 57.

60. Hopkins: *Ibid.*

61. Dowson: *Ibid.* § *Yama*

62. Bühler: *Ibid.*

63. *Anguttara Nikāya,* iii, 35 H.C. Warren: *Buddhism in Translations* § 51. See also *Devadūta Sutta* in the *Majjhima Nikāya* iii, 180-188. Chalmers (tr.) *Further Dialogues of the Buddha,* Vol. II, (London 1927).

64. *Acāradinakara* paying obeisance to Yama called him *dharmarāja* and endowed with *daṇḍa* (rod of justice). The only difference is that in Jainism Yama's wife is Chāyā, who is the wife of the Sun God in Hindu mythology. B.C. Bhattacharya: *The Jaina Iconography,* (Delhi, 2nd Edition, 1974), p. 110, f.n.1.

65. Śabara in his *Bhāṣya* on *Jaimini Mīmāṁsā Sūtras* 16-17 states that expiations *(prāyaścittas)* are of two kinds (a) for correcting defects arising from individual omission of what has been enjoined and commission of what has been prohibited and (b) expiations to be performed in certain contingencies in which sacrifices to be performed are not fulfilled such as offering rice to Mitra for failure to perform Agnihotra before Sun rise.

66. The *mahāpātakas* are heinous crimes like murder, especially of a Brahmin, theft, adultery, especially incest and sexual intercourse with a *Guru's* wife, intoxication through drinking.

67. The *upapātakas* are minor sins like neglecting the sacred fires, offending the *guru,* killing a cow, not repaying a debt, failing to undergo the *upanayaṇa* (sacred thread) ceremony at the prescribed age etc. etc. The number of *upapātakas* varies greatly in different texts.

68. G. Bühler (tr): *The Sacred Laws of the Āryas* (*S.B.E.*, Vol. II)

69. Bühler (tr): *S.B.E.,* Vol. XIV.

70. Bühler *Ibid: S.B.E.,* Vol. XIV.

71. Bühler *Ibid.*

72. Bühler: *The Laws of Manu, S.B.E.* Vol. XXV. The *Māhābhārata* XII, 34, 2, makes identical observations about *prāyaścitta*

73. J. Jolly: *The Institutes of Viṣṇu* XLVIII, XLIX and LV, *S.B.E.* Vol. XXXIII.

74. Bühler *Ibid.*

75. Bühler *Ibid.*

76. Cited by P.V. Kane: *History of Dharmaśāstra,* Vol. III, pp. 183-184.

77. P.V. Kane: *Ibid,* Vol. III. pp. 172-173 and footnote 411.

78. *The Sacred Laws of the Aryas* as taught in the school of Yājñavalkya and explained by Vijñāneśvara in his commentary.

79. The *Mitākṣarā,* Vol. III (tr.) S.N. Naraharayya. (Allahabad, 1913).

80. An *upapurāṇa.* Quoted from Kane: *Ibid.* Vol. IV, p. 76, footnote 182.

81. *Garuḍa Purāṇa* (800-1000 A.D.) CV quoted Yajñavalkya,. "For commission of heinous and infamous acts and omission of doing what is good and commendable, a person is sure to be condemned to the torments of hell. An unbridled gratification of the senses paves one's way to the gates of hell. Hence rites of expiation should be performed both for the cleansing of the spirit and the body...".

    M.N. Dutt: (tr.) The *Garuḍa Purāṇam,* (Chowkhamba Sanskrit Series Office, Varanasi, 1968).

    The *Agnipurāṇa* (9th century A.D.) CLXVIII to CLXXI describes various penances for expiating sins.

    M.N. Dutt: (tr) *Agni Purāṇam* Vol. II (Chowkhamba Sanskrit Series Offices Varanasi. 1967).

82. Quoted by Kane: *Ibid.* Vol. IV, p. 178 and fn. 421.

83. *Manusmṛti* XI. 73 with the *Manubhāṣya* of Medhātithi (tr. G. Jha, Calcutta, 1926) speaks of *prāyaścitta* for murder of a brahmin being undergone by one's own will. Again, certain law digests as *Prāyaścittasāra* and *Madanapārijāta* recognise that the *prāyaścittas* prescribed for *Mahāpātaka* or grave sins as ending one's life by entering fire, or drinking boiling water were to be undergone volunatrily. Kane: *Ibid.* Vol. IV, p. 76, and fn. 183.

84. Bühler *Ibid.*

85. Jacobi (tr.) *S.B.E.* Vol. XLV, p. 166.

86. Kane: *Ibid.* Vol IV, p. 561-62

87. Kane: *Ibid.* Vol IV, pp. 563 fn. 1265.

88. Kane: *Ibid.* Vol IV, p. 563 fn. 1266. The *Matsyapurāṇa* 184.18 and the *Kūrmapurāṇa* (*pūrvārdha* 29, 30), maintain that pilgrimage to Benares destroys all sins. Kane: *Ibid.* Vol IV, p. 55 fn. 134 and fn. 135.

89. D. C. Sircar: *Inscriptions of A'soka,* (New Delhi 1956).

90. Bühler: *Ibid.*

91. Jolly: *Ibid.*

9

Contribution of Buddhism to Art

All forms of art, according to the orthodox interpretation of the teachings of the Master, the Lord Buddha, are derived from and minister to *tanha* and *vasana,* desire and nostalgia; they are instruments of attachment, of enjoyment of the senses and of exercise of the intellect, they relate themselves to the world of name and form of *nama* and *rupa,* and are, therefore, to be shunned by one who aspires after *nirvana, sunyata or prajna.* The Buddhist position in this respect is not, therefore, unlike that of the Vedanta.

Paradoxically, however, the world of *nama and* rupa, which is the world of art, had its full play in Buddhism, not in India alone but wherever the life and message of the Master extended itself. Ever in history, organised and institutionalised religions found in art, visual and otherwise, a most potent and powerful instrument for communication and dissemination of their ideas and ideologies, their myths and legends, their creeds and rituals. Buddhism was no exception to this general picture of the history of ancient and mediaeval religions. Communication calls for concretisation of personal visions, ideas and experiences, and in its process recreates the world of 'name' and 'form', which deliverance is sought from, or in other words, annihilation is sought of. Whatever was the theoretical position of the Lord Buddha Himself in this respect, organised Buddhism in order to teach people the transitoriness of the world of name and form, was obliged to admit that very world into the realm of one of their significant activities. Indeed, art helped to extend the physical horizons of Buddhism, deepen its most subtle and sublime ideas thoughts, and concretise its most elusive, abstract and subjective visions to an extent which is no less that what was achieved by the texts, canonical and otherwise, of the religion and by the life and activities of the *achariya-parampara* or succession of venerable *theras*.

Yet, strictly speaking, it would be incorrect to refer to the arts employed and patronised by the votaries of Buddhism, or as a matter of that, of Brahmanism of Jainism, as Buddhist, Brahmanical or Jaina art. All that is connoted by such phrases are the respective forms and styles of traditional and contemporary expression of a given region, that were pressed to the service of the respective religions just referred to. But, since the religions were different, which means that their creeds, rituals, myths, legends, ideas and ideologies were different, the contents of the respective arts too, had therefore, to be different. The validity of such a statement would be evident, it is believed, when one analyses the forms, styles and contents of the art employed by Buddhism and Brahmanism in a given time and space, say, of the Ganga-Yamuna valley of the fifth and sixth centuries, or of Eastern Indian during the early mediaeval centuries, or of the Buddhist bas-reliefs of the *stupa* of Borobudur and the Brahmanical bas-reliefs of the temples of Pranbanam, both of Java. In all these instances, forms and styles of art are characteristically the same, the contents alone, of necessity, being different. This was only in the nature of things, since an artists, irrespective of the religion he subscribed to, belonged to a class of craftsmen organised in guilds and worked within the framework of a flowing tradition; it was against this background that he served the demands of his patrons and clients, Buddhist, Brahmanical or Jain, whose sole concern was the content of their creed, not the means by and the manners in which it was served for or before them. While there was thus a Buddhist or Brahmanical or Jain iconography, there was no art that could specially and exclusively be called Buddhist or Brahmanical or Jaina art.

Since the Lord Buddha did not recognise any divinity external to men, Buddhism in its essence did not fall in line with the early Brahmanical position that art was but a manifestation of a divine purpose, or in other words, of a natural law, as stated in the *Aitareya*, the *Satapatha* and the *Taittiriya Brahmanas*. The Lord Buddha seems to have held that art was the product of human thinking and imagination. Thus, in respect of a class of painting called *charana chinititam*, that the *charana-chitra* was indeed conceived by the mind *(Samyutta*, Khandha-Samyutta, 5.8., quoted in the *Atthasalini, p. 64)*. Elsewhere, with reference to a statue or bust, the Buddha is said to have stated that it is to be judged only as an expression of the mind *(manamattaka),* which is commemorative or referential *(uddesika)* and without any positive basis, oravatthuka (Kalingabodhi Jataka). Commenting on the above statement of the *Samyutta-Nikaya,* Buddhaghosa, centuries later, states: "In the world there is no finer artmanship than what is displayed in a piece of painting, and of paintings the one called *charana* is admittedly the best. In drawing this class of paintings the thought arises in the mind of the painters, 'such and such kinds of figures are to be drawn in this picture'. Following this thought, the drawing of outline, colouring, polishing and such other detail works of drawing result: as a consequence a wonderful figure appears on the *charana-chitra.* 'Let that go above this figure let this go below,' and then the finishing touch is given to the painting, and all these according to the thought of the artist. Similarly whatever products of art there are in the world all are wrought by the mind" (*Saratthapakasini* Ceylonese edn. pp. 469 ff). The view that art was a product of the mind that is, this psychological view of art, seems to have been an important contribution of Buddhism to the total Indian approach to art in general. Later, in the Mahayana and Vajrayana schools of Buddhism as much as in Brahmanism one only find confirmation of the original position. Indeed, the Brahmaical *dhyanas* the Buddhist *sadhanas,* supported by texts on *slipa* and *pratimalakshana,* leave no room for doubt as to the Indian position that art, in its essence, was an activity of the mental faculties, that is, an intellectual operation.

Though Asoka Maurya in particular and the Maurya court (c. 326—180 B.C.) in general helped fix Indian art in permanent materials, that is, gave currency to the use of stone in sculptural and architectural activities, and made use of certain significant Buddhist symbols in the art patronised by them, Buddhist art, that is, an art with a specific Buddhist content, does not come to view before the middle of the second century before Christ. This is already about four hundred years later than the great event of the Dharmachakarapravarttana, and belongs to a time, when the organised sangha had grown to large proportions and divided itself into several contending schools, each with a wide circle of lay adherents for support, and the religion had spread itself even beyond the frontiers of India.

Yet, when an art with a specific Buddhist content does at last come to view—one must not forget that with the exception of Maurya court art, the earliest chapter of Buddhist art is also the earliest chapter of Indian art that can be linked up along the arrow line of time with the later art of India—the impress on it of earlier and contemporary art activities in relatively impermanent or semi-permanent materials, is too strong to be missed. Indeed, in form and technique it still retains a great deal of the grammar and idiom of art practices in wood, clay and other materials. A most significant idiom is that of the arrangement of the bas-reliefs themselves of such monuments as those of Barhut, Sanchi, Bodhgaya, Mathura, Amaravati and other places, an idiom which was nothing but a translation in terms of stone and the third dimension of what was practised on textile and in the second dimension in what was called charanachitras or pata-chitras, a practice that survives to this day in the villages of Eastern India. There is no doubt that this and many other forms and idioms were survivals from an ethnically primitive and autocthonus culture.

Equally evident is the fact that this early art (c. 150 B.C. to C. 250 A.D.) was to a very large extent socially conditioned and had a much wider appeal and a much larger clientele than the art that served Buddhism of a later period. First, it was frankly narrative and representational in character and whatever symbols it employed they were easily recognisable to the multitude, in shape, form and significance. Their primary function was to tell a story, edificatory, didactic, or otherwise, of the life of the historical Buddha or of His previous lives, to represent the gods and demi-gods of popular beliefs— yakshas and yakshinis, gandharvas, kinnars and others— accepted in and recognised by Buddhism, and to do all this simply and directly, even naively, as one narrates a folk-tale. The folk-tale character is also evident in the way in which men, animals and trees and plants are all endowed with the same qualities and invested with the same significance. The technique employed is also equally simple and direct; for example, things happening at different places and on different occasions, that is, the sequences of a given narrative are shown as happening at one and same time and at one and the same place. Men and women and animals move and have their being in a shy and halting manner and with a very modest and humble bearing.

But as one marches with time and meets the finally evolved phases at Sanchi, at Mathura and in the countless reliefs of the Buddhist monuments of the Godavari-Krishna valley one notices that vegetal nature and the animal world gradually recede into the background and man becomes the pivot of the art; slow movements become quicker, and the increasing quickening of life brings about a faster tempo of the compositional scheme; a simple, humble and modest life is increasingly transformed into a complex and consciously sophisticated existence indulging in all the sweet pleasures of the senses. The human body, which was considered by early Buddhism as the source of kama, desire, and hence of evil, becomes the central object of love, adoration and adulation. Indeed, in the reliefs of the Vengi or Andhra School, the artist bestows all his caressing care in bringing out the fullest charm of the human figure. The adequacy of the technique is also correspondingly brought up-to-date to express in full the quickened and sophisticated way of life fostered by a rich maritime trade and a fast-growing urban economy in the inland emporiums and coastal ports.

Epigraphic records prove that though the sangha took the initiative, the material wherewithal of this art as of the monastic establishments themselves, came from a much wider circle of classes and communities and hence had a much wider social basis than it is possible to speak of in respect of later schools and periods of Indian art.

The story-telling or narrative and representational quality of this art is a distinct contribution to the history of Indian and Asian art, and its formal character has interesting parallel in mediaeval Christian sculpture and Indian Renaissance painting. With a certain thinning of the original impulse this narrative quality of early Buddhist art can be witnessed in the bas-reliefs of the great Borobudur stupa and in some of the temples of Pagan in Burma, but a certain monotony of style and treatment waters down the intensity of the narration.

The international content of Buddhism contributed directly and indirectly to its adoption and integration of art forms and styles from diverse ethnic and cultural sources, and gave it plasticity and resilience enough to allow its indigenous forms to be adopted and integrated by alien art forms and styles. Within the borders of India, along her north-western territories and at Mathura, on the banks of the Yamuna, Buddhism during the early centuries of the Christian era, helped to bring into existence an eclectic school of art in which Bactrian-Hellenistic, Roman early Christian, nomadic Central Asian, Scythian and Achaemenian art forms, styles and symbols were interwoven into a common pattern. In this a direct reflection of the sociological pattern of Buddhism in these regions, is difficult to brush aside. The same artistic pattern, at a later date (c. 400-500 A.D.), came to be impregnated with the form, style and ideology of contemporary Buddhist art of the Ganga-Yamuna valley, and this gave a creative interpretation to the mechanistic and eclectic Gandhara form and idiom of the earlier centuries, which is particularly marked in the interpretation of the Buddha images of the school of the fourth and fifth centuries.

On the other hand, when Buddhism, borne on the shoulders of the sreshthis, sarthavahas and bhikshus, penetrated the rugged plains and hills of Afghanistan, the desert sands of Central Asia and the river valleys of China, and then Korea and Japan, it acted as a fertilising agent everywhere and infused new life into the traditional and contemporary art of the respective regions. There in Afghanistan and Central Asia, such diverse people as the Iranians and Uigur Turks, the Sassanians and Manichiaen Christians, the Scythians, Central Asian and the Chinese, became converts to, or ardent adherents of Buddhism and evolved diverse forms and patterns of art in which were echoed forms, styles and idioms from as far as Sanchi and Amaravati, the valleys of the Ganga and Yamuna, and Ajanta, for example. In China and Japan, the characteristic Buddhist conceptions of *bodhi* or enlightenment and *karuna* or compassion, Gupta plasticity of volume and abstract treatment of modelling, the boldly flowing and modelled line of the Paintings of Ajanta, their tonal quality and refined consistency of colour as well as the total colour scheme of the Indian Classical School of painting, brought about a new phase sculpture and painting. Indeed, art proved to be a great carrier and exponent of Buddhism, and wherever Buddhism extended itself, it acted as a lever to the mind, imagination and sensibilities of men and inspired them to express themselves in art as much as in other activities of life. Converts to a new faith and a new way of life, these alien peoples—some of them of nomadic pastoral way of life—seem to have been touched by a new energy that expressed itself in endless varieties of form.

But perhaps the most significant contribution of Buddhism to art is the concertisation in visual form of such abstract and elusive conceptions as *bodhi* and *karuna and prajna,* and finding for them a human habitation in the image of the Buddha and the Bodhisattvas.

Indeed, this is an achievement which at its finally evolved phase has hardly any parallel in the history of art. One need not in this connection enter into or even refer to the much debated question of the origin of the Buddha image, since it is a purely iconographic question. In early Buddhism, the Lord Buddha was a historical person, but even before the Christian era He came to be invested with divinity. The idea behind the term Buddha the Enlightened One, slowly and steadily and with deepening experience, began to yield deeper and subtler meanings and came to mean Enlightenment in the abstract, into which was integrated the subtly sensuous and emotional idea of *Karuna*—both interpreted in terms of the evolved system of *Yogachara*. By about the fourth, fifth and sixth centuries, the idea took a concrete shape and form and resulted in evolving a form of the Buddha and Bodhisattvas which, artistically speaking, had but little to do with the earliest Buddha-Bodhisattva images of either Gandhara or Mathura. Both responded equally satifactorily to the iconographic requirements of the Buddha icon and to the more well-known *mahapurushalakshanas*. While Gandhara evolved an electric type composed mechanically of Hellenistic inspiration and Indian Buddhist literary and iconographic tradition, Mathura simply translated the heavy, earthy and suprahuman Yaksha figures in Buddhist terms and called them Buddhas or Bodhisattvas. Both the types were equally innocent of the meaning of what the term Buddha meant and of the deeper experiences that the historical Buddha must have gone through before and at the final stage of realisation of Enlightenment. Early Buddha and Bodhisattva figures even of the Mathura type are, therefore, of heavy proportions, earthbound and of supra human size, energy and strength, all understood in a purely temporal context. Their eyes, wide open, look out into the world of externals. Gradually, by about the third century of the Christian era they begin to look inwards and wear a contemplative appearance (c.f. the image at Anuradhapura, for example). In the next two centuries, there is clearly noticeable a progressive attempt to shed the body of its earthy weight and heavy proportions as well as to give an increasingly subtler and simpler interpretation to the plastic quality of the volume. By about the end of the fifth and beginning of the sixth century, principally at Sarnath, but to an extent also at Mathura and in Eastern India, we see the emergence of a physiognomical form which is slender and very much lighter in proportion, an unspeakably subtle and abstract plastic treatment of volume that makes the texture of the body meltingly tender and softly luminous, and an over-all attitude of absolute calm, complete detachment, rapt concentration and perfect contemplativeness. The weightlessness of the body is the concretisation off the conquest of matter, the luminosity of the plastic treatment is the concretisation of Enlightenment itself, the melting tenderness, of compassion or *karuna,* and the absolute detachment and concentrated inwardness of attitude is the concretisation of the inner meaning of *yoga.* Yet, be it remembered, all this was achieved with the hammer and chisel of the sculptor and the brush of the painter. Enlightenment and *karuna* and yoga are things of experience and realisation; but art is 'making' or 'doing'. For the artists to make an experience of the kind connoted by the term Buddha, take shape and form and meaning in terms of line and volume and depth and surface, is also an experience of supreme spiritual significance.

It was this evolved idea and image of the Buddha and Bodhisattva that inspired the artists of Borobudur and Candi Mendut in Java, those of the T'ang period in China, of the Nara period and the Horiyuji Temple in Japan, of Dvaravati and Sukhotaya in Thailand, for example.

It is in the sphere of architecture that it is possible to speak of a specific Buddhist architecture as such, architecture being the art that by its very nature has to respond a great deal to practical requirements. Religious architecture has, therefore, to answer the demands of the religion it is called upon to serve, and to express its ideology. Buddhist architecture has been no exception.

Whatever the origins of the *stupa* from it cannot be doubted that Buddhism gave it a new interpretation and imparted to it, judging by the best examples, a majesty of shape and form, at the same time utilising it for popularising the symbols, myths and legends of the religion. A stupendous hemispherical dome crowned by a *harmika* and a number of receding *chhatras,* and surrounded by a magnificent railing with two or four stupendous gates on all of which are unfolded a long panorama of life, must have made a deep and undying impression on contemporary minds. Even today, far away from the life of those spacious days, the great *stupa* at Sanchi or still greater *stupa* of Borobudur in Java have an overpowering appeal in the dignified majesty of form and their largeness of conception and execution.

The *chaitya* and the *vihara,* two other unique architectural types that Buddhism evolved to serve its requirements, both in their rock-cut and structural forms, are distinct contributions of Buddhism to the art of architecture, not only in India but in Asia and the world. Beginning from the primitive and rude rock-cut single-cell residence chamber of the monk to the elaborate structural monastic university establishments of such centres as Nalanda for example, the story of *vihara*-architecture in India, Burma, Ceylon and Central Asia, is indeed an unique one, and follows the history of the evolution of the Buddhist sangha, and its rich and active monastic life which has a fine parallel in the monastic life and monasteries of mediaeval Christendom. The *chaitya* which served the purpose of congregational worship has also an interesting story of evolution and is a fine example of how religious requirements conditioned the evolution of its form from simple and modest beginnings to such a refined and elegant edifice, so finely organised as that of the *chaitya* at Sanchi. Indeed, in elegance and refinement the *chaitya* form of architecture is a definite contribution the history of architecture in the East.

It is not so much accidence of preservation but social and historical circumstances which destined that Buddhism should contribute, by and large, the early chapters of the history of art in India when some of the basic principles of form and style were evolved for the first time and certain techniques laid down—principles and techniques that persisted through centuries in Indian and Asian art. Buddhism as the one and only civilizing factor, also contributed practically the entire history of the art of such countries as Ceylon, Burma and Thailand. It also contributed significant chapters of the story of Chinese sculpture and painting of Japanese painting, of Central Asian sculpture, painting and architecture and of the sculptures and bronzes of Java and Sumatra. Art was, indeed, one of the stronger threads with which Buddhism bound these Asian countries in one common fraternity of faith.

—*N.R. Roy*

10

Some Sayings of the Buddha

The Going Forth of Cotama[1]

'Now I, brethren, before my enlightenment, when I was not yet a perfected Buddha, but was a Bodhisatta, being myself still of nature to be born again,—I sought after things that are of nature to be reborn. Being myself of nature to decay, being subject to disease and death, being myself subject to sorrow, to the impurities, I sought after things of like nature.

Then there came to me the thought: "Why do I, being of nature to be reborn, being subject to death, to sorrow, to the impurities...thus search after things of like nature? What if I, being myself...of such nature, and seeing the disadvantage of what is subject to rebirth, were to search after the unsurpassed, perfect security, which is Nibbana? Being myself subject to decay, disease, death, sorrow, and the impurities, and seeing the disadvantage. (of what is subject to these things), what if I were to search after the untainted, unsurpassed, perfect security, which is Nibbana?

Then I, brethren, some time after this, when I was a young lad, a black-haired stripling, endowed with happy youth,[2] in the first flush of manhood, against my mother's and my father's wish, who lamented with tearful eyes, I had the hair of head and face shaved off, I donned the saffron robes, and I went forth from my home to the homeless life.

Thus become a wanderer and a searcher for what is good, searching after the unsurpassed, peaceful state most excellent, I approached Alara Kalama, and drawing near I said to Alara Kalama: "Friend Alara, I desire to live the holy life in this Norm-Discipline (of yours)..."

(He then soon acquired all that Alara Kalama had to teach, the path of yoga for reaching in meditation the Realm of the Void, but no further, so leaving him he went to Rama, who took him a step further, to the realm where there is no more perception of anything. Dissatisfied with this he went to Uddaka, disciple of Rama, who professed to go a little further, but who, confessing that he could not go beyond a certain point, himself accepted Gotama as his master. So Gotama resolves to struggle on alone to reach the Goal, the 'incomparable security which is Nibbana.')

The Attainment of Nibbana by Gotama

'So I, brethren, thinking lightly of that teaching (of Alara and the others), being averse from that doctrine, went away.

Then, I, brethren, in my search for what is good, searching after the unsurpassed state of peace most excellent, while roaming about among the folk of Magadha, came to Uruvela, a suburb of the Captain of the Host. There I beheld a lovely spot, a pleasant forest grove and a river of clear water flowing by, easy of access and delightful, and hard by was a village where I could beg my food. Then, brethren, I thought thus:

"Delightful in truth is this spot, pleasant this forest grove and this river of pure water flowing by, easy of assess and delightful, and this village hard by where I can beg my food! Truly a proper place is this for a clansman bent on striving for his welfare, to strive therein!"

SO, brethren, there and then I sat down, saying to myself: "A proper place is this for striving in!"

Then I, being of nature to be reborn, perceived the disadvantage of things of like nature... *(as above)*...and searching after the unsurpassed state of security, that is Nibbana, free from the impurities, I did attain unto the utter peace of Nibbana that is free from the impurities, so that the Knowledge arose in me, the Insight arose in me thus: "Sure is my release. This is my last birth. There is no more birth for me!"'

Majjhima Nikaya, i. I66.

Hard is the Truth to Discern

'Then, brethren, I had this thought:

"This Reality[3] that I have reached is profound, hard to see, hard to understand, excellent, pre-eminent, beyond the sphere for thinking, subtle, and to be penetrated by the wise alone.

But this world of men is attached to what it clings to, takes pleasure in what it clings to, delights in what it clings to. Since then this world is thus attached (to things) ... a hard task it is for them (to grasp) ... namely, the Originating of things by Dependence on Couses.[4] A hard task it is for them to see the meaning of the fact that all activities may be set at rest, that all the bases of being may be left behind, the destruction of craving, Passionlessness, Cessation, which is Nibbana.

Verily, if I were to teach them the Truth, this Reality, others would not understand, and that would be labour in vain for me, vexatious would it be to me."'

(Then Brahma Sahampati, the great Deva, appeared and begged the Buddha to preach the Truth for the sake of a few.)

For the Sake of a Few, But the Profit of the Many

Then said Brahma Sahampati:

'Let my Lord the Exalted One teach the Truth: let the Happy One teach the Truth. For there are some creatures whose sight is but little clouded with dust. They are perishing through not hearing the Truth. They will become knowers of the Truth.' So spake Brahma Sahampati, and so saying added this further:

In Magadha was hitherto a Norm—
A Norm not pure, by minds impure thought out.
Open this Door to what is 'Deathless' called:
Let men hear *this* Norm by the Pure discerned.

As. Standing on a rocky mountain-peak,
One may look down upon the folk below:
So, Wise One, climbing up the Norm-built steps,
Do thou, with eye that seeth all around,
Look down upon the folk in sorrow plunged—
Thou who art freed from sorrow—O look down
On folk by birth, age and decay o'erwhelmed.

Rise up, brave heart, victorious in battle,
Debt-freed, Band-Leader, roam through all the world!
Let the Exalted One show us the Norm.
Hearing it, men shall come to understand.

Vin, *i*, *4* = M. *i*, 168.

Cf. Dhammapada, 28:

Lo! The sage that drives away
The cloud of sloth by heedfulness,
Climbing up the heights of wisdom
Sorrowless looks down upon
All the miserable beings,
As a hillman on the plains.

All Sorts and Conditions of Men

'Then I, brethren, seeing the wish of Brahma Sahampati, out of compassion for all beings, looked down upon the world with the eye of a Buddha. And as I looked down upon the world with a Buddha's eye, I beheld beings eyes were but little clouded with dust, also beings whose eyes were much clouded with dust: beings of sharp wits and beings of dull wits, beings of good and beings of evil natures: beings docile and beings of stubborn sort, and some of these abode in understanding of the danger of lives to come and fear of evil deeds.

As in a pond of lotuses blue and red and white, some plants which spring and grow in the water come not to the surface, but flourish underneath; and some spring and grow in the water and reach up to the surface; and yet others in like manner push up above the surface and are not wetted by the water,—even so, brethren, did I, looking over the world with a Buddha's eye, behold beings whose eyes were but little clouded with dust....

> Then, brethren, did I make answer to Brahma Sahampati in verse:
> Open for such is the Door to the Deathless State.
> Ye that have ears, renounce the creed ye hold.[5]
> Conscious of danger, in its depth, Brahma,
> I would not preach the Norm of Norms to men.'[6]

The First Sermon

Thus have I heard: Once the Exalted One was dwelling near Benares, at Isipatana, in the Deer-Park.

Then the Exalted One thus spake unto the company of Five Brethren:

'These two extremes brethren, should not be followed by one who has gone forth as a wanderer:

Devotion to the pleasures of sense—a low and pagan practice, unworthy, unprofitable, the way of the world (on the one hand), and on the other hand devotion to self-mortification, which is painful, unworthy, unprofitable.

By avoiding these two extremes he who hath won the Truth (the Buddha) has gained knowledge of that *Middle Path* which giveth Vision which giveth Knowledge, which causeth Calm, Insight, Enlightenment, and Nibbana.

And what, brethren, is *Middle Path* which giveth Vision, which giveth Knowledge, which causeth Calm, Insight, Enlightenment. And Nibbana?

Verily it is this Ariyan Eightfold Path, that is to say:

Right View, Right aim, right speech, right action, bright living, right effort, right mindfulness, right contemplation.

This, brethren, is that *Middle Path,* which giveth Vision, which giveth knowledge, which causeth Calm, Insight, Enlightenment, and Nibbana?

Now this, brethren, is the Ariyan Truth about *Suffering:*

Birth is Suffering, Decay is Suffering, Sickness is Suffering, Death is Suffering, likewise Sorrow and Grief, Woe, Lamentation and Despair. To be conjoined with things which we dislike, to be separated from things which we like—that also is Suffering. Not to get what one wants—that also is Suffering. In a word, this Body, this fivefold Mass which is based on *Grasping,* that is Suffering.

Now this, brethren, is the Ariyan Truth about *The Origin of Suffering:*

It is that *Craving* that leads downwards to birth, along with the Lure and the Lust that lingers longingly now here, now there: namely, that Craving for Sensation, the Craving to be born again, the Craving to have done with rebirth. Such brethren, is the Ariyan Truth about *The Origin of Suffering.*

And this, brethren, is the Ariyan Truth about *The Ceasing of Suffering:*

Verily it is the utter passionless cessation of, the giving up, the for-saking, the release from, the absence of longing for, this *Craving.*

Now this, brethren, is the Ariyan Truth about *The Way leading to the Ceasing of Suffering.* Verily it is this Ariyan Eightfold Path, That is:

> Right view, right aim, right speech, right action, right living, right effort, right mindfulness, right contemplation.

At the thought, brethren, of this Ariyan Truth of Suffering, concerning things unlearnt before, there arose in me Vision, Insight, Understanding: there arose in me Wisdom, there arose in me Light.

At the throught, brethren, "this Ariyan Truth about the Origin of Suffering is to be understood," concerning things unlearnt before, there arose in me Vision, Insight, Understanding: there arose in me Wisdom, there arose in me Light.

At the thought, brethren, "this Ariyan Truth of Suffering has been understood," concerning things unlearnt before, there arose in me Vision, Insight, Understanding: there arose in me Wisdom, there arose in me Light.

Again, at the thought, brethren, of this Ariyan Truth of the Origin of Suffering, concerning things unlearnt before, there arose in me Vision, Insight, Understanding: there arose me Wisdom, there arose in me Light.

At the thought, brethren, the Origin of Suffering must be put away," concerning things unlearnt before, there arose in me Vision, insight, Understanding: there arose in me Wisdom, there arose in me Light.

So also at the thought "The Origin of Suffering has been put away"...there arose in me Light.

Again, at the thought, brethren, of this Ariyan Truth of the Ceasing of Suffering...there arose in me Light.

At the thought, brethren, "the Ceasing of Suffering must be realized" ...there arose in me Light.

At the thought, brethren, "the Ceasing of Suffering has been realized" ...there arose in me Light.

Finally, brethren, at the though of This Ariyan Way leading to the Ceasing of Suffering... there arose in me Light.

At the thought, brethren, "the Way leading to the Ceasing of Suffering has been developed" ... there arose in me Light.

At the thought, brethren, "the Way leading to the Ceasing of Suffering has been developed"... concerning things unlearnt before, there arose in me Vision. Insight, Understanding: there arose in me Wisdom, there arose in me Light.

Now so long, brethren, as my knowledge and my insight of these thrice-revolved twelvefold Ariyan Truths, in their essential nature, were not quite purified,—so long was I not sure that in this world, together with the devas, the Maras, the Brahmas, among the hosts of recluses and brahmi of devas and mankind, there was one enlightened with supreme enlightenment.

But so soon, brethren, as my knowledge and my insight of these thrice-revolved twelvefold Arivan Truths, in their essential nature, were quire purified,—then, brethren, was I assured what it is to be enlightened with supreme enlightenment with regard to the world and its devas, Maras, and Brahmas, and with regard to the hosts of recluses and brahmins, of devas and mankind.

But now Knowledge and Insight have arisen in me, so that I know, "Sure is my heart's release. This is my last birth. There is no more becoming for me."'

Samyutta Nikaya v. 421-3.

Analysis of the Eightfold Path

And the Exalted One said:

'Now what, brethren, is Right View?

The knowledge about ill, the Arising of ill, Ceasing of ill, and the Way leading to the Ceasing of ill,—that, brethren, is called Right View.

And what, brethren, is called Right Aim?

The being set on Renunciation, on Non-resentment, on Harmlessness,—that, brethren, is called Right Aim.

And what, brethren, is Right Speech?

Abstinence from lying speech, from backbiting and abusive speech, and from idle babble,—That, brethren, is called Right Speech.

And What, brethren, is Right Action?

Abstinence from taking life, from taking what is not given, from wrong doing in sexual passions,—that, brethren, is called Right Action.

And what, brethren, is Right Living?

Herein, brethren, the Ariyan disciple, by giving up wrong living, gets his livelihood right living,—that, brethren, is called Right Living.

And What, brethren, is Right Effort?

Herein, brethren, a brother generates the will to inhibit the arising of evil immoral conditions that have not yet arisen: he makes an effort, he sets energy afoot, he applies his mind and struggles. Likewise (he does the same) to reject evil immoral conditions that have already arisen. Likewise (he does the same) to cause the arising of good conditions that have not yet arisen. Likewise he does the same to establish, to prevent the corruption, to cause the increase, the practice, the fulfilment of good conditions that have already arisen. This, brethren, is called Right Effort.

And what, brethren, is Right Mindfulness?

Herein, brethren, a brother dwells regarding body as a compound, he dwells ardent, self-possessed, recollected, by controlling the covetousness and dejection that are in the world. So also with regard to Feelings, with regard to Perception, with regard to the Activities ...what regard to Thought. This, brethren, is called Right Mind-Fulness.

And what, brethren, is Right Contemplation?

The Four Jhanas

Herein, brethren, a brother, remote from sensual appetites, remote from evil conditions, enters upon and abides in the First Musing, which is accompanied by directed thought and sustained thought (on an object). It is born of solitude, full of zest and happiness.

Then, by the sinking down of thought directed and sustained, he enters on and abides in the Second Musing, which is an inner calming, a raising up of the will. In it there is no directed thought, no sustained thought. It is born of contemplation, full of zest and happiness.

Then again, brethren, by the fading away of the zest, be becomes balanced (indifferent) and remains mindful and self-possessed, and while still in the body he experiences the happiness of which the Ariyans aver "the balanced thoughtful man dwells happily." Thus he enters on the Third Musing and abides therein.

The again, brethren, rejecting pleasure and pain, by the coming to an end of the joy and sorrow which he had before, he enters on and remains in the Fourth Musing, which is free from pain and free from pleasure, but is a state of perfect purity of balance and equanimity. This is called Right Contemplation.

This, brethren, is called the Ariyan Truth of the Way leading to the Ceasing of Woe.[17]

Digha Nikaya, ii, 312.

The Cause of Ill

Now the Exalted One thus addressed the brethren:

'Through not understanding, though not penetrating the Four Ariyan Truths, brethren, we have run on and wandered round this long journey (of rebirth), both you and I. What are those four?

The Ariyan Truth of Ill: the Ariyan Truth of the Arising of Ill: The Ariyan Truth of the Way reading to the Ceasing of Ill.

But, brethren, when these Four Ariyan Truths are understood and penetrated, then is uprooted the craving for existence, cut off is the thread that leadeth to rebirth, then is there no more coming to be.'

Thus spake the Exalted One. When the Happy One had thus spoken, the Master added this further:

> Blind to the Fourfold Ariyan Truths of things,
> And blind to see things as they really are,
> Long was our journeying thro divers births.
> Gone is the cord of life when these are seen.
> No More becoming when Ill's root is cut.

D.N. ii. 90.

Early Struggles for Light

(Before attaining the Middle Way, Gotama Followed every known ascetic practice. In his old age he related his Experiences to Sariputta.)

'I can recall, Sariputta, how I practised the four-square practice of the holy life. Thus: I was a penance-worker, outdoing others in penance: I was a rough-liver, outdoing others in roughing it: I was scrupulous, outdoing others in my scruples: a solitary was I, outdoing others in solitude.

Thus far, Sariputta, did I go in my penance.

I went without clothes. I licked my food from my hands. I was no complier with invitations of "Come in, your reverence! Stay, your reverence!" I took no food that was brought, or meant specially for me. I accepted no invitations to a meal. I took no alms from pot or dish. I took no food from within a threshold, or through window-bars, or within the pounding-place, nor from two people eating together, nor from a pregnant woman, nor from a women suckling a child, nor from one in intercourse, nor from food collected here and there; nor food where a dog stood by, nor from places where flies were swarming, not fish nor flesh, nor drink fermented, nor drink distilled, nor yet sour gruel did I drink.

I ate from just one house, and just one morsel from that. Or else I ate from two houses only and just two morsels thence: or I ate from seven houses only, and just one morsel from each house. I kept my self going on food from just one pot, or just two pots, or just seven pots at a time. I took food only once a day or once in two days or once in seven days. Thus did I dwell given to the practice of taking food by rule, at stated intervals of half a month.

I lived on vegetables, on millet, on wild paddy, on *daddula,* on watercress, on paddy-husk, on scum of rice, on ground sesamum on gross, on cowdung. I lived on toots and fruits of the forest, on casual fruits [that had fallen] I existed.

I was one who wore coarse clothes, I wore hemp woven in with other things, grave-cloths, dustheap rags, a dress made of bark: I wore antelope-skin, a dress made of shreds of antelope skin, I wore *kusa* fibre bark fibre, clothes made of shavings, a hair shirt of human hair, a hair shirt of horsehair, or made of owl's feathers.

I plucked out and beard, and kept the practice up. I stood always, refusing to sit down. I was a squatter on my heels, struggling by the method of squatting. I was a thorn-bed man and lay upon a bed of thorns. I lived given to the habit of bathing thrice a day, going down into the water.

Thus in divers ways did I dwell given to tormenting and again tormenting the body. To that extent, Sariputta, was I given to penance.

And thus far did I go in roughing it, Sariputta.––The dirt of many seasons gathered on my body just like the outer crust of tree-bark. Just like the stump of a *tinduka*-tree was I, Sariputta, covered with the outer crust of bark gathered through countless seasons. But never once did I think to myself: "O to wipe off this dirt and dust with my hand," or "O that others might do so for me!" I never thought of such a thing. Thus far, Sariputta, did I go in roughing it.

And thus far, Sariputta, did I go in scrupulosity.—Mindful was I in going and in coming. Even to a drop of water was charity established in me, thus: "May I not be guilty of violence in harming tiny living things (therein)." Thus far, Sariputta, did I go in my scrupulosity.

And thus far did I go in solitude—I used to resort to some forest domain, plunge into it and dwell therein. When I saw a cow-keeper or a herd or a grass-gatherer, or a gatherer of sticks, or a forester, then from forest to forest, from jungle to jungle, from marshland to marshland, from upland to upland I fled away. And why? Lest they should see me or I should see them. Even as, Sariputta a wild creature of the forest on beholding man flees away from forest to forest jungle to jungle, from marshland to marshland, from upland to upland.—even so did I flee and flee away, lest they should see me, lest I should see them. Thus far did I go in the practice of the solitary, life.

Then, Sariputta, where there were cowpens and cows penned therein, when the cowherds had gone away, I drew near with my water-pot and gathered up the droppings of calves and young calves and sucking calves. So long as my own excrements lasted Sariputta, I lived even on mine own excrements. To such extremes did I go, Sariputta, as to live on filth for food.

Then, Sariputta, I plunged into a fearsome forest thicket and dwelt therein. Such was the fearsome horror of that dread forest thicket that anyone whose passions were not stilled and entered there,—the very hairs of his body would stand on end.

Then those cold frosty nights between the eighths [of the lunar month], on nights when the snow was falling, those nights did I pass in the open air, and the days I spent in the forest covert. And in the last month of the hot season, by day I dwelt in the open air, by night in forest covert. So that, Sariputta, these verses never heard before, these curious verses, occurred to me:

Scorched, frozen, and alone,
In fearsome forest dwelling,
Naked, no fire to warm,
Bent on the quest is the Sage.

Then again, Sariputta, in a charnel-field I lay down to rest upon bones of corpses. And the cowherds came up to me, even spat upon me and even made water upon me, spattered me with mud, even poked straws into my ears. Yet, Sariputta, I cannot call to mind that a single evil thought against them arose in me. Thus far was I gone in forbearance, Sariputta.

M.N. i. 77-9.

Panic Fear and Dread

(The Master describes his early experiences of the struggles, mentioned above, to the brahmin Janussoni.)

"Then, brahmin, I thought, "Suppose now that on those nights that are notable and well marked, the fifteenth and eight (of the lunar month),—suppose I spend them in shrines of forest, park, or tree, fearsome and hair-raising as they are, making such shrines my lodging for the night, that I may behold for myself the panic fear and horror of it all."

So, brahmin, when the next time came round I did so, and made such shrines my lodging for the night. As I stayed there, a deer maybe came up to me, or a peacock threw down a twig, or else a breeze stirred a heap of fallen leaves. Then thought I, "here it is! Here comes that panic fear and horror." Then, brahmin, there came to me this thought: "Why do I remain thus is constant fear and apprehension? Let my bend down to my will that panic fear and horror, just as I am, and just as it had come to be." So as I was walking to and for that panic fear and horror came upon me. Then I neither stood still nor sat nor lay down, but just walking up and down I bent to my will that panic fear and horror.

Again, as I was standing still, it came upon me. But I neither walked up and down, nor sat nor lay, but just standing bent it down to my will. And yet again, as I was sitting, it came upon me. But I neither stood up nor walked up and down, nor lay down, but, just sitting as I was, I bent it to my will. Then as I lay it came upon me. But I sat not up nor stood up nor walked up and down, but, just lying as I was, I bent that panic fear and horror to my will.'

M.N. i. 20-1.

Struggles More Terrible

Here he describes to Saccaka, the Jain, whom he calls by his title, his further struggles for the Light.)

(a) The Suspension of Breath

'Then I said to myself: "How now if, setting my teeth and pressing my palate with my tongue, I were to hold down and force down my mind by will and so destroy it?"

So, Aggivessana, I set my teeth and pressing tongue to palate by an effort of will I strove to hold down, to force down my mind and so destroy it. And as I struggled, Aggivessana, with the effort the sweat burst forth from my arm-pits.

Just as if a strong man were to seize a weaker man by head and shoulders, and try to hold him down, press him down and break him in,—even so did I struggle.

Thus, Aggivessana, was my energy strenuous and unyielding. Mindfulness was thus indeed established undisturbed, but my body was perturbed; it was not calmed thereby, because I was overpowered by the stress of my painful struggling. But even such painful feeling as then arose could not lay hold of and control my mind.

Then, Aggivessana, I sad to myself: "Suppose now I practise the musing of breath suppressed."

Accordingly I checked the breathing in and out from mouth and nostrils. Then with mouth and nostrils stopped, in my ears arose a sparing noise of the escaping vital airs. Just as the sound of a smith's bellows being blown, even such was the roaring noise in my ears of the vital airs that struggled to escape when I had stopped mouth and nostrils.

Then, Aggivessana, was my energy strenuous and unyielding indeed. Mindfulness was indeed established undisturbed, but yet my body was perturbed: it was not made calm thereby, because I was overpowered by the stress of my painful struggling. But even such painful feeling as then arose could not lay hold of and control my mind.

Then, Aggivessana, I said to myself: "Suppose I practise still further the musing of breath suppressed." Accordingly I stopped my breathing in and out from mouth and nostrils, and I closed my ears.

Then, just as if a strong man with a sharp-pointed sword should crash into the brain, so did the rush of air, all outlets being stopped, crash into my brain. Then was my energy strenuous (*as before*).

...Yet such painful feelings as arose could not lay hold of and control my mind.

Then I thought: " Suppose I practise the musing of breath suppressed still further." So I closed all outlets of the breath.... Then did dreadful head-pains come in my head. Just as if a strong man should twist a stout leathern though round the head, even so did violent pains assail my head.... Yet even so, Aggivessana, could not such painful feeling as then arose lay hold of and control my mind.

Then I thought: "Suppose I practise the musing of breath suppressed still further." So I closed all outlets for the breath... Then just as a skilful butcher or butcher's 'prentice with a sharp butcher's knife might rip up the belly of an ox, even so did violent pains assault my belly.... Yet even so did not ... (*as before*) ... control my mind.

Then I thought: "Suppose I carry the practise further still." So I closed all outlets (*as before*).... Then, just as if two strong men should lay hold of some weaker man, seizing him each by an arm, and scorch and burn him in a pit of glowing charcoal, even so, because of the closing of all outlets of the breath, did a burning pervade my body.... Then, Aggivessana, was my energy strenuous and unyielding, and mindfulness was established undisturbed. Yet my body was perturbed. It was not made calm thereby, because I was overpowered by the stress of my painful struggling. Yet even such painful feelings as then arose could not lay hold of and control my mind.

Thereupon certain devas beholding me exclaimed: "Gotama the recluse is dead!" But some devas said, "Gotama the recluse is not dead yet, but he is nearing his end." Yet other devas said, "Gotama the recluse is neither dead nor nearing his end. An Arahant is Gotama the recluse. Such is the way an Arahant doth abide!"'

(b) Abstinence from Food

After that, Aggivessana, I thought to myself: "Now suppose I practise for the utter abstinence from food."

Then certain devas approached me and said: "Do not thou, good sir, practise for the utter abstinence from food. Yet if thou dost so practise, we will pour heavenly sustenance through the body's pores, and by that shalt thou be sustained."

Then thought I: "If I proceed to utter abstinence from food and these devas pour heavenly sustenance through my body's pores and I am sustained thereby, that would be a fraud in me." So I rejected the offer of those davas, saying "Let be."

Then, Aggivessana, I thought thus: "Suppose I feed myself on just a little food, a mere handful now and then, such as the juice of (chewed) beans or vetch or lentils or peas."

And I did so. And my body reached a state of utter exhaustion. Just like knot-grass or bulrush, so did every several joint of it become, through that lack of sustenance. Just like a bison's hoof became my hinder parts through that same lack of sustenance. Just like a row of reed-knots my backbone stood out through that lack of sustenance. Just as the rafters of a tottering house fall in this way and that, so did my ribs fall in this way and that through that lack of sustenance. Just as in a deep, deep well the sparkle of the waters may be seen sunk in the deeps below, so in the depths of their sockets did the lustre of my eyes seem sunk, through that same lack of sustenance. Just as a bitter gourd, cut of unripened from the stalk, is shrivelled and withered by wind and sun, so was the very skin of my head shriveled and withered through lack of food.

Then that same I, Aggivessana, saying to myself. "I will touch my belly's skin," I seized instead my backbone. And saying, "I will touch my backbone", I seized instead my belly's skin: for so it was, Aggivessana, that the one clung to the other through that same lack of sustenance.

Then that same I, Aggivessana, saying to myself, "I will go to ease myself," there on the spot I stumbled and fell down for that same want to food. And that same I, Aggivessana, Saying to myself. "I will ease my body with my hand," when with my hand I stroked my limbs, rotten at the very roots my body's hairs fell of from my body through that same lack of sustenance.

And those who beheld me said, "Gotama the recluse is a black man." But some said, "Nay, he is dusky-hued." But yet others said, "Not so. Gotama the recluse is neither black nor dusky. Sallow is the skin of Gotama the recluse." Thus were the utter purity and clearness of my complexion spoiled by that same lack of sustenance.

Then thought I: "All the feelings, sharp, painful grievous, and bitter, that recluses and brahmins in past times have felt,—surely these pains of mine go far beyond them all. All the feelings to be thus borne in future times, surely these painful feelings of mine go far beyond them all. All the feelings that are now thus borne, surely these of mine surpass them all. Yet by all this bitter, woeful way do I not achieve the truly Ariyan excellence of knowledge and insight surpassing mortal things. Maybe there is some other way to the Wisdom.

(c) *The Saner Way*

Then, Aggivessana, I thought: "I call to mind how when the Sakyan my father was ploughing I sat in the cool shade of the rose-apple tree, remote from sensual desires and ill conditions, and entered upon and abode in the First Musing, that accompanied by thought directed and sustained, which is born of solitude, full of zestful ease."

And I said then, "Is this, I wonder, the Way to the Wisdom?" And on that occasion there came to me the consciousness that follows thought composed, "Yes, this is the Way to the Wisdom."

Then, Aggivessana, I thought, "Why am I afraid of that state of ease, that ease which is apart from sensual desires and ill conditions?"

Then I thought: "No. I am not afraid of that state of ease".... Then I said, "But it is not easy for one to reach that state of ease with a body thus utterly exhausted. Suppose now I take some substantial food, some rice gruel." And so I did, Aggivessana.

Now at that time I had with me five brethren attending me, who thought, "Whatever truth Gotama the recluse shall arrive at, that will he impart to us." But, as soon as I took to eating food substantial, those five brethren were disgusted and went away, saying, ""Luxurious is Gotama the recluse become! He wavers in his purpose; he has turned back to the life luxurious."

M.N. i. 242-7.

'Then I, Aggivessana, after taking food substantial got back my strength: and remote from sensual desires, remote from ill conditions, I entered and abode in the First Musing ... the second Musing ...The Third Musing... the Fourth Musing (*as described above in the section on the Four Jhanas*): but in each case the blissful feelings that arose failed to lay hold of and control my mind.

Then with thought steadied, perfectly purified, and made perfectly translucent, free from blemish, purged of taint, made supple and pliable, fit for wielding, established and immovable, I bent down my mind to the recalling of my former existences. I recalled divers births... evolutions and involutions of aeons... conditions of births... and experiences in such... the rise and full of beings and their characteristics in the different worlds with the eye divine.

Then I perceived the Four Ariyan Truths... the destruction of the asavas... and I knew this: "Destroyed is rebirth for me. Lived is the holy life. Done is my task. For life in these conditions there is no hereafter."

Thus on that night, in the last watch of the night, the Threefold Knowledge was attained by me: knowledge arose, darkness was overcome, light arose, as it does for him that abides earnest, ardent and of set purpose. Yet did not the blissful feeling that arose lay hold of and control my mind.

M.N. i. 247-8.

All These Things Avail Not

Not nakedness, nor matted hair, nor filth,
Nor fasting long, nor lying on the ground,
Not dust and dirt, nor squatting on the heels,
Can cleanse the mortal that is full of doubt.

But one that lives a calm and tranquil life,
Though gaily decked,—if tamed, restrained he live,
Walking the holy path in righteousness,
Laying aside all harm to living things,—
True mendicant, ascetic, Brahmin he.

Dhammapada, vv. 141—2.

References

1. Note from Majjhima Nikaya, i. 163 (Ariyapariyesana-sutta or The Sutta of the Ariyan Searching).

   The popular legend of the Great Renunciation is not in the Pali Tipitaka, but is based on the story of the young noble Yasa (*Vinaya, i.7*) and is expanded in *Lalita Vistara* and the late *Commentary of the Jataka Tales.*
2. This statement about early youth does not harmonize with the account given in the Maha-Parinibbana-Sutta (See end of this book), where the Buddha says he was twenty-nine years old at the time.
3. *Dhamma,* The Norm, The Law, The Truth.
4. *Paticca-samuppada.*

5. *Pamuncantu Saddham*— a much discussed phrase and wrongly translated by the early Pali scholars by 'give faith,' 'put forth belief,' etc.—but it undoubtedly means 'put away.'

6. Note.—In other passages the Buddha has pointed out that if a Buddha give out occult truth to an unbelieving generation, harm befalls the man who rejects it. E.g. *Samyutta Nikaya,* ii. 261: 'I also, brethren, have seen these things before, yet I did not reveal them. I might have revealed it, and others would not have believed it. Now, had they not believed me, it would have been to their loss and sorrow.'

7. Note.—After the Fourth Step, the walker on the Path is termed 'disciple,' and after the Fifth Step, 'brother (*bhikkhu*), lit. 'begger,' one who has renounced the world.

11

The Stability of Societies

Conditions of Communal Stability

Now at that time the venerable Ananda was standing behind the Exalted One and fanning him. And the Exalted One said to the venerable Ananda:

'How now, Ananda? Have you ever heard that the Vajjians repeatedly assemble together and in large numbers?

'I have heard so, Lord.'

'Well; Ananda, so long as the Vajjians shall assemble repeatedly and in large numbers, just so long may the prosperity of the Vajjians be looked for and not their decay.

So long, Ananda, as the Vajjians assemble in harmony and disperse in harmony: so long as they do their business in harmony: so long as they introduce no revolutionary ordinance, or break up no established ordinance, but abide by the old-time Vajjian Norm, as ordained: so long as they honour, reverence, esteem, and worship the elders among the Vajjians and deem them worthy of listening to: so long as the women and maidens of the families dwell without being forced or abducted: so long as they honour, revere, esteem, and worship the Vajjian shrines, both the inner and the outer: so long as they allow not the customary offerings, given and performed, to be neglected: so long as the customary watch and ward over the Arahants that are among them is well kept, so that they may have free access to the realm and having entered may dwell pleasantly therein: just so long as they do these things, Ananda, may the prosperity of the Vajjians be looked for and not their decay.'

D.N. ii.73.

Conditions of the Stability of the Order

1

Then the Exalted One the brethren, saying:

'I will teach you, brethren, seven things that prevent decay. Do ye listen to it carefully. Apply your minds, and I will speak.'

'Even so, Lord,' replied those brethren to the Exalted One, who then said:

'So long, brethren, as the brethren shall assemble repeatedly and in large numbers, the prosperity of the brethren may be looked for and not their decay. So long as the brethren assemble in harmony and disperse in harmony, so long as they do the business of the Order in harmony. So long as they introduce no revolutionary ordinance, break up no established ordinance, but live in accordance with the appointed charges,—

So long as the elder brethren, men of many days and long ordained, fathers of the Order, men of standing in the Order,—so long as these are honoured, reverenced, esteemed, and deferred to,—

So long as brethren do not fall subject to that craving which arises and leads back to rebirth,—

So long as there shall be brethren who are fond of the forest life and lodging,—

So long as brethren shall establish themselves in mindfulness, with this thought, "Let goodly co-mates in the righteous life come hither in the future, and let those that have already come live happily,—"

So long, brethren, as these seven things that prevent decay shall stand fast among the brethren, so long as the brethren shall be instructed therein,—just so long may the prosperity of the brethren be looked for, and not their decay.'

2

'Brethren, I will teach you seven other conditions that prevent decay. Do you listen to it. Apply your minds carefully. I will speak.

'Even so, Lord,' raplied those brethren to the Exalted One. The Exalted One said:

'So long as the brethren do not delight in (worldly) activities, are not busybodies nor devoted to activities,—

So long as the brethren are not gossipers, not delighting in gossip, not devoted to gossip,—

So long as the brethren are not sluggish, not delighting in sleep, not given to somnolence,—

So long as the brethren are not given to company, not delighting in company, not devoted to company,—

So long as the brethren are not slaves of evil desires,—

So long as the brethren are not the friends, comrades, and associates of men of evil ways,—

So long as the brethren shall not come to a stop upon the Way by the attainment of lesser excellence,—

Just so long, brethren, as these seven conditions that prevent decay shall be established and the brethren are instructed in them,—so long may the prosperity of the brethren be looked for, not their decay.'

3

'I will teach you, brethren, seven other conditions that prevent decay....

So long as the brethren are faithful, modest, and conscientious, of wide knowledge, of ardent energy, of steady mindfulness, and full of wisdom,—just so long may the prosperity of the brethren be looked for and not their decay.'

4

'Seven[1] other (like) conditions will I teach you, brethren...

So long as the brethren shall practise the limb of wisdom which is mindfulness, the limb of wisdom which is searching into things, energy, zest, calm, contemplation, and equanimity... so long may their prosperity and not their decay be looked for.

5

'Seven other conditions, brethren, will I teach you that prevent decay....

So long as the brethren shall practise the perception of Impermanence, of the Unreality of Self, of Impurity, of the Besetting Dangers, of Abandonment, of Passionlessness, of Cessation,—just so long may their prosperity be looked for, not their decay.'

6

'I will teach you six condition brethren, which prevent decay....

So long as brethrens shall provide themselves with (the habit of) kindly deeds, kindly words, and kindly thoughts, whether in secret or openly,—

So long as the brethren shall be impartial sharers and dividers of whatsoever lawful gains and profits may accrue to them,—even to the more contents of the begging-bowl,—and shall share them with their virtuous co-mates in the righteous life,—

So long as the brethren shall dwell keeping unbroken, undivided, unvaried, and unsoiled those practices which set one free, which are praised by the wise, which are not used for a wrong purpose, which conduce to contemplation,—so long as they shall dwell endowed with the virtue of such practices along with their co-mates in the righteous life, whether in secret or openly,—

So long as the brethren shall dwell endowed with right views, that is, the Ariyan View which leads to salvation, which leads one who acts accordantly to the utter destruction of Ill,—along with their co-mates in the righteous life, whether in secret or openly,—

So long may the prosperity of the brethren be looked for, not their decay.'

D.N. ii. 79-80.

Now when the Exalted One was dwelling near Rajagaha on the Hill called Vulture's Peak, he gave to the brethren this pious talk about things that include each other:

'Such is Right Practice, such is Contemplation, such is Insight.

Contemplation when compassed about by Right Practice is of great fruit, of great profit.

Insight compassed about by Contemplation is of great fruit, of great profit.

The Mind when compassed about by insight is utterly freed from the *asavas,* namely, the *asava* of sensual lust, wrong view, and ignorance"[2]

*D.N.*ii.81.

Instructions to the Brethren

Then the Exalted One said:

'Wherefore, Cunda, do ye to whom have been shown the things that I have penetrated, do ye one and all meet together and rehearse them together, comparing meaning with meaning and expression with expression, not wrangling over them: so that this way of holy living may be lasting and long-standing, for the profit of many, for the bliss of many, out of compassion for the world, for the use, for the profit, for the bliss of devas and mankind.

And what, Cunda, are those things which I have penetrated and shown into you, and which ye should so rehearse together...?

They are The Four Ways of Establishing Mindfulness. The Four Best Efforts, The Four Ways of Will, The Five Controlling Faculties, The Five Powers, The Seven Factors of Wisdom, and The Ariyan Eightfold Path.

These, Cunda, are the things that I have penetrated and shown unto you, which ye should rehearse together... as I have said ... for the bliss of devas and mankind.'

D.N. iii. 127.

Excess of Merriment

'In the Ariyan discipline, brethren, music is lamentation. In the Ariyan discipline, dancing is sheer madness. In the Ariyan discipline, laughing that displays the teeth is childishness.

Wherefore, brethren, do ye break down the bridge that causes music, dancing, laughter. Enough for you just to smile if you have any cause to show your pleasure.

Ang. Nik. i. 26I

Mindful and Self-possessed

Now at Vesali the Exalted One way staying in Ambapali's Grove. On that occasion the Exalted One called to the brethren and said:

'Brethren, let a brother dwell mindful and self-possessed. This is my advice to you. And how, brethren, is a brother mindful?

Herein, brethren, a brother, realising, body as a compound, remains ardent, composed, mindful, by controlling that covetousness and discontent that are in the world. That, brethren, is how a brother is mindful.

And how, brethren, is a brother self-possessed?

Herein, brethren, a brother, both in his going forth and in his home-returning, acts composedly. In looking forward and in looking back he acts composedly. In bending or stretching (arm or body) he acts composedly. In wearing his robes and bearing bowl and robe: in eating, drinking, chewing, swallowing: in relieving nature's needs: in going, standing, sitting, sleeping, waking, speaking keeping Silence, he acts composedly. That, brethren, is how a brother is self-possessed?

Then let a brother dwell mindful and self-possessed. This is my advice to you, brethren.

D.N. ii. 94-5.

By faith and virtue, energy and mind
In perfect balance, searching of the Norm,
Perfect in knowledge and good practices,
Perfect in concentration of your thoughts,
Ye shall strike off this multitude of woes.

Dhammapada, v. 144.

Confession of Faults

(*Certain brethren had expelled another wrongfully, and came to the Master to confess their fault.*)

Then those brethren rising from their seats threw their robes over one shoulder, fell at the feet of the Exalted One, and said to him:

Transgression, Lord, overcame us: such was our folly, such was our stupidity, such was our wrong-doing, in that we expelled a brother who was pure and faultless without ground and without reason. May the Exalted One, O Lord, accept this (our confession of) guilt as such, for our self-restraint in future.'

'Truly, brethren, transgression overcame you, such was your folly, such was your stupidity, such was your wrong-doing, in having expelled a brother who was pure and faultless, without ground and without reason.

Nevertheless, brethren. As you have seen your transgression as transgression, and have made confession as is fit and proper, I do accept it from you. For this, brethren, is growth in the Ariyan Discipline when, having seen our transgression as such, we make confession as it fit and proper, for the future practice of self-restraint.'

Vinaya. Mahavagga, 9. 1.

Falling Away

(The Exalted One said:)

'Once upon a time, brethren, a cat was standing in a dust-bin, on a dust-heap, watching for a mouse (and said), "As soon as a mouse comes out in search of food, I will catch and swallow it."

Well, brethren, that mouse came out in search of food, the cat pounced suddenly upon it, caught and swallowed it. But the mouse gnawed away at his inside and gnawed his bowels, as a result of which the cat came by his death and mortal pain.

Even so, brethren, such and such a brother rises up at an early hour, robes himself, and, taking bowl and robe, enters a village or suburb to beg for alms, with bodily senses unguarded, with mindfulness unsteadied, and senses unrestrained.

There he catches sight of some womenfolk, lightly clad or incompletely clad, and on seeing womenfolk thus clad passion torments his mind. With his mind thus tormented by the stings of passion, he comes by his death or else by mortal pain.

Now, herein, brethren, "death" means to desert the training of the Ariyan discipline and to return to the lower life (of the world): "mortal pain," brethren, means to fall into some grievous offence, (but) an offence of such a sort that recovery from it can be made.

Therefore, brethren, thus must ye train yourselves: "Guarded in body-senses, in speech and in mind, with mindfulness established and senses restrained will we enter a village or suburb to beg for alms."

Even so, brethren, must ye train yourselves.'

S.N. ii. 123.

The Simple Life

The Exalted One said:

'A new teaching, Cunda, do I show you for the control of the *asavas* which belong to this life, Nay, I do not show you a teaching for the prevention of the *asavas* of some future life, but for the control of them here and now, as well as for the prevention of them in the future.

Wherefore, Cunda, as to the robe I have permitted you,—let that be enough for you to keep off cold, to keep off heat, to prevent the touch of gnats and stinging flies, of wind and sun and snakes, and for modesty.

As to the food you beg, permitted me,—let that be enough for the setting up, for the keeping up, for the safeguarding of the body, and for the adoption of the holy life, bearing this in mind: "Thus do I destroy my old feeling and produce no new feeling, so that I shall be blameless and may live at ease."

And as to the lodging that I have permitted, let that be enough to keep off cold, to keep off heat, to keep of the touch of gnats and stinging flies, and wind and sun and bite of snakes,—just enough to provide shelter from the stress of seasons and for solitude.

And as to the supply of drugs and requisites in case of sickness, which I have permitted,—let those be enough to keep off the pains of sickness that have arisen and as a bare sufficiency of relief.'

D.N. iii. 130.

The Pith of the Matter

"Suppose, brethren, a man in need of sound timber, in quest of sound timber, going about searching for sound timber, should come upon a mighty tree, upstanding, all sound timber, and pass it by; but should cut away that outer wood and bark and take that along with him, thinking it to be sound timber.

Then a discerning man might say thus: "This fellow surely cannot tell the difference between sound timber and outer wood and bark, branch-wood and twigs: but being in need of sound timber…he passes it by and goes off with the outer wood and bark, thinking it to be sound timber. Now such a way of dealing with sound timber will never serve his need."

Thus, brethren, the essentials of the holy life do not consist in the profits of gain, honour, and good name: nor yet in the profits of observing moral rules: nor yet in the profits of knowledge and insight: but the sure heart's release, brethren—that, brethren, is the meaning that is the essence, that is the goal of living the holy life.'

M. N. i. 194.

How to Reprimand a Brother

'First, a brother must be warned (if he be a wrong-doer): and when he has been duly warned, let him again be reminded: and when he has been reminded, let him be definitely charged with wrong-doing. When he has been charged with wrong-doing, let some discreet and able brother bring the matter before the Order.

A brother, Upali, who is about to admonish another must realize within himself five qualities before doing so, (that he may be able to say), thus: "In due season will I speak, not out of season. In truth will I speak, not in falsehood. Gently will I speak, not harshly. To his profit will I speak, not to his loss. With kindly intent will I speak, not in anger."

Vinaya, ii. 9.

Treatment of a Brother

'Now when ye have thus met together, Cunda, in friendly guise one to another and without wrangling, ye should practise yourselves in these things.

It a co-mate in the holy life should say a thing in the Company, then, if ye think thus: "This venerable one has wrongly grasped the meaning (of the Norm) and wrongly interpreted the letter of it," yet ye should not agree with him nor yet think scorn of him therefor. But without agreement with him or thinking scorn of him, thus should be your speech to him: "of this meaning, friend, the letters are either these or those. Which is the better of the two?" or "Of these letters either this or that is the right meaning. Which is the better meaning of the two?"

And if he should say: "Of this meaning, friends, it is exactly these renderings (of mine) which are the better: and of these expressions, exactly this meaning (which I give) is the better": then in such case ye should not wave him aside nor yet abuse him: but without rejection or abuse, he must carefully be made to understand by paying attention to that meaning and those expressions.

And again, if a co-mate in the holy life should say a thing in the Company, and if ye judge thus: "This venerable one has wrongly grasped the meaning, but he is right in the expression," then ye should neither agree with him nor yet thank scorn of him therefor. But without agreement with him or thinking scorn of him, thus should be your speech to him: "Of these expressions, friend, either this or that is the meaning. Now which is the better of the two?"

Then if he reply, "Of these expressions it is exactly this (one of mine) that is the better meaning," then he should not be waved aside nor yet abused, but without doing either ye must carefully make him to understand by paying attention to that meaning.

But if, on the other hand, he rightly grasp the meaning but give a wrong expression to it, in the same way...ye must set him right in the expression of it.

But if he be right in both meaning and letter (of expression), then should ye say: "Well said!" and so agree with him and be pleased with what he says. And with the words "Well said!" and so forth, ye should say thus: "It is a gain for us, friend: it is a think well gotten by us, that we behold such a venerable one as our co-mate in the holy life, one thus well versed both in the spirit and in the letter (of the Norm).'"

D. N. iii. 127-8.

The Master's Robes of Rags

Then the venerable Kassapa the Great said to the venerable Ananda: ...'I; friend, am one who has shaved his head and beard, donned the saffron robes, and gone forth from the household to the homeless life... I do not admit to acknowledge any other teacher save that Exalted One, the Arahant who is perfectly enlightened.

In former days, friend, when I was still living the household life, this thought occurred to me: "Oppressive is the household life, a path for the dust of passion[3]: an open-air life is the wanderer's: not easy is it four him who dwells in a house to live the holy life in its entire fulfilment, in its entire purity, made clean and white. What if get my hair and beard shaved off, don the saffron robes, give up my home, and go forth to the homeless life!"

Will! Some time later I made me an under-robe of rags, and taking as my pattern those Noble Ones in the world, I had my hair and beard shaved off, donned the saffron robes, left my home, and went forth to homeless life.

Thus become a wanderer, as I tramped along the high road, I saw the Exalted One,—between Rajagaha and Naland it was,—seated by a wayside shrine,[4] and when I saw him I thought: "To think that I should behold the Teacher, that I should behold the Exalted One, the Happy One, who is the Exalted One, that I should behold the fully-enlightened One, the Exalted One!"

Thereupon, friend, I fell with my head at the Exalted One's feet and said to him: "The Exalted One is my teacher, Lord! I am the Exalted One's disciple!"

At these words of mine, friend, the Exalted One thus spake: "Whosoever, Kassapa, not knowing a disciple thus full endowed with the power of will should say 'I know,' or not seeing such an one should say 'I see,' his head would split as under. Now I, Kassapa, knowing such, 'I know'; seeing such, I say 'I see.'

Therefore, Kassapa, thus must you train yourself: 'There must be the strictest conscientiousness and discretion present in senior brethren, in novices, and in those of medium standing.' Even so must you train yourself.

Therefore, Kassapa, thus also must you train yourself: 'Whatever teaching of the Norm I hear which is attended by profit, realizing that and paying attention to it, considering it with my mind, I will listen to that teaching with a ready ear.' Even so, Kassapa, must you train yourself.

Therefore also, Kassapa, thus must you train yourself: 'Heedfulness and cheerfulness as regards body shall never desert me.' So must your train yourself."

Then, friend, the Exalted One, having thus exhorted me, rose from his seat and went away.

For seven days, friend, I ate the country food and was still in bond age to the flesh: but on the eighth day insight arose in me. After that, when the Exalted One, stepping off the high road, was approaching the root of a certain tree, folding my under-robe of rags in four, I said to the Exalted One: "Let the Exalted One be seated here, Lord, that it may be for my profit and happiness for many a day."

So, friend, the Exalted One sat down upon the seat I had prepared, and so seated he thus spake: "Soft, indeed, Kassapa, is this your under-robe of rags."

"May the Exalted One deign to accept this under-robe of rags out of compassion for me."

"Then, Kassapa, will you wear my coarse patchwork cast-off robes?"

"I will indeed, Lord, wear the Exalted One's coarse patchwork cost-off robes."

So, friend, I gave the Exalted One my under-robe of rags, and I myself put on the Exalted One's coarse patchwork cast-off robes.

Therefore, friend, if one would say the truth of me, with truth might he say of me that I am a true son of the Exalted One, born of his lips, born of the Norm, begotten by the Norm, a kinsman of the Norm, one who accepted his coarse patchwork cast-off robes.

I, friend, when I so desire, remote from passions can reach and dwell in each of the nine *jhanas* and I have the five supernormal powers.

And I, friend, by the destruction of the *asavas,* have entered on and abide in that emancipation of mind which is free from the *asavas,* having realized it by mine own super-knowledge even in this present life.

Wherefore, friend, he who should think that I can conceal the six supernormal powers might just as well think that an elephant, seven or eight cubits high, could be hidden by a bit of palm-leaf.

S.N. ii. 220.

The Admission of Women to the Order

Now at that time the Exalted One, the Buddha, dwelt among the Sakyas at Kapilavasthu, in the Banyan Park.

Then did Maha-Pajapati, the Gotamid, go to where the Exalted One was, and coming there she bowed before the Exalted One and stood at one side As she thus stood, she said unto the Exalted One: Well were it, Lord, if women were permitted to go forth from the home unto the homeless life under the Norm-Discipline set forth by the Tathagata.'

'Enough, O Gotamid! Long not that women be permitted to go forth from the home unto the homeless life under the Norm-Discipline set forth by the Tathagata.'

Then a second and yet a third time did Maha-Pajapati, the Gotamid, make the same petition and get the same reply from the Exalted One.

Then Maha-Pajapati, the Gotamid, at the thought: 'The Exalted One permits not that women should go forth' ... sad sorrowful, tearful, and wailing, saluted the Exalted One by the right and went away.

Then the Exalted One, when he had dwelt at Kapilavasthu as long as it pleased him, set out on a journey towards Vesali, and wandering on from place to place he cam unto Vesali, And there at Vesali the Exalted One dwelt in Grove, at the Hall of the Peaked Gable.

Now Maha-Pajapati, the Gotamid, got her hair cut off, donned saffron robes, and started off with a number of women of the Sakyan clan to Vesali: and wandering on from place to place, she drew near to Vesali, to Great Grove and the Hall of the Peaked Gable. And there she took her stand outside the porch, her feet all swollen and dust-begrimed, sad, sorrowful, tearful, and wailing.

Now the venerable Ananda beheld her so standing, and he said into her: 'Wherefore, O Gotamid, dost thou stand there outside the porch with feet all swollen and dust-begrimed, sad, sorrowful, weeping, and wailing?'

'O my lard Ananda, it is because the Exalted One permits not that women go forth form the home unto the homeless life under the Norm-Discipline set forth by the Tathagata.'

Thereupon the venerable Ananda went unto the place where the Exalted One was, bowed down before him, and sat down at one side. So seated the venerable Ananda said unto the Exalted One: 'Lord here is Maha-Pajapati, the Gotamid, standing outside the porch... weeping and wailing ... because women are not permitted by the Exalted One to go forth... under the Norm-Discipline set forth by the Tathagata. Well were it, Lord, if women were permitted so to do!'

'Enough, Ananda ! Long not that women be permitted so to do.'

Then a second and yet a third time did the venerable Ananda make the same request and get the same reply from the Exalted One.

Then the venerable Ananda thought: 'The Exalted One permits not that women go forth... to the homeless life... How now if by some other method I were to request the Exalted One to grant permission... so to do?' Then the venerable Ananda said to the Exalted One:

'Lord, are women capable, after going forth from the home unto the homeless life under the Norm-Discipline set forth by the Tathagata,—are they capable of realizing the Fruit of Stream-winning, of Once-returning, of Never-returning, of Arahantship?'

'Women are capable ... of doing so, Ananda.'

'Then, Lord, if women are capable ... of so doing, inasmuch as Maha-Pajapati, the Gotamid, was of great service to the Exalted One,—for she was aunt, nourisher, and milk-giver, on the death of his mother she suckled the Exalted One,—well were it, Lord, if women were permitted to go forth from home unto the homeless life under the Norm-Discipline set forth by the Tathagata.'

'Well then, Ananda, if Maha-Pajapati, the Gotamid, will undertake to keep Eight Important Rules, let that be reckoned unto her as full ordination. Those rules are these:

A sister, even if she be an hundred years in the robes, shall salute, shall rise up before, shall bow down before, shall perform all duties of respect unto a brother, even if that brother have only just taken the robes. Let this rule never be broken, but be honoured, esteemed, reverenced, and observed as long as life doth last.

Secondly, a sister shall not spend the rainy season in a district where there is no brother residing Let this rule never be broken, but be honoured, esteemed, reverenced, and observed as long as life doth last.

Thirdly, at the half-month let a sister await two things from the Order of Brethren, namely, the appointing of the Sabbath and the coming of a brother to preach the sermon. Let this rule never be broken....

Fourthly, at the end of keeping the rainy season let a sister, in presence of both Orders, of Brethren and of Sisters, invite inquiry in respect of three things, namely, of things seen, heard, and suspected. Let this rule never be broken....

Fifthly, a sister guilty of serious wrong-doing shall do penance for the half-month to both Orders. Let this rule never be broken...

Sixthly, when a sister has passed two seasons in the practice of the Six Rules she may ask full orders from both Orders. Let this rule never be broken....

Seventhly, a sister shall not in any case abuse or censure a brother. Let this rule never be broken....

Eighthly, henceforth is forbidden the right of a sister to have speech among brethren, but not forbidden is the speaking of brethren unto sisters. Let this rule never be broken, but be honoured, esteemed, reverenced, and observed as long as life doth last.

Now, Ananda, if Maha-Pajapati, the Gotamid, will undertake to keep these Eight Important Rules, let that be reckoned unto her as full ordination.'

Then the venerable Ananda having received from the Exalted One these Eight Important Rules, went to Maha-Pajapati, the Gotamid [and told her all that the Exalted One had said], and she replied:

'Just as, lord Ananda, a women or a man, youthful, of tender age, found of self-adornment, having washed the head and gotten a wreath of blue lotus or of jasmine or of scented-creeper flowers, should take it with both hands and place it atop of the head,—even so do I, lord Ananda, take upon me these Eight Important Rules, never to be broken so long as life doth last.'

Thereupon the venerable Ananda went back to the Exalted One, bowed down before him, and sat down at one side. So seated, the venerable Ananda said to the Exalted One: 'Lord, Maha-Pajapati, the Gotamid, has undertaken the Eight Important Rules. Fully ordained is the sister of the Exalted One's mother.'

(Then the Master replied:)

'Ananda, if women had not been permitted to go forth from the home unto the homeless life under the Norm-Discipline set forth by the Tathagata, then would the righteous life last long, the Good Norm would last, Ananda, a thousand years, But now, Ananda, since women have been permitted to go forth from the home unto the homeless life... not for long will the righteous life prevail; only for five hundred years, Ananda, will the Good Norm stand fast.[5]

Just as, Ananda, whatsoever families have many women and few men are easily molested by robbers and pot-thieves, even so, Ananda, under whatsoever Norm-Discipline womenfolk get permission to wander forth from the home unto the homeless life, not for long does that righteous life prevail.

Just as, Ananda, when the blight called mildew falls upon a blooming paddy-field, that paddy-field does not last for long, even so, Ananda, under whatsoever Norm-Discipline womenfolk get permission to wander froth from the home unto the home unto the homeless life, not for long does that righteous life prevail.

Just as, Ananda, when the blight called red-rust falls upon a blooming field of sugar-cane, that filed of sugar-cane does not last long,—even so, Ananda, under whatsoever Norm-Discipline... that righteous life does not long prevail.

Now just as, Ananda, a man should cautiously build an embankment to a great waterworks, to prevent the water from flowing out,—even so, Ananda, have I cautiously proclaimed 'these Eight Important Rules, not to be broken as long as life shall last.'

Vinaya, ii. x.

Thus have I heard. Once the Exalted One was staying at Kimbili in Bamboo Grove. Then that brother Kimbila came to the Exalted One, sat down. And said:

'What, Lord, is the reason, what is the cause why, when the Tathagata has finally passed away, the Good Norm lasts not for long?'

'With regard to this, Kimbila, when the Tathagata has finally passed away, the brethren, the sisters, the sisters, the lay-brethren and lay-sisters dwell regardless of the Master, and disobedient to him, regardless of the Norm do they dwell and disobedient to the Norm, regardless of the Order do they dwell and disobedient to the Order: they dwell regardless of the Training and pay no attention to it, and so also with regard to concentration of mind, earnestness, and friendly feeling.

That, brethren, is the reason, that is the cause why, after the final passing away of the Tathagata the Good Norm does not last for long.

Ang. Nik. iv. 84.

Teacher and Pupil

'The teacher, brethren, should regard the pupil as his son. The pupil should regard the teacher as his father. Thus these two, by mutual reverence and deference joined, dwelling in community of life, will win increase, growth, progress in this Norm-Discipline.

I do enjoin, brethren, that ye live ten years in charge of a teacher. Then he who has completed his tenth year of discipleship may have a charge himself.'

Vin. Pit. Mahavagga, iii. 1.

Keeping the Rainy Season

Now at that time the Exalted One dwelt near Rajagaha, in the Bamboo Grave, at the Squirrels' Feeding-Ground. And at that time the Retreat during the rainy season was not yet appointed for the brethren by the Exalted One. So the brethren went a-roaming in the cold, the hot, and the rainy seasons alike.

Thus folk were vexed and murmured angrily, saying: What! Are the recluses who are the sons of the Sakyan to roam about in the cold, the hot, and the rainy season alike? They tread down the green grass, they crush the living thing that has one sense,[1] they trample to death many a tiny life.

Are the recluses of the heretical sects, who follow a Norm ill-preached—are they to settle down and live retired during the rains? Are birds to build their nests on the tree-tops and take shelter in the rains and live retired, and yet are the recluses who are the sons of the Sakyan to go a-roaming in the cold, the hot, and the rainy season alike, treading down the green grass, crushing the living thing that has one sense, trampling to death many a tiny life.

Now some brethren heard those folk who were vexed and murmured angrily this, and they told the thing to the Exalted One.

Therefore in this connexion and on this occasion, the Exalted One, after pious talk, thus spake unto the brethren:

'I enjoin on you, brethren, that ye observe the retreat during the rains.'

Vin. Pit. Mahavagga, iii. 1.

Rules of Etiquette

'Brethren, I appoint this rule for the guidance of newly arrived brethren.

A newly arrived brother, brethren, with the thought "I will now enter the residence," having taken off his sandals, should turn them down, beat them together, take them up again, lay down his umbrella, uncover his head, put his upper robe over one shoulder, then enter the residence heedfully and without undue haste.

On entering he should consider where the resident brethren have retired, and, wherever they have gone, whether to the service-hall or to the pavilion or to the foot of a tree, thither going let him lay aside bowland robe, select a proper seat, and so sit down.

Then let him ask about water for drinking and water for use, and inquire which is which. If he need drinking water, let him take and drink it. If he need water for use, let him take and wash his feet therewith.

In washing his feet, let him hold the water with one hand and rub down his feet with the other hand. Let him not do so with the hand that holds the water.

Then let him ask for rags to wipe his sandals, and do so. In wiping his sandals let him first dust them with a dry cloth, and then wipe them with a damp cloth. Then he should rinse the rags and lay them aside.

If the resident brother be an elder, let him salute him. If he be a junior, he should salute the newcomer.[2] Then let him ask about lodging, saying, "What lodging is allotted me? Is it occupied or unoccupied?" And he must ask about his district for begging food, and what district is out of bounds, what families are to be considered as educated. He should inquire where are the privies and urinals, about drinking water and water for use, about walking staves, the meeting halls of the Order, about time to go in and time to go out.

If (When he arrives) there is no one at home, let him knock on the door, then wait a while, then slip the bolt, open the door, and look in while he still stands outside.'

Vin. Pit. ii. 8.

Conversion, Ordination, Attainment of the Goal

Thereupon (when the Master had spoken) Sabhiya, the Wanderer, bowed his head at the feet of the Exalted One and said: 'Excellent, O Lord! Excellent,. O Lord! Even as one raises what is overthrown or shows forth what is hidden, or points the way to him that wandereth astray, or holds up a light in the darkness that they who have eyes may see objects,—even so in divers ways hath the Norm been set forth by the venerable Gotama. To the venerable Gotama I go for refuge, to the Norm and to the Order of Brethren. I would take ordination at the hands of the Exalted One, I would take full orders at the hands of the Exalted One.'

(The Master said:)

'He who, formerly being of another faith, Sabhiya, desires ordination, desires full orders[3] in this Norm and Discipline,—he remains on trial for four months. At the end of four months brethren of established heart give him full ordination in the Brother's Rule. Yet do I recognize a difference of persons.'

(Sabhiya said:)

'If it be so (even as the Exalted One hath said), then I too will remain on trial for four months; and, when they are past, let brethren of established heard give me ordination, give me full orders in the Brother's Rule.'

So Sabhiya, the Wanderer, received ordination and full orders from the hands of the Exalted One; and the venerable Sabhiya, not long after taking orders, living alone, remote, earnest, ardent, and resolute, in no long time came to realize for himself in that very life, by his own powers of mind, that Goal unsurpassed of holy living, to win which the clansmen duly wander forth from home; so that he knew for sure: 'Destroyed is rebirth (for me), lived is the holy life, done is my task: there is no more life for me on terms like these.'[4]

And the venerable Sabhiya was yet another of the Arahants.

The only Way

(i) *The contemplation of Body*

Thus have I heard:

On the Exalted One was staying among the Kurus,—there is a suburb of the Kurus called Kammassa-dhamma, There the Exalted One called to the brethren and said, 'Brethren!' 'Yes, Lord!' replied those brethren to the Exalted One. Then the exalted One thus spake:

'This is the Only way, brethren, that leads to the purification of beings, to passing beyond Sorrow and lamentation, to the destruction of grief and despair, to the attainment of the Method, to the realizing of Nibbana, thus: The four Ways of Establishing Mindfulness.[5]

What are the four?

Herein, brethren, a brother abides regarding Body (as a compound): he is ardent, self-possessed, and concentrated by controlling the covetousness and dejection that are in the world. So also with regard to feelings, the Thought, and Mental States (Ideas).

And how, brethren, does a brother abide regarding body (as a compound)?

In this method, brethren, a brother goes to the forest or to the foot of a tree or to a lonely place and there sits down cross-legged and holds his body straight, establishing concentration in front of him.[6] Then he breathes in mindfully, and mindfully breathes out. As he draws a long breath he knows, "A long breath I draw in. As he breathes out a long breath he knows, "A long breath I breathe out." As he draws in a short breath he knows, " A short breath I draw in. As he breathes out a short breath he knows, " A short breath I breathe out."

With the thought "In full body-consciousness will I breathe in" he trains himself. With the thought "In full body-consciousness will I breathe out" he trains himself. With the thought "Calming down my body-compound I will breathe in" he trains himself. With the thought "Calming down my body-compound I will breathe out" he trains himself.

Just as, brethren a clever turner or turner's 'prentice, when he gives a long pull [to his lathe-string] is aware "I am giving a long pull," or when he gives a short pull is aware "I am giving a short pull,"—even so does a brother train himself (by conscious in-breathing and out-breathing).

Thus he abides regarding body either in its inner or in its outer state or in both. He abides observing either the rise or the fall of things in body, or the rise-and-fall of things in body. Or else, with the thought "It is body." His mindfulness of body is established, just sufficiently for him to know its existence and to become concentrated. Thus he abides detached, and he grasps at nothing at all in the world.

Thus, brethren, does a brother abide in the Contemplation of Body.

Then again, brethren, a brother when he walks in conscious "I am walking," or when he stands still he is conscious "I am standing still." When he sits, or lies, he is conscious of so doing: and whatever the posture of the body he is aware of it. Thus he abides in Contemplation of body, inwardly or outwardly or both... and grasps at nothing at all in the world....

Then again, brethren, both in advancing a retreating he acts mindfully. In looking forward or backward, in bending or straightening, in wearing his robes or carrying bowl and robe, he acts mindfully. In eating, drinking, chewing, or tasting, in his bodily functions, he acts mindfully. In going, standing, sitting, sleeping, waking, speaking, or keeping silence he acts mindfully. Thus does he contemplate body, inwardly or outwardly or both... and grasps at nothing at all in the world. Thus does a brother dwell in the Contemplation of Body.

Then again, brethren, a brother examines this same body upwards from the soles of his feet to the top of his head. He regards it as something enclosed by skin, and filled with contents of divers kinds, as a thing impure: saying, "Here in this body are hairs of the head, hairs of the body, nails, teeth, skin, flesh, sinews, bones, and marrow: kidney, heart, liver, tissue, spleen, lungs, stomach, bowels, intestines: excrement, bile, phlegm, matter, blood, sweat, fat, tears, serum, saliva, mucus, lubricants, and urine." Just as if, brethren, there were a bag of samples, open at each end, full of grains. of divers sorts, such as rice, paddy, beans, pulse, sesamum, or husked rice: and a sharp-sighted man were to loose the ends and examine the contents, saying, "This is rice, this is paddy," and so on. Even so, brethren, does a brother examine the body, from the soles of the feet upwards to the top of the head: regards it as closed with skin, and filled with contents of divers kinds, as something impure.... Thus does he dwell in Contemplation of Body.

Then again, brethren, a brother considers this same body, however placed or however disposed, by way of its essential properties, thus: "There are in this body the elements of earth, water, "heat, and air."

Just as if, brethren, a clever butcher or butcher's 'prentice, on slaving a steer, cuts it up bit by bit and sits with it at the four crosswind. Even so does a brother consider this same body, however placed and however disposed, by way of its essential properties of earth, water, heat, and air.... So does he abide in the Contemplation of Body.

Then again, brethren, suppose a brother sees a dead body, thrown away in a charnel-field, one day or two days or three days dead,—bloated, black and blue, decomposing: and he compares his own body with that, saying to himself: "Here is this body of mine, it is of such a nature as that, it has come to be like that, it has not gone beyond that!" And so does he consider body inwardly or outwardly or both...and grasps at nothing at all in the world. So does he abide Contemplating Body.

Then again, brethren, a brother might see a dead body thrown away in the charnel-field, being devoured by crows, devoured by kites, by vultures, or-dogs or jackals or divers sorts of worms. Then he compares this body of his with that, saying (as before).... Thus does he abide Contemplating Body.

Then again, brethren, suppose a brother sees a body thrown away in the charnel-field, just a chain of bones, with flesh and blood, and held together by tendons: or else just a chain of bones with the flesh gone, blood-bedabbled and held together with tendons: or else just a chain of bones, with flesh and blood both gone, just held together with tendons. Or he sees bones only, without any connecting links, bones scattered in all directions: here lies a foot-bone, there a leg-bone, here a thigh-bone, there a hip-bone or a backbone or a skull. Then he compares his own body with those, thinking: "Here is this body of mine: it is of such a nature as that, it has come to be like that, it has not gone beyond that!" And so does he consider body inwardly or outwardly or both...and abides Contemplating Body.

Or again, brethren, a brother might see body thrown away in the charnel-field,—just whitened bones, something like sea-shells, or just bones in a heap, over a year old, or bones that are crumbling away to dust. Then he compares his own body with that, saying: "This body of mine is just of such a nature, thus come-to-be, not gone beyond that!"

Thus inwardly contemplating body, or outwardly or both, does he abide. He abides contemplating the rise of things, or the fall of things, or the rise-and-fa'l of things in body. With the thought "It is body" his mindfulness of body is established, just sufficiently for him to know its existence and to become concentrated. Thus he abides detached, and he grasps a nothing at all in the world.

That, brethren, is how a brother abides in the Contemplation of Body.

(ii) The Contemplation of Feelings

'In this method, brethren, a brother when feeling a pleasant feeling is aware "I feel a pleasant feeling": or when feeling a painful feeling is aware "I am feeling a painful feeling": or when the feeling is neither pleasant nor painful is aware "I am feeling a neutral feeling."

Or in the same way, when affected by a pleasant or painful or neutral feeling regarding material things, or when so affected by a feeling regarding immaterial things, he is aware of his feelings in like manner.

Thus, inwardly or outwardly or both, he abides contemplating his feelings. He abides contemplating the rise of things in feelings or the fall of things in feelings or the rise-and-fall or things in feelings. He says to himself, "It is feeling," and thus his mindfulness of feelings is established, just sufficiently for him to know their existence and to become concentrated. Thus he abides detached and he grasps at nothing at all in the world.

That, brethren, is how a brother abides in the Contemplation of Feelings.'

(iii) The Contemplation of Thought

'And how, brethren, does a brother abide in the Contemplation of Thought as such? In this method, a brother is aware of a passionate thought that it is passionate: of a dispassionate through that it is dispassionate. Of a hateful thought he is aware that it is hateful: of a thought free from hate he is aware that it is so. Of a confused thought he is aware that it is confused, and of a clear thought he is aware that it is clear. Of a concentrated thought he is aware that it is concentrated, and of a diffuse thought he is aware that it is diffuse. Of a lofty thought he is aware that it is lofty, of a low thought he is aware that it is low. Of a through concerned with the higher he is aware that it is so: of a thought concerned with the lower he is also aware. Of a thought composed or discomposed, of one that is liberated or bound, in each case he is aware that it is so.

Thus, either inwardly or outwardly or both inwardly and outwardly he abides contemplating thought. He contemplates the rise of things in thought or the fall of things in thought, or the rise-and-fall of things in thought. Thinking "It is thought" his mindfulness about thought is established, just sufficiently for him to know its existence and to become concentrated. Thus does he abide detached and he grasps at nothing at all in the world.

That is how, brethren, a brother abides, as regards thought, in the Contemplation of Thought.'

(iv) The Contemplation of Ideas

'And how, brethren, does a brother, as regards ideas, abide in the Contemplation of Ideas?

In this method, brethren, a brother abides in the Contemplation of Ideas by way of the Five Hindrances.

And how does he so contemplate Ideas?

In this method, brethren, a brother is aware of an inner sensual desire that it is sensual, and when he has no inner sensual desire he is aware of it. When there arises in him a sensual desire not felt before, he is aware of it. When there is a rejection of a sensual desire that has arisen, he is aware of it. Also he is aware that when he has rejected such a desire it will not rise up again.

So also with regard to Ill-will, Sloth and Torpor, Excitement and Worry, and Wavering. Of each of these he is aware in the same way, that it is present or absent, of the arising of such when not felt before, of its rejection when felt, and of its never rising again when once rejected.

Thus, inwardly or outwardly or both, he abides in the Contemplation of Ideas ... and grasps at nothing at all in the world.

That, brethren, is how a brother abides in the Contemplation of Ideas by way of the Five Hindrances.'

The Five Grasping-groups

'Then again, brethren, as regards Ideas, a brother abides in the Contemplation of Ideas by way of the Five Grasping-groups. And how does he so abide?

In this method, brethren, a brother reflects: "Such is body, such is the arising of body, such is the passing away of body. Such are feelings, such is the arising of feelings, and so forth. Such is perception, such is the arising of perception, and so forth. Such are the activities.... Such is consciousness, such is the arising of consciousness, such is the passing away of consciousness." Thus inwardly or outwardly (as before)... does a brother abide in the Contemplation of Ideas by way of the Five Grasping-groups.'

The Six Spheres of Sense

'Then again, brethren, as regards Ideas, a brother abides in the Contemplation of Ideas by way of the Six Inner and Outer Spheres of Sense. And how does he so abide?

In this method, brethren, a brother is aware of the eye and objects of the eye: and whatsoever fetter is effected by the conjunction of these two, he is aware of that. He is aware how a fetter arises that has not arisen before: how he rejects a fetter which has already arisen: how there is no more arising again in the future of a fetter which he has rejected.

The same with regard to ear and sound: with regard to nose and scent: with regard to tongue and taste: with regard to body and tangibles: with regard to mind and mental images....Thus, brethren, does a brother abide in the Contemplation of Ideas by way of the Six Inner and Outer Spheres of Sense.'

The Seven Factors of Wisdom

'Then again, brethren, with regard to Ideas, a brother abides in the Contemplation of Ideas by way of the Seven Factors of Wisdom. How does he so abide?

In this method, brethren, if in a brother there exist Inner (subjective) Mindfulness as a Factor of Wisdom, he is aware of it: if such be absent, he is aware of it. He is (as before) aware of the arising of such mindfulness not hitherto arisen, and of its perfect development when it has arisen...And in the same way as regards the other Factors of Wisdom, namely: Searching of the Norm Energy, Zest, Serenity, Concentration, and Mental Balance (or Equanimity) as Factors of Wisdom.

In each case he is aware of their inner or subjective presence or absence, of the arising of each one of then which has not arisen before, and of the perfect development of each one of them when arisen.

That is how, brethren, a brother abides in the Contemplation of Ideas by way of the Seven Factors of Wisdom.'

The Four Ariyan Truths

Then lastly, brethren. with regard to Ideas, a brother abides in the Contemplation of Ideas by way of the Four Ariyan Truths. "And how does he so abide?

In this method, brethren, a brother is aware, as it really is, "This is Ill. This is the arising of Ill, as it really is. This is the Ceasing of Ill, as really is. This is the Way to the Ceasing of Ill, as it really is."'

(The Digha Nikaya account then proceeds with the analysis of Ill, described elsewhere. The Majjhima Nikaya account ends as follows:)

'Now whosoever, brethren, shall thus practise these Four Ways of Establishing Mindfulness for seven years (as most), may look to win one of two fruits: either in this very life he wins the Knowledge, or, if there be still a residue of him, he wins the Fruit of Not-returning.

But let alone seven years, brethren, whosoever shall thus practise the Four Ways of Establishing Mindfulness for six years, for five four, three, two, one year,—nay, whosoever shall thus practise them for seven months, for even one month, for half a month, nay, even for seven days,—he shall win one of two Fruits: either in this very life he shall win the Knowledge, or, if there be still a residue of him, he shall win the Fruits of Not-returning.

This, brethren, is what I meant when I said before, "This is the Only Way that leads to the purification of beings, to passing beyond sorrow and lamentation, to the destruction of grief and despair, to the attainment of the Method, to the realizing of Nibbana, namely: The Four Ways of Establishing Mindfulness."'

Thus spake the Exalted One. And those brethren were pleased with what was spoken by the Exalted One and took delight therein.

D.N. ii. 314-15; *M.N.* i. 62.

The Elements

Thus have I heard. Once the Exalted One was dwelling near Savatthi, in Jeta Grove, at Anathapindika's Park. Then the Exalted One, robing himself early, and taking bowl and robe, went forth to Savatthi to beg. And the venerable Rahula[7] also, robing himself early, and taking bowl and robe, followed after the Exalted One, keeping close behind him.

Then the Exalted One, looking behind, said to the venerable Rahula: 'Whatsoever form Rahula, be it past, future, or present, inward or outward, gross or subtle, low or high, whether far or near, every form must be regarded thus, as it really is, by perfect insight: "This is not mine: not this am I: herein is not the self of me."'

'It is just form only, Exalted One? Is it just from only?'

'Nay, Rahula: form and feeling too, Rahula: and perception, Rahula: the activities, Rahula: and consciousness too, Rahula.'

Then thought the venerable Rahula: 'Who could go to a village in quest of alms to-day, after being given a warning face to face with the Exalted One?'

So thinking, he turned back again and sat down at the root of a certain tree cross-legged, and holding his body straight sét mindfulness before him as his task.

Now the venerable Sariputta saw the venerable Rahula so seated, and called to him: 'Practise the practice of mindfulness by breathing in and out, Rahula: for that practice, if made to grow, is of great fruit and profit.'

Now the venerable Rahula, rising from his solitude at eventide, went to the Exalted One and, coming into his presence, saluted him and sat down at one side. So seated, the venerable Rahula thus addressed the Exalted One: 'Lord, pray how is the practice of mindfulness by breathing in and out of great fruit and profit, when enlarged?'

'Whatsoever hard, solid matter, Rahula, ahs gathered in yourself, personally, such as the hair of the head, the hair of the body, nails, teeth, skin, flesh, sinews, bones, marrow, kidneys, heart, liver, pleura, spleen, lungs, intestines, mesentery, stomach, excrements, that, Rahula, is called the personal element of earth. Bot the personal earth-element and the external earth-element are called by that name of "earth-element." That you must regard thus, as it really is, by perfect insight: "This is not mine: not this am I: herein is not the self of me." So regarding it one is repelled by the earth-element, and cleanses his heart of it.

And what, Rahula, is the Element of Water?

It may be the personal element of water, and it may be the external element of water. But what, Rahula, is the personal element of water?

Whatsoever water, whatsoever fluid, has gathered in yourself personally, such as bile, phlegm, pus, blood, sweat, lymph, tears, lubricant, saliva, mucus, oil, urine,—whatsoever of a liquid nature has gathered in yourself personally, Rahula,—that is called the personal element of water. Both that personal element of water and the external element of water are called by the name water-element, and it must be regarded (as I have told you) in the same way as the earth-element. So regarding it one is repelled by the water-element, and cleanses his heart of it.

And what, Rahula, is the Element of Heat?

It may be the personal element and it may be the external element of heat.

Now what, Rahula, is the personal element of heat?

Whatsoever heat, or whatsoever is of the nature of burning, has gathered in yourself personally, such as that by which there is warming, digesting, consuming: that by which what is eaten, drunk, chewed, tasted goes to perfect digestion,—whatsoever else of like nature is gathered in yourself personally, that, Rahula, is called that personal element of heat. That and the external element of heat go by the same name of heat-element. That also is to be regarded as I have told you.

And what, Rahula, is the Element of Air?

It may be the personal or the external element of air.

And what, Rahula, is the personal element of air?

Whatsoever air, whatsoever is of a windy nature, is gathered in yourself personally; such as, the upgoing and down-going breath, the wind of the belly, wind of the intestines, the vital airs that pervade the limbs, air inbreathed and outbreathed,—all such are called by the name of personal air-element. Both this and the external air-element are called by the same name of air-element. That also must be regarded as I have shown you.

And what, Rahula, is the Element of Space?
It may be the personal or the external element of space.
Now what, Rahula, is the personal element of space?

Whatever empty space or what is of the nature of void is included in yourself personally, such as, the cavities of ear and nose and mouth, the cavities by which food enters, wherein food is stored, the cavities by which it is extruded,—all such cavities are called by the same name of element of space. Both these and the external element of space are called by the same name of element of space. That also must be regarded as I have shown you.

Now, Rahula, make your practice of meditation like the earth. If you so practise, all delightful contacts will not seize hold of and be established in your mind. Just as on the earth men throw down what is fair and foul alike, and excrements of dung and urine, saliva, pus, and blood: and yet earth is not worried or troubled or disgusted thereat,—so also do you make your practice like unto the earth, Rahula. So practising all delightful delightful contacts will not seize hold of and be established in your mind.

And so with water: make your practice of mediation like water. For just as in water men wash things fair and foul alike (as before stated with regard to earth), yet water is not worried or troubled or disgusted thereat. So also do you make your practice like water.

And so with fire...For just as fire burns up fair and foul alike, but is not worried or troubled or disgusted threat (but burns up all alike), so do you make your practice like fire.

And so with air....For just as the wind carries away things fair and foul alike, but is not worried or troubled or disgusted thereat ... so do you make your practice like the air.

And so with space....For just as space is not established anywhere, so [unattached] do you make your practice....So practising, Rahula, all delightful contacts will not seize upon or be established in your mind.

Practise the practice of kindliness, Rahula, for by so practising all enmity will be abandoned. Practise the practice of compassion, Rahula, for so will all vexation be abandoned. Practise the practice of sympathy, Rahula, for so will all aversion be abandoned. Practise the practice of equanimity, Rahula, for so will all repulsion be abandoned. Likewise meditate on the ugly, for so will lust be abandoned. Meditate on the impermanent, for so will pride-of-self be abandoned.'[8]

M.N. i. 420-5 *(condensing repetitions)*

To Those of Other Faiths

(*Nigrodha, the ascetic, thinks that the Master wishes to overthrow the views and practices of other sects. He is shown that the Norm is of universal application.*)

'Now this is what I say to you, Nigrodha: "Let any intelligent man come to me, any man who is also without guile, not a deceiver, but an upright man. I will teach him. I will show him the Norm. And if he practises according to my instructions, to know and realize for himself even in this very life that unsurpassed holy life for the sake of which clansmen go forth from home to the homeless in its perfection, he too shall know and realize in seven years. Do I say seven years? Why Nigrodha, even if he do so, as I have said, for six, five, four, three, two years, even one year, half, a year; five, four, three two months, even one month...nay, if he so practise for seven days, Nigrodha... such a man coming to me shall so realize....

Now this I say, Nigrodha, not desiring to win pupils, not wishing to make others fall from their religious vows, not wishing to make others give up their ways of life, not wishing to establish you in wrong ways or to make you give up ways that are good. Not so!

But, Nigrodha, there are bad things not put away, things that have to do with corruption, things that draw one down again to rebirth, things causing suffering, having Ill for their fruit, things concerned with rebirth, decay, and death in time to come. It is for the rejection of these things that I teach you the Norm, walking according to which these things that are concerned with corruption shall be put away by you, and wholesome-things shall be brought to increase; by which even in this present life by his own abnormal powers a man shall realize and abide in the full knowledge and realization of perfect wisdom."'

D.N. iii. 56-7.

References

1. These are the Seven Limbs of Wisdom or the *Sattabojjhanga*.
2. A fourth *asava* (Taint or Intoxicant or Drug) is sometimes added, viz. *bhav'asava*, desire for continued existence.
3. *Rajapatha*—so explained by Buddhaghosa: but it may mean simply 'a stuffy life.'
4. *Bahuputte cetiye*—it was called 'the Shrine of the Many Children.'

5. After the Master's death, the Order charged Ananda with this offence, among others, of introducing women to the Order, and so causing its decay.

6. The vegetable world.

   In North India the rainy seasons were two, an early and a late. The early date for keeping *Vassa* (the rainy season) was the day after the *Asalha* (June-July) full moon, the date of the first Sermon: the later, a month after the same full moon, Probably these were the dates of the ancient Vedic festivals.

7. Doubt about seniority is solved by asking 'How many *vassa* (rainy seasons) has your reverence kept?' ... that is, 'How long have you been in the robes?'

8. *Mahavagga of Sutta Nipata,* and *Majjhima Nikaya,* i. 391. *Pabbajja* and *upasampada.*

9. I.e. rebirth in every conceivable condition.

10. Cattaro Sat Vahana.

11. Concentrating between the eyebrows.

12. The Master's own son.

13. The further section on breathing, about which Rahula asks, is given on p. 49.

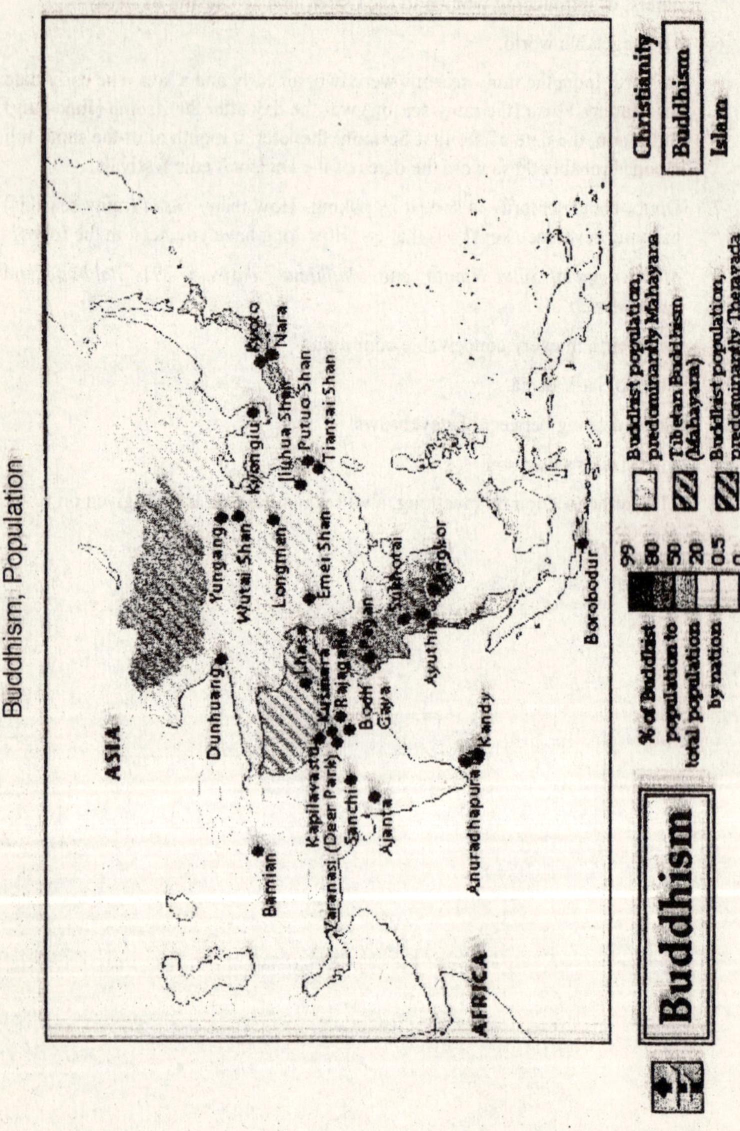
Buddhism; Population
ASIA
AFRICA
Bamian
Dunhuang
Yungang
Wutai Shan
Longmen
Emei Shan
Jiuhua Shan
Putuo Shan
Tiantai Shan
Kyongju
Kyoto
Nara
Lhasa
Kapilavastu
Varanasi (Deer Park)
Sanchi
Ajanta
Bodh Gaya
Sukhothai
Angkor
Anuradhapura
Kandy
Borobodur
% of Buddhist population to total population by nation
99
80
50
20
0.5
0
Buddhist population, predominantly Mahayana
Tibetan Buddhism (Mahayana)
Buddhist population, predominantly Theravada
Christianity
Buddhism
Islam
Buddhism

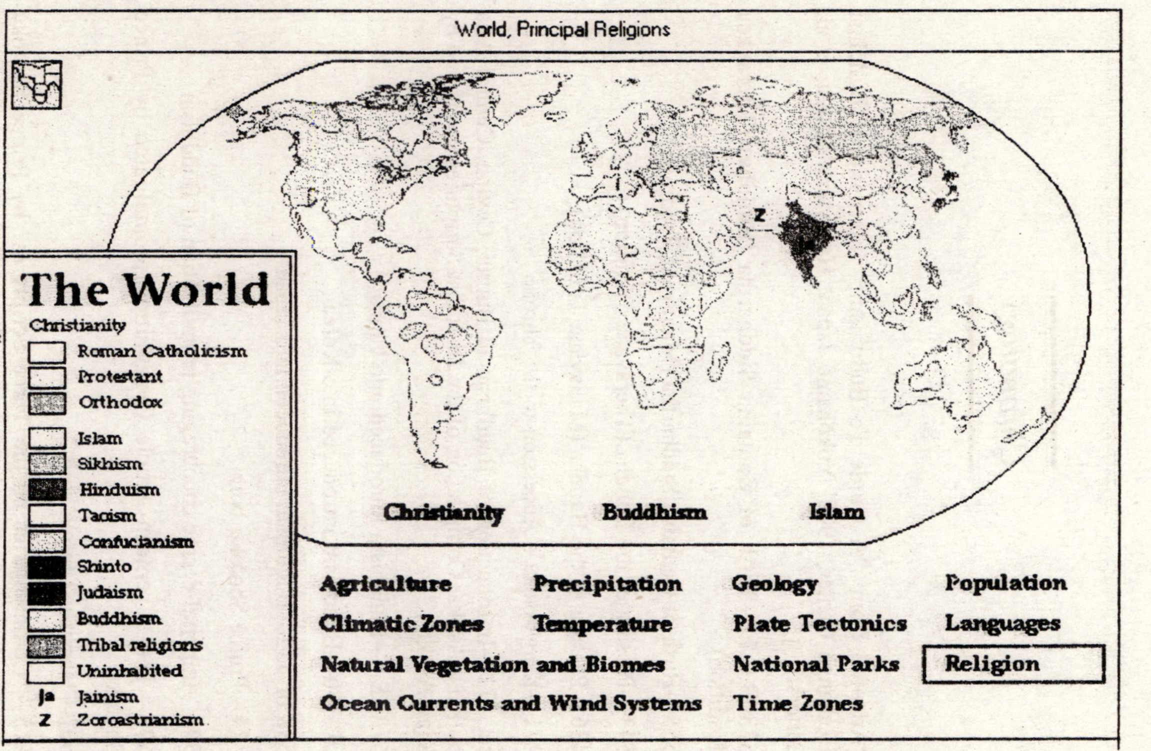
World, Principal Religions
The World
Christianity
Roman Catholicism
Protestant
Orthodox
Islam
Sikhism
Hinduism
Taoism
Confucianism
Shinto
Judaism
Buddhism
Tribal religions
Uninhabited
Ja Jainism
Z Zoroastrianism
Z
Christianity
Buddhism
Islam
Agriculture
Precipitation
Geology
Population
Climatic Zones
Temperature
Plate Tectonics
Languages
Natural Vegetation and Biomes
National Parks
Religion
Ocean Currents and Wind Systems
Time Zones

Chronology

(Adapted from: "A Guide To Buddhism," International Buddhist Exchange Center, 1970, Yokohama Japan. Hanayama Shoyu, et al, editors.)

623 B.C.E.—Birth of Gautama Siddhartha (Buddha) (Theravada Tradition)

565—Birth of Gautama Siddhartha (Mahayana Tradition)

543—Passing of the Buddha (Theravada Tradition)

486—Passing of the Buddha (Mahayana Tradition)

271—King Asoka's Accession to the Throne

ca. 271—Introduction of Buddhism to Burma, Ceylon, Central Asia by King Asoka; Compilation of the Buddhist Scriptures sponsored by King Asoka

67 C.E. —Buddhism introduced into China

ca. 350—Buddhism introduced into Korea

538 or 552—Buddhism introduced into Japan

574—Prince Shotoku born

594—Imperial decree encouraging promulgation of Buddhism

604—The Seventeen-Article Constitution promulgated by Prince Shotoku

607—Horyu-ji Temple built

615—"Commentaries on the Three Scriptures" by Prince Shotoku completed

621 or 622—Prince Shotoku died

712—The Kojiki (Ancient Chronicle) composed

720—The Nihon-shoki (Chronicles of Japan) composed

752—The Huge Statue of the Vairocana Buddha of the Todai-ji Temple of Nara completed

770—One Million Miniature Stupas (Pagodas) built

794—Capital moved from Nara to Kyoto

805—Saicho (767-822) established Tendai Buddhism

806—Kukai (774-835) established Shingon Buddhism

822—Mahayana Disciplines established

972—Kuya (b. 903), an advocator of the Pure Land Faith, died

985—Genshin (944-1017) wrote the 0-jo-yo-shu ("Collection of Essential Documents to Attain the Birth in the Pure Land")

1224—Ryonin (1072-1132) founded the Yuzu-gatari

1275—Honen (1133-1212) founded the Jodo Denomination

1191—Eisai (1141-1215) founded Rinzai Zen Buddhism

1124—Shinran (1173-1262) founded the Jodo-Shin Denomination

1127—Dogen (1200-53) founded Soto Zen

1252—The Huge Image of Amida Buddha at Kamakura cast

1253—Nichiren (1222-82) founded Nichiren Buddhism

1274—The First Mongolian Invasion

1275—Ippen (1239-89) founded the Ji Denomination

1281—The Second Mongolian Invasion

1336—Muromachi Shogunate established

1339—The Moss-garden of the Saiho-ji Temple in Kyoto built

1384—Kan-ami (b. 1333), a writer of Noh Dharma, died

1397—The Kinkaku-ji Temple or the Golden Pavilion in Kyoto built

1499—The Rock-garden of the Ryoan-ji Temple in Kyoto built; Rennyo (b. 1415), restorer of Jodo-Shin Buddhism, died

1543—Portuguese landed on Tanega-shima Island, and rifles introduced

1549—Christianity introduced by Francis Xavier

1582—Christian Youths Delegates started for Rome

1586—Toyotomi Hideyoshi became Japanese Prime Minister

1591—Sen-no-rikyu (b. 1520), founded of the Tea Ceremony, died

1602—The Jodo-Shin Denomination Split into the Higashi (East) and the Nishi (West) Hongan-ji Schools

1603—Tokugawa Iyeyasu established Edo Shogunate

1613—The Danka System or the Family-temple system formed

1639—Japan closed the door to foreigners

1654—Ingen or Yin-yuan (1592-1673) introduced the Obaku Denomination of Zen Buddhism

1681—Buddhist Scriptures in Chinese Version published by Tetsugen

1687—The killing of animals prohibited by Law

1853—Commodore Perry came to Japan

1868—Buddhism suppressed by the Shintoists, the Meiji Restoration and Nationalists; capital moved

1872—Celibacy and vegetarianism given up by governmental permission, Ban on Christianity cancelled; women admitted to any Buddhist temple.

1873—Religions in Japan put under government control

1894-95—The Sino-Japanese War

1904-95—The Russo-Japanese War

1934—Taisho Edition of the Buddhist Scriptures in Chinese version completed in 100 volumes

1941—World War II begins

1945—Japan surrendered to the Allied Powers

1946—The New Constitution of Japan promulgated; franchise given to women.

1951—The Religious Juridical Persons Law; Japan's Peace Treaty enforced

1952—The Second World Buddhists' Conference held in Tokyo

1959—Buddha Jayanti held in Japan

1968—International Buddhist Exchange Center incorporated (HANAYAMA).

Glossary

A

Agadas
adj.: healthy: n.: antidote, panacea, universal remedy.

Agamas
Generic term applied to a collection of traditional doctrines and precepts; also means the home or collecting-place of the law or truth; the peerless law; the ultimate absolute truth. The Four Agamas are as follows: (1) Dirghagama, "law treatises on cosmogony; (2) Madhyamagama, "middle" treatises on metaphysics; (3) Samyuktagama, "miscellaneous" treatises on abstract contemplation; (4) Edottaragama, "numerical" treatises on subject treated numerically. The sutras of Theravada are referred to at times as the Agamas.

Agara
House, dwelling, receptacle; also, used in the sense of a Bodily organ, e.g., the ear for sound, etc.

Agaru/Aguru
Sandalwood incense.

Alaya Consciousness
The fundamental consciousness of all sentient beings. As defined by the Yogacara School, Alaya means the "storehouse". Implying that this consciousness contains and preserves all past memories and potential psychic energy within its fold; it is the reservoir of all ideas, memories and desires and is also the fundamental cause of both Samsara and Nirvana.

Almsgiving
see charity.

Amitabha (Amida, Amita, Amitayus)
Amitabha is the most commonly used name for the Buddha of Infinite Light and Infinite Life. A transhistorical Buddha venerated by

all Mahayana schools (T'ien T'ai, Esoteric. Zen …) and, particularly, Pure Land, Presides over the Western Pure Land (Land of Ultimate Bliss), where anyone can be reborn through utterly sincere recitation of His name, particularly at the time of death.

Amitabha Buddha at the highest or noumenon level represents that True Mind, the Self-Nature common to the Buddhas and sentient beings – all encompassing and all-inclusive. This deeper understanding provides the rationale for the harmonization of Zen and Pure Land, two of the most popular schools of Mahayana Buddhism. See also "Buddha Reatation," "Mind," "Pure Land."

Amitabha Sutra

See "Three Pure land Sutras."

Anasrava

(Skt.) Opposite of asrava.

Anuttara-Samayak-Sambodhi

The incomparably, completely and fully awakened mind; it is the attribute of buddhas.

Apaya-bhumi

States of woe: the three realms of existence characterized by extreme discomfort and delusion—i.e., hell-states, animal-birth and the hungry ghosts, or pretas.

Arhat

Arhatship is the highest rank attained by Sravakas. An Arhat is a Buddhist saint who has attained liberation from the cycle of Birth and Death, generally through living a monastic life in accordance with the Buddhas' teachings. This is the goal of Theravadin practice, as contrasted with Bodhisattvahood in Mahayana practice. (A Dictionary of Buddhism.) The stage is preceded by three others: 1. Stream Winner, 2. Once-Returner, 3. Non-Returner. See also "Sravakas."

Arthakrtya

One of the Four All-Embracing Virtues: performance of conduct profitable to others in order to lead them toward the truth.

Arya

Any individual ennobled by his/her own continuing effort on the path to enlightenment.

Asamkhiya (kalpa)

Term related to the Buddhist metaphysics of time. Each of the periodic manifestations and dissolutions of universes which go on eternally has four parts, called asamkhiya kalpas.

Asrava

(Skt.) Pain causing impurity, defilement.

Asura

Titanic demons, enemies of the gods, with whom-especially Indra-they wage war.

Attachment

In the Four Noble truths, Buddha Shakyamuni taught that attachment to self is the root cause of suffering:

> From craving [attachment] springs grief, from craving springs fear; For him who is wholly free from craving, there is no grief, much less fear, (Dhammapada Sutra. In Narada Maha Thera, The Buddha and His Teachings.)
>
> If you don't have attachments, naturally you're liberated ... In ancient times, there was an old cultivator who asked for instructions from a monk, "Great Monk, let me ask you, how can I attain liberation?" The Great monk said, "Who tied you up?" This old cultivator answered, "Nobody tied me up." The monk said, The monk said, "Then who do you seek liberation?" (Hsuan Hua, tr., Flower Adornment Sutra, "Pure Conduct," chap. 11.)

For the seasoned practitioner, even the Dharma must not become an attachment. As an analogy, to clean one's shirt, it is necessary to use soap. However, if the soap is not then rinsed out, the garment will not be truly clean. Similarly, the practitioner's mind will not be fully liberated until he severs attachment to everything, including the Dharma itself.

Avalokitesvara

The name is a compound of Ishwara, meaning Lord, and avalokita, looked upon or seen, and is usually translated as the Lord Who Observes (the cries of the world); the Buddhist embodiment of compassion as formulated in the Mahayana Dharma. Also called Kuan Yin, the Bodhisattva of Compassion. Guan Yin is one of the triad of Amitabha Buddha, represented on his left, Usually recognizable by the small Buddha adorning Her crown. Guan Yin can transform into many different forms in order to cross over to the beings. Guan Yin is one of the most popular Bodhisattva in China.

Avatamsaka (Flower Ornament) Sutra

The basic text of the Avatamsaka School. It is one of the longest sutras in the Buddhist Canon and records the highest teaching of Buddha Shakyamuni, immediately after Enlightenment. It is traditionally believed that the Sutra was taught to the Bodhisattvas and other high spiritual beings while the Buddha was in samadhi. The Sutra has been described as the "epitome of Buddhist thought, Buddhist sentiment and Buddhist experience" and is quoted by all schools of Mahayana Buddhism, in particular, Pure Land and Zen.

Awakening vs. Enlightenment

A clear distinction should be made between awakening to the Way (Great Awakening) and attaining the Way (attaining Enlightenment). (Note: There are many degrees of Awakening and Enlightenment. Attaining the Enlightenment of the Arhats, Pratyeka Buddhas, Bodhisattvas, etc. is different from attaining Supreme Enlightenment, i.e., Buddhahood.)

To experience a Great Awakening is to achieve (through Zen meditation, Buddha Recitation, etc.) a complete and deep realization of what is means to be a Buddha and how to reach Buddhahood. It is to see one's Nature, comprehend the True Nature of things, the Truth. However, only after becoming a Buddha can one be said to have truly attained Supreme Enlightenment (attained the Way). A metaphor appearing in the sutras is that of a glass of water containing sediments. As long as the glass is undisturbed, the sediments remain at the bottom and the water is clear. However, as soon as the glass is shaken, the water becomes turbid. Likewise, when a practitioner experiences a Great Awakening (awakens to the Way), his afflictions (greed, anger and delusion) are temporarily suppressed but not yet eliminated. To achieve Supreme Enlightenment (i.e., to be rid of all afflictions, to discard all sediments) is the ultimate goal. Only then can he completely trust his mind and actions. Before then, he should adhere to the precepts, keep a close watch on his mind and thoughts, like a cat stalking a mouse, ready to pounce on evil thoughts as soon as they arise. To do otherwise is to court certain failure, as stories upon stories of errant monks, roshis and gurus demonstrate.

Awakening of the Faith (Treatise)

A major commentary by the Patriarch Asvaghosha (1st/2nd cent.), which presents the fundamental principles of Mahayana Buddhism. Several translations exist in English.

B

Ban T'o

Suddhidanthaka in Sanskrit. Ban T'o was a disciple of Buddha, and he was very forgetful; for when the Buddha taught him the second sentence of a gatha of a sutra he would forget the first one, and when he was taught the third one he would forget the second one. Ultimately, however, with persistence he become an Arhat.

Bardo

The intermediate existence between death and reincarnation — a stage varying from seven to forty-nine days, after which the Karmic body from previous lives will certainly be reborn.

Bhiksu

Religious mendicant; Buddhist fully ordained monk. Bhiksuni is the equivalent term designating a women.

Bhadanta

"Most virtuous"; honorific title apllied to a Buddha.

Bhaisajyaguru

Sanskrit word, the Buddha of Medicine, who quells all diseases and lengthens life. His is the Buddha in the Pure Land of the Paradise of the East.

Bhutatathata

The true character of reality. The real as thus, always or eternally so. True Suchness.

Bodhi

Sanskrit for Enlightenment. Also Perfect knowledge or wisdom by which a person becomes a Buddha.

Bodhi-Tao

Bodhi-path: The way or path to the Supreme Enlightenment of Buddhahood.

Bodhi Mind (Bodhicitta, Great Mind)

The spirit of Enlightenment, the aspiration to achieve it, the Mind set on Enlightenment. It involves two parallel aspects: i) the determination to achieve Buddhahood and ii) the aspiration to rescue all sentient beings.

Bodhimandala

Truth-plot, holy sits, place of Enlightenment, the place where the Buddha attained Enlightenment.

Bodhisattvas

Those who aspire to Supreme Enlightenment and Buddhahood for themselves and all beings. The word Bodhisattva can therefore stand for a realized being such as Avalokitesvara or Samantabhadra but also for anyone who has developed the Bodhi Mind, the aspiration to save oneself and others.

Bodhisattva-Tao

The way of the practitioner of Mahayana Buddhism. One following this path aspires to the attainment of Enlightenment for the sake and benefit of all sentient beings.

Brahma Net Sutra (Brahmajala Sutra)

This is a sutra of major significance in Mahayana Buddhism. In addition to containing the ten major precepts of Mahayana (not to kill, steal, lie, etc.) the Sutra also contains forty-eight less important injunctions. These fifty-eight major and minor precepts constitute the Bodhisattva Precepts, taken by most Mahayana monks and nuns and certain advanced lay practitioners.

Brahmacarya

Lit., Brahma or purified life, usually connoting the practice of celibacy.

Brahmajala

Or Indra's net, characterized by holding a luminous gem in every one of its eyes. (Hindu mythology).

Brahmin

The highest of the four Castes in Hinduism. They served Brahma, his offering, the keepers of the Vedas, i.e. priestly.

Buddha

Lit., the Awakened One; one who through aeons of spiritual development has attained Anuttara-Samyak-Sambodhi. This epithet usually refers to Sakyamuni Buddha, who lived and taught in India some 2,600 years ago.

Buddha Nature

The following terms refer to the same thing: Self-Nature, True Nature, Original Nature, Dharma Nature, True Mark, True Mind, True Emptiness, True Thusness, Dharma Body, Original Face, Emptiness, Prajna, Nirvana, etc.

> According to the Mahayana view, [buddha-nature] is the true, immutable, and eternal nature of all beings. Since all beings possess buddha-nature, it is possible for them to attain enlightenment and become a Buddha, regardless of what level of existence they occupy ... The answer to the question whether Buddha-nature is immanent in beings is an essential determining factor for the association of a giving school with Theravada or Mahayana, the two great currents within Buddhism. In Theravada this notion is unknown; here the potential to become a Buddha is not ascribed to every being. By contrast the Mahayana sees the attainment of buddhahood as the highest goal; it can be attained through the inherent Buddha-nature of every being through appropriate spiritual practice. (The Shambhala Dictionary of Buddhism and Zen.)

See also "Dharma Nature."

Buddha Recitation

See "Buddha-Remembrance".

Buddha-Remembrance

General term for a number of practices such as *(i)* oral recitation of Amitabha Buddha's name and *(ii)* visualization/contemplation of His auspicious marks and those of the Pure Land.

> In reciting the Buddha-name you use your one mind to be mindful of your own true self: how could this be considered seeking outside yourself?

> Reciting the buddha-name proceeds from the mind. The mind remembers Buddha and does not forget. That's why it is called Buddha remembrance, or reciting the Buddha-name mindfully.

The most common Pure Land technique is recitation of Amitabha Buddha's name. See also "Amitabha," "Pure Land."

Buddhadharma

Lit., Teaching of Enlightenment. Originally apllied to designate of Shakyamuni Buddha; supplanted by the term "Buddhism" in its later historical development.

Buddharupa

A statue or Image of the Buddha, used for devotional purposes.

C

Caitya

Tumulus, a mausoleum; a place where the relics of Buddha were collected; hence, a place where the sutras or images are placed.

Cakravala

The nine cakravala or concentric mountain ranges or continents, separated by eight seas, of a universe.

Candana

White candana, or white sandalwood.

Chan

See Zen.

Ch'an-Ting

Lit., mind still and quiet: the Chinese translation of the Sanskrit terms Dhyana-Samadhi, meaning deep contemplative practice or yogic absorption.

Charity

Or almsgiving, the first Paramitas. There are three kinds of charity in terms of goods, teaching (Dharma) and courage (fearlessness). Out of the three, the merits and virtues of the teaching of the Buddha Dharma is the most surpassing. Charity done for no reward here and hereafter is called pure or unsullied, while the sullied charity is done for the purpose of personal benefits. In Buddhism, the merits and virtues of pure charity is the best.

Chiliocosm

Countless Universes.

Chih-Kuan

In practice there are three contemplations; seeing such abstractions: (1) by fixing the mind on the nose, navel, etc. (2) by stopping every thought as it arises; (3) by dwelling on the thought that no thing exists of itself, but from a preceding cause.

Chung Yin Shen

See Bardo.

Cintamani

The talismanic pearl, a symbol of bestowing fortune and capable of fulfilling every wish.

Citta

Mind or heart. The two terms being synonymous in Asian religious philosophy.

Conditioned (compounded)

Describes all the various phenomena in the world – made up of separate, discrete elements, "with outflows," with no intrinsic nature of their own. Conditioned merits and virtues lead to rebirth within samsara, whereas unconditioned merits and virtues are the causes of liberation from Birth and Death. See also "Unconditioned."

D

Dana

The practice of generosity or charity: one of the Paramitas as well as one of the All-Embracing Virtues, where it means, in the latter, giving others what they want just to lead them towards the truth.

Dedication of Merit

See "Transference of Merit."

Delusion (Ignorance)

"Delusion refers to belief in something that contradicts reality. In Buddhism, delusion is ... a lack of awareness of the true nature or Buddha nature of things, or of the true meaning of existence. "According to the Buddhist outlook, we are deluded by our senses—among which intellect (discriminating, discursive through) is included as a sixth sense. Consciousness, attached to the senses, leads us into error by causing us to take the world of appearances for the world of reality, whereas in fact it is only a limited and fleeting aspect of reality." (The Shambhala Dictionary of Buddhism and Zen.)

Demons

Evil influences which hinder cultivation. These can take an infinite number of forms, including evil beings or hallucinations. Disease and death, as well as the three poisons of greed, anger and delusion are also equated to demons, as they disturb the mind.

The Nirvana Sutra lists four types of demon: (i) greed, anger and delusion; (ii) the five skandas, or obstructions caused by physical and mental functions; (iii) death; (iv) the demon of the Sixth Heaven (Realm of Desire).

The Self-Nature has been described in Mahayana sutras as a house full of gold and jewellrry. To preserve the riches, i.e., to keep the mind calm, empty and still, we should shut the doors to the three thieves of greed, anger and delusion. Letting the mind wander opens the house to "demons," that is, hallucinations and harm. Thus, Zen practitioners are taught that, while in meditation, "Encountering demons, kill the demons, encountering Buddhas, kill the Buddhas," Both demons and Buddhas are mind-made, Mind-Only.

For a detailed discussion of demons, see Master Thich Thien Tam, Buddhism of Wisdom and' Faith, sect. 51.

Devakanya

Goddess in general attendance on the regents of the sun and moon.

Deva

Lit., "A shining one". An inhabitant of the heavenly realms, which is characterized by long life, joyous surroundings and blissful states of mind. In the Buddhist tradition, these states are understood to be impermanent, not eternal.

Deva King

The four Deva Kings in the first, or lowest, Devaloka on its four sides are the following: East-Dhrtarastra; South-Virodhaka; West-Viropaksa; North-Dhanada, or Vaisravana.

Dharini

Extended mantra used in esoteric branch of Buddhism to focus and expand the mind. Its words, or sounds, should not communicate any recognizable meaning.

Dharma

(a) The teachings of the Buddhas (generally capitalized in English);

(b) duty, law, doctrine;

(c) things, events, phenomena, everything.

Dharma-dhatu

The Law-doctrine that is the reality behind being and non-being. It is interpenetrate and all-inclusive, just as the rotation of the earth holds both night and day.

Dharma-Ending Age, Degenerate Age, Last Age

The present spiritually degenerate era, twenty-six centuries after the demise of Shakyamuni Buddha. The concept of decline, dissension and schism within the Dharma after the passing of the Buddha. is a general teaching of Buddhism and a corollary to the Truth of Impermanence. See, for example, the Diamond Sutra (sect. 6 in the translation by A.F. Price and Wong Mou-lam). The time following Buddha Shakyamuni's demise is divided into three periods; (i) the Perfect Age of the Dharma, lasting 500 years, when the Buddha's teaching (usually mediation) was correctly practiced and Enlightenment often attained; (ii) the Dharma Semblance Age, lasting about, 1,000 years, when a form of the teaching was practised but Enlightenment seldom attained; (iii) the Dharma-Ending Age, lasting some ten thousand years, when a diluted from of the teaching exists and Enlightenment is rarely attained.

Dharma Gate

School, method, tradition.

Dharma Nature

The intrinsic nature of all things. Used interchangeably with "emptiness," "reality." See also "Buddha Nature."

Dharmakara

The Bodhisattva who later become Amitabha Buddha, as related in the Longer Amitabha Sutra. The Bodhisattva Dharmakara is famous for forty-eight Vows, particularly the eighteenth, which promises rebirth in the Pure Land to anyone who recites His name with utmost sincerity and faith at the time of death.

Dharmakaya

See "Three bodies of the Buddha."

Dhyana

The practice of concentration—i.e., meditation. Also, more specifically, the four form concentrations and the four formless concentrations.

Diamond Sutra

"An independent part of the Prajnaparamita Sutra, which attained great importance, particularly in East Asia. It shows that all phenomenal appearances are not ultimate reality but rather illusions, projections of one's own mind ... The work is called Diamond Sutra because it is 'sharp like a diamond that cuts away all unnecessary conceptualizations and brings one to the further shore of enlightenment.'" (The Shambhala Dictionary of Buddhism and Zen.)

Difficult Path of Practice (Path of the Sages, Self-Power Path)

According to Pure Land teaching, all conventional Buddhist ways of practice and cultivation (Zen, Theravada, the Vinaya School ...), which emphasize self-power and self-reliance. This is contrasted to the East Path of Practice, that is, the Pure Land method, which relies on both self-power and other-power and assistance of the Buddhas and Bodhisattvas).

Five Corruptions

See "Five Turbidities."

Five Desires (Five Sensual Pleasures)

Desires connected with the five senses, i.e., form, sound, aroma, taste and touch.

Five Eyes

1. human eye; 2. devine eye; 3. dharma eye; 4. wisdom eye; 5. Buddha eye.

Five Fundamental Conditions of Passions and Delusions

1. Wrong views which are common to triloka; 2. Clinging or attachment in the desire realm; 3. Clinging or attachment in the form realm: 4. Clinging or attachment in the formless realm which is still mortal; 5. The state of unenlightenment which is the root-cause of all distressful delusion.

Five Natures

The natures of (1) Bodhisattvas, (2) Sravakas and Pratyekabuddhas, (3) ordinary good people, (4) agnostics, (5) heretics.

Five Offenses

The five rebellious acts or deadly sins: (1) parricide; (2) matricide; (3) killing an arhat; (4) shedding the blood of a Buddha; (5) destroying the harmony of the sangha, or fraternity.

Five Precepts

The precepts taken by lay Buddhists, prohibiting i) killing, ii) stealing iii) lying, iv) sexual misconduct, v) ingesting intoxicants. See also "Ten Precepts."

Five Skandhas

The five groups of elements (Dharmas) into which all existences are classified in early Buddhism. The five are: Rupa (matter), Vedana (feeling), Sanjna (ideation); Samskara (forces or drives) Vijnana (consciousness or sensation). Group, heap, aggregate; the five constituents of the personality; form, feeling, perception, impulses, consciousness; the five factors constituting the individual person.

Five Turbidities (Corruptions, Defilements, Depravities, Filths, Impurities)

They are. 1. The defilement of views, when incorrect, perverse thoughts and ideas are predominant; 2. The defilement of passions, when all kinds of transgressions are exalted; 3. The defilement of the human condition, when people are usually dissatisfied and unhappy; 4. The defilement of the life-span, when the human life-span as a whole decreases; S. the defilement of the world-age, when war and natural disasters are rife. These conditions, viewed from a Buddhist angle, however, can constitute aids to Enlightenment, as they may spur practitioners to more earnest cultivation.

Flower Store World

The entire cosmos, consisting of worlds upon worlds and infinitum, as described in the Avatamsaka Sutra. It is the realm of Vairocana Buddha, the transcendental aspect of Buddha Shakyamuni and of all Buddhas. The Saha World, the Western Pure Land and, for that matter, all lands and realms are within the Flower Store World.

Four Aspects (of Buddha Dharma)

(1) the teaching; (2) the principle; (3) the practice; (4) the fruit/reward/result.

Four Elements

All matters are formed and are composed by four conditioned causes: (1) earth, which is characterized by solidity and durability; (2) water, which is characterized by liquid/fluid and moisture; (3) fire, which is characterized by energy and warmth; (4) wind, which is characterized by gas/air movement.

Four Fruits of the Arhat

See under Arhat entry.

Four Great Bodhisattva

The represent the four major characters of Bodhisattva:

1. Manjusri – Universal Great Wisdon Bodhisattva.
2. Samantabhadra – Universal Worthy Great Conduct Bodhisattva;
3. Ksitigarbha – Earth Store King Great Vow Bodhisattva;
4. Avalokitesvara – Guan Shr Yin Great Compassion Bodhisattva.

Four Great Vows (Four Universal Vows)

The four vows held by all Bodhisattvas. There vows are called great because of the wondrous and inconceivable compassion involved in fulfilling them. They are as follows: *Sentient beings without number we vow to enlighten; Vexations without end we vow to eradicate; Limitless approaches to Dharma we vow to master; The Supreme Awakening we vow to achieve.*

Four Noble Truths

1) Sufferings; 2) Cause of Sufferings; 3) Cessation of sufferings; 4) The Path leading to the cessation of sufferings.

Four Pure Lands

A classification by the Pure Land and T'ien T'ai schools of the pure realms subsumed under the Land of Amitabha Buddha, as described in the sutras. They are:

(i) the Land of Common Residence of Beings and Saints (Land Where Saints and Ordinary Beings Dwell Together), where all beings, from the six lower worlds (hells, hungry ghosts ...) to the Buddhas and Bodhisattvas, live together (further divided into two, the Common Residence Pure Land and Common Residence Impure Land);

(ii) the Land of Expediency (Land of Expedient Liberation), inhabited by Arhats and lesser Bodhisattvas;

(iii) the Land of Real Reward, inhabited by the highest Bodhisattvas;

(iv) the Land of Eternally Quiescent Light, in which the Buddhas dwell.

These distinctions are at the phenomenal level. At the noumenon level, there is, of course, no difference among them.

Four Reliance (to learning Buddhist Dharma)

The four standards of Right Dharma which buddhist should rely on or abide by:

1. to abide by the Dharma, not the person;
2. to abide by the sutras of ultimate truth, not the sutras of incomplete truth;
3. to abide by the meaning, not the word;
4. to abide by the wisdom, not the consciousness.

Four Unlimited Mind

The mind of Bodhisattva: 1. Kindness; 2. Compassion; 3. Delight; 4. Renunciation.

Four Virtues

The four Nirvanic virtues: (1) Eternity or permanence; (2) Joy; (3) Personality; (4) Purity.

These four important virtues are affirmed by the sutra in the transcendental or nirvanarealm.

Four Ways (of learning Buddhist Dharma)

(1) Belief/faith; (2) Interpretation/discernment; (3) Practice/performance; (4) Verification/assurance. These are the cyclic process in learning a truth.

Four Wisdom

The forms of wisdom of Buddha. (1) the Great-Mirror wisdom of Aksobhya; (2) the Universal Wisdom of Ratnaketu; (3) the Profound Observing Wisdom of Amitabha; (4) the Perfecting Wisdom of Amoghsiddhi.

Fourfold Assembly

Or the Four Varga (groups) are bhiksu, bhiksuni, upasaka and upasika, i.e. monks, nuns, male and female devotees.

G

Good Spiritual Advisor

Guru, virtuous friend, wise person, Bodhisattva, Buddha—anyone (even an evil being!) who can help the practitioner progress along the path to Enlightenment. This notwithstanding, wisdom should be the primary factor in the selection of such an advisor: the advisor must have wisdom, and both advisor and practitioner must exercise wisdom in selecting one another.

Great Awakening

See "Awakening vs. Enlightenment."

Great Vehicle

See Mahayana.

H

Hua T'ou

Lit., ante word, The reality prior to the arising of thought.

Heaven of the Thirty-Three

A heaven in the Realm of Desire, with thirty-two god-kings presided over by Indra, thus totaling thirty-three, located at the summit of Mt. Sumeru (G.C.C. Chang).

Heretical views

The sutras usually refer to sixty-two such views. They are the externalist (non-Buddhist) views prevalent in Buddha Shakyamuni's time.

Hinayana

The Lesser Vehicle; a term applied by the Mahayana to those schools of Buddhism that practice to attain the fruits of Sravakayana and Pratyekabuddhayana and do not attempt to attain the Anuttara-Samyak-Sambodhi of Buddha.

Holy One

Holy or Saintly One; One who has started on the path to Nirvana.

I

Icchantika

One who has no interest in the path to Awakening, or one whose good roots are completely covered.

J

Jambunada-suvarna

Jambu River gold; the golden sand of the Jambu river.

Jetavana

A park near the city of Sravasti, said to have been obtained from Prince Jeta by Anathapindika, in which monasterial building were erected; the favourite resort of Sakyamuni.

Jewel Net of Indra

This is a net said to hang in the palace of Indra, the king of the gods. At each interstice of the net is a reflecting jewel, which mirrors not only the adjacent jewels but the multiple images reflected in them. This famous image is meant to describe the unimpeded interpenetration of all and everything.

K

Kalpa

Periodic manifestations and dissolutions of universes which go on etemally, Great kalpas consist of four asamkhiya kalpas corresponding to childhood. Maturity, old age and the death of the universe.

Karma

Volition, volitional or intentional activity. Karma is always following by its fruit, Vipaka.

Karma and Vipaka are oftentimes referred to as the law of causality, a cardinal concern in the Teaching of the Buddha.

Common karma: the difference between personal and common karma can be seen in the following example: Supposes a country goes to war to gain certain economic advantages and in the process, numerous soldiers and civilians are killed or maimed. If a particular citizen volunteers for military service and actually participates in the carnage, he commits a personal karma of killing. Other citizens, however, even if opposed to the war, may benefit directly or indirectly (e.g., through economic gain). They are thus said to share in the common karma of killing of their country.

Fixed karma: in principle, all karma is subject to change. Fixed karma. however, is karma which can only be changed in extraordinary circumstances, because it derives from an evil act committed simultaneously with mind, speech and body. An example of fixed karma would be a premeditated crime (versus a crime of passion).

Kasaya

The monk's robe, or cassock.

Ksana

An inconceivably short mind-moment.

Ksanti

Patience or forbearance, one of the Six Paramitas.

Ksatriya

The second of the four Hindi Castes at the time of Shakyamuni, they were the royal caste, the noble landlord, the warriors and the ruling castes.

L

Laksana

A distinctive mark, sign, indication, characteristic or designation. A Buddha is recognized by his thirty-two characteristic physiological marks.

Lankavatara Sutra

The only sutra recommended by Bodhidharma, the First Zen Patriarch in China. It is a key Zen text, along with the Diamond Sutra (recommended by the Sixth Patriarch), the Surangama Sutra, the Vimalakiti Sutra, the Avatamsaka Sutra... The last for sutras are referred to frequently in Pure Land commentaries.

Last Age

See "Dharma-Ending Age."

Law of Interdependent Causation

It states that all phenomena arise depending upon a number of casual factors. In other world, a phenomenon exists in condition that the other exist; it has in condition that others have; it extinguishes in condition that others extinguish; it has not in condition that others have not. For existence, there are twelve links in the chain:

- Ignorance is the condition for karmic activity:
- karmic activity is the condition for consciousness;
- Consciousness is the condition for the name and form;
- Name and form is the condition for the six sense organs;
- Six sense organs are the condition for contact;
- Contact is the condition for feeling;
- Feeling is the condition for emotional love/craving;
- Emotional love/craving is the condition for grasping;
- Grasping is the condition for existing;
- Existing is the condition for birth;
- Birth is the condition for old age and death;
- Old age and death is the condition for ignorance; and so on.

Lesser Vehicle

The early Buddhism. A term coined by Mahayanists to distinguish this school of Buddhism [whose modern descendent is Theravada] from Mahayana. It is so called because the teaching of this school puts emphasis on one's own liberation, whereas the teaching of Mahayana stresses the attainment of Buddhahood for all sentient beings. Theravada is now prevalent in southeast Asia, while Mahayana has spread over the northern area (China, Vietnam, Korea, Japan...) (G.C.C. Chang).

Lotus Grades

The nine possible degrees of rebirth in the Western pure Land. The more merits and virtues the practitioner accumulates, the higher the grade.

Lotus Sect

A Buddhist sect founded by the great Master Hui Yuan about 390 A.D. at his monastery on Mount Lu in Kiangsi Province in China.

The Lotus Sect believes in and honours Amitabha Buddha and declares that, through the chanting of his name and by purifying and finally ridding oneself of desire, one can be reborn in the Pure Land. There one is born of a lotus, and depending on one's degree of purification and practice, one is born into one of the nine grades of the lotus: upper superior, middle superior, lower superior, etc.

Lotus Sutra

Or Saddarma-pundarika, Dharma Flower, or "The Lotus of the True Law." The sutra is the basis for the Lotus sect (Tien-t'ai in Chinese). Among the sutras of the Mahayana canon.

> One of the earliest and most richly descriptive of the Mahayana sutras of Indian origin. It became important for the shaping of the Buddhist tradition in East Asia, in particular because of its teaching of the One Vehicle under which are subsumed the usual Hinayana [Theravada] and Mahayana divisions. It is the main text of the Tendai [T'ien Tai] school. (Joji Okazaki.)

This School has a historically close relationship with the Pure Land School. Thus, Master T'ai Hsu taught that the Lotus Sutra and the Amitabha Sutras were closely connected, differing only in length.

Lotus Treasury World

See "Ocean-Wide Lotus Assembly."

M

Maha-Bodhisattva

Also, Mahasattva; a great Bodhisattva who has reached the advanced stage of Enlightenment.

Mahakaruna

Great compression.

Mahakasyapa

Also, Kasyapa; one of Buddha's disciples. The Ch'an Sect, according to its tradition. Claims him is its first patriarch.

Maharaja

A great or superior king.

Mahayama

The mother of Shakaymuni. She was a Koliyan Princess and married to Suddhodana.

Mahayana

Lit., great vehicle; the dominant Buddhist tradition of East Asia. Special characteristics of Mahayana are 1. Emphasis on Bodhisattva ideal, 2. The accession of the Buddha to a superhuman status, 3. The development of extensive philosophical inquiry to counter Brahmanical and other scholarly argument, 4. The development of elaborate devotional practice.

Mahasattva

See Maha-Bodhisattva.

Mahasthamaprapta (Shih Chih, Seishi)

One of the three sages in Pure Land Buddhism recognizable by the water Jar (jeweled pitcher) adorning Her crown. Usually represented in female form in East Asian iconography. Amitabha Buddha is frequently depicted standing between the Bodhisattvas Avalokitesvara and Mahasthamaprapta.

Maitreya

Sanskrit word, literally means friendly and benevolent. He will be the next Buddha in our world. He is now preaching in Tusita Heaven. In China, he is usually represented as the fat laughing Buddha.

Maitri

Loving-kindness.

Manas

The name of the seventh of the eight consciousnesses. I refers to the faculty of thought, the intellectual function of consciousness.

Mani

A jewel, gem, precious stone; especially a pearl bead or other globular ornament.

Mantra

A syllable, word or verse which has been revealed to a seer in meditation, embodiment in sound of a deity; spell or incantation.

Marks

Characteristics, forms, physiognomy. Marks are contrasted with essence, in the same way that phenomena are contrasted with noumenon. True mark stands for True Form, True Nature, Buddha Nature, always unchanging. The True Mark of all phenomena is like space: always existing but really empty; although empty, really existing. The True Mark of the Triple World is No-Birth/No-Death, not existent/not non-existent, not like this/not like that. True Mark is also called "Self-Nature," "Dharma Body," The "Unconditioned,"

"True Thusness, " Nirvana," "Dharma Realm.11 See also "Noumenon/ Phenomena."

Meditation Sutra

One of the three core sutras of the Pure Land school. It teaches sixteen methods of visualizing Amitabha Buddha, the Bodhisattvas and the Pure Land. This sutra stresses the element of mediation in Pure Land. See also "Three Pure Land Sutras," "Vaidehi." "Visualization."

Merit and Virtue

These two terms are sometimes used interchangeably. However, there is a crucial difference: merits are the blessings (wealth, intelligence, etc.) of the human and celestial realms; therefore, they are temporary and subject to Birth and Death. Virtues, on the other hand, transcend Birth and Death and lead to Buddhadood. Four virtues are mentioned in Pure Land Buddhism: eternity; happiness; True Self; purity. An identical action (e.g., charity) can lead either to merit or virtue, depending on the mind of the practitioner, that is, on whether he is seeking mundane rewards (merit) or transcendence (virtue). Thus, the Pure Land cultivator should not seek merits for by doing so, he would, in effect, be choosing to remain within samsara. This would be counter to his very with to escape Birth and Death.

Middle Vehicle

Also called Middle Doctrine School or Madhyarnika; on of the two main schools of Mahayana thought; it upholds the Void as the only really real or independent, unconditioned Reality.

Mind

Key concept in all Buddhist Teaching.

> Frequent term in Zen, used in two senses: (1) the mind-ground, the One Mind... the Buddha-mind, the mind of thusness...(2) false mind, the ordinary mind dominated by conditioning, desire, aversion, ignorance, and false sense of self, the mind of delusion...(J.C. Cleary, A Buddha from Korea.)

The ordinary, deluded mind (thought) includes feelings, impressions, conceptions, consciousness, etc. The Self-Nature True Mind is the fundamental nature, the Original Face, reality, etc. As an analogy, the Self-Nature True Mind is to mind what water is to waves – the two cannot be dissociated. They are the same but they are also different. To approach the sutras "making discriminations and nurturing attachments is no different from the Zen allegory of a person attempting to lift a chair while seated on it. If he would only get off the chair, he could raise it easily. Similarly, the practitioner truly understands the Dharma only to the extent that he "suspends the operation of the discriminating intellect, the faculty of the internal dialogue through which people from moment to moment define and perpetuate their customary world of perception. "(See this book, Introduction.)

See also the following passage:

> The mind... "creates" the world in the sense that it invests the phenomenal world with value. The remedy to this situation, according to Buddhism, is to still the mind, to stop it from making discriminations and nurturing attachments toward certain phenomena and feelings of aversion toward others. When this state of calmness of mind is achieved, the darkness of ignorance and passion will be dispelled and the mind can perceive the underlying unity of the absolute. The individual will then have achieved the state of enlightenment and will be freed from the cycle of birth and death, because such a person is now totally indifferent to them both. (Burton Watson, The Zen Teachings of Master Lin-Chi.)

Mindfulness of the Buddha

Synonymous with Buddha Recitation. See "Buddha Recitation."

Mount Sumeru

The central mountain of every universe. Also called Wonderful Height, Wonderful Brilliancy, etc.

N

Nagarjuna (2nd/3rd cent.)

"One of the most important philosophers of Buddhism and the founder of the Madhyamika school. Nagarjuna's major accomplishment was his systematization of the teaching presented in the Prajnaparamita Sutras. Nagarjuna's methodological approach of rejecting all opposites is the basis of the Middle Way (Shambhala Dictionary of Buddhism and Zen).

Narayana

Name of a deva, a strong, manly hero having divine power.

Nirmanakaya

See "Three bodies of the Buddha."

Nirvana

The deathless; the cessation of all suffering. The very opposite of the Wheel of Birth-and-Death; it is what those in the Buddhist tradition aspire to experience. The Absolute, which transcends designation and mundane characterization.

Nirvana Sutra

The last of the sutras in the Mahayana canon. It emphasizes the importance of Buddha-nature, which is the same as Self-Nature.

Non-Birth (No-Birth)

"A term used to describe the nature of Nirvana. In Mahayana Buddhism generally, No-Birth signifies the 'extinction' of the discursive thinking by which we conceive of things as arising and perishing, forming attachments to them." (Ryukoku University.) See also "Tolerance of Non-Birth."

O

Ocean-wide Lotus Assembly

The Lotus Assembly represents the gathering of Buddha Amitabha, the Bodhisattvas, the sages and saints and all other superior beings in the Land of Ultimate Bliss. This Assembly is "Ocean-wide" as the participants are infinite in number — spreading as far and wide as the ocean. The term Ocean-wide Assembly is generally associated with the Avatamsaka Sutra, a text particularly prized by the Pure Land and Zen schools alike.

Once-returner

A sage who has only one rebirth left before reaching Arhatship and escaping birth and death.

One-Life Bodhisattva

The one Yana, the vehicle of Oneness. The One Buddhayana, the One Vehicle, i.e., Mahayana, which contains the final or complete Law of the Buddha and not merely a part, or preliminary stage, as in Hinayana.

Other-Power

The issue of other-power (Buddhas' power) is often misunderstood and glossed over by many Buddhists. However, it must be pointed out that, in Buddhism, other-power is absolutely necessary if a Bodhisattva is to attain Ultimate Enlightenment. The Lankavatara Sutra (The only sutra recommended by Bodhidharma) and the Avatamsaka Sutra (described by D.T. Suzuki as the epitome of Buddhist thought) are emphatically clear on this point:

> As long as [conversion] is as experience and not more understanding, it is evident that self-discipline plays in important role in the Buddhist life. But.. we must not forget the fact that the Lanka [Lankavatara Sutra] also emphasizes the necessity of the Buddha's power being added to the Bodhisattvas', in their upward course of spiritual development and in the accomplishment of their great task of world salvation. (Daisetz Teitaro Suzuki, tr.. The Lankavatara Sutra, p. xviii.)

The Avatamsaka Sutra states:

> Having purified wisdom and means in the seventh stage...
> The great sages attain acceptance of non-origination...
> On the basis of their previous resolution, be Buddhas further exhort them...
> "Though you have extinguished the burning of the fore of affliction,
> Having seen the world still afflicted, remember your past vows;
> Having thought of the welfare of the world, work in quest Of the cause of knowledge, for the liberation of the world."
> (T. Cleary, tr., The Flower Ornament Sutra, Vol II, p. 86)

See also "Easy Path of Practice."

P

Parajika

Lit., defeat or the conditions leading to the defeat of the Bodhicitta. Also the conditions leading to the defeat of the Bhiksu's life.

Paramita

Refers to the six practices, the perfection of which ferries one beyond the sea of suffering and mortality to Nirvana. The six Paramitas are the following: (I) Dana, Charity or giving, including the bestowing of truth on others; (2) Sila, keeping the discipline; (3) Ksanti, patience under suffering and insult; (4) Virya, zeal and progress; (5) Dhyana, meditation or contemplation; (6) Prajna, wisdom, the power to discern reality or truth. It is the perfection of the last one — Prajna — that ferries sentient beings across the ocean of Samsara (the sea of incarnate life) to the shores of Nirvana.

Parinirvana

The Buddha's final Nirvana, entered by him at the time of death.

Polar Mountain

In Buddhist cosmology, the universe is composed of worlds upon worlds 7 ad infinitum. (Our earth is only a small part of one of these worlds). The Polar Mountain is the central mountain of each world.

Polaris

The North Star, polestar; star of the second magnitude, standing alone and forming the end of the tail of the constellation Ursa Minor; it marks very nearly the position of the north celestial pole.

Prajna

True or transcendental wisdom. Last of the paramitas. One of the highest attainments of Buddhist Practice.

Pratyeka Buddha

A solitary Buddha; one who has achieved Awakening through insight into the dependent origination of mind and body. Pratyekabuddhas lead only solitary lives, and they do not teach the Dharma to others not do they have any desire to do so.

Pretas

Hungry ghosts. Who are tormented by continual and unsatisfied cravings. The preta-realm is one of the three states of woe (apaya-bhumi) and one of the six realms of existence.

Priyavacana

Lit,. loving or affectionate speech. This beautiful and affectionate speech is one of the four All-Embracing Virtues and is used to lead sentient beings toward the truth.

Pure Land

Generic term for the realms of the Buddhas. In this text it denotes the Land of Ultimate Bliss or Western Land of Amitabha Buddha. It is not a realm of enjoyment, but rather an ideal place of cultivation, beyond the Triple Realm and samsara, where those who are reborn are no longer subject to retrogression. This is the key distinction between the Western Pure Land and such realms as the Tusita Heaven. There are two conceptions of the Pure Land: as different and apart from the Saha World and as one with and the same as the Saha World. When the mind is pure and undefiled, any land or environment becomes a pure land (Vimalakirti, Avatamsaka Sutras...). See also "Tripe Realm."

Pure Land School

When Mahayana Buddhism spread to China, Pure Land ideas found fertile ground for development. In the fourth century, the movement crystallized with the formation of the Lotus Society, founded by Master Hui Yuan (334-416), the first Pure Land Patriach.

The school was formalized under the Patriarchs T'an Luan (Donran) and Shan Tao (Zendo). Master Shan Tao's teachings, in particular, greatly influenced the development of Japanese Pure Land, associated with Honen Shonin (Jodo school) and his disciple, Shinran Shonin (Jodo Shinshu School) in the 12th and 13th centuries. Jodo Shinshu, or Shin Buddhism places overwhelming emphasis on the element of faith.

> [Pure Land comprises the schools] of East Asia which emphasize aspects of Mahayana Buddhism stressing faith in Amida, meditation on and recitation of his name, and the religious goal of being reborn in his "Pure Land" or "Western Paradise." (Keith Crim.)

Note: An early form of Buddha Recitation can be found in the Nikayas of the Pali Canon:

> In the Nikayas, the Buddha... advised his disciples to think of him and his virtues as if they saw his body before their eyes, whereby they would be enabled to accumulate merit and attain Nirvana or be saved from transmigrating in the evil paths... (D.T. Suzuki, The Eastern Buddhist, Vol 3, No. 4, p.317).

Pure Land Sutras

See "Three Pure Land Sutras."

S

Saddharma-pundarika

See entry under Lotus Sutra.

Saha World

World of Endurance. Refers to this world of ours, filled with suffering and afflictions, yet gladly endured by its inhabitants.

Sakra

God of the sky who fights the demons with his vajra, or thunderbolt.

Sage

A wise and virtuous person, an accomplished one who is second in rank to a saint.

Sala

Or Salavana, the grove of sal(teak) trees near Kusinagara, the place of the Buddha's death.

Samadhi

Deep concentration: the state of one-pointedness of mind

characterized by pace and imperturbability. Samadhi is also one of the Paramitas and is indispensable on the path to Bodhi.

Samanarthata

Cooperation with and adaptation to others for the sake of leading them towards the truth. Samanarthata is one of the Four All-Embracing Virtues.

Samantabhadra

Also called Universal Worthy or, in Japanese, Fugen. A major Bodhisattva, who personifies the transcendental practices and vows of the Buddhas (as compared to the Bodhisattva Manjusri, who represents transcendental wisdom). Usually depicted seated on an elephant with six tusks (six paramitas). Best known for his "Ten Great Vows."

Samatha

Quiet, tranquility, calmness of mind, absence of mind.

Sambhogakaya

See "Three bodies of the Buddha."

Samsara

Cycle of rebirths; realms of Birth and Death.

Sangha

Lit., harmonious community. In the Buddhadharma, Sangha means the order of Bhiksus, Bhiksunis, Sramaneras and Sramanerikas. Another meaning is the Arya Sangha, made up of those individuals, lay or monastic, who have attained one of the four stages of sanctity. Also, the Bodhisattva Sangha.

Sangharama Body

A monastery with its garden or grove, a universal body.

Sanskrit

Learned language of India. Canonical texts of Mahayana Buddhism in its Indian stage were written in Sanskrit.

Sariputra

Major disciple of Shakyamuni Buddha, foremost in wisdom among His Arhat disciples.

Sastra

Commentary; the commentaries constitute one of the three parts of the Buddhist canonical scrptures.

Self-Nature

One's own Original Nature, one's own Buddha Nature.

Self-Power

See "Difficult Path of Practice."

Seven Treasures

Gold, silver, lapis lazuli, crystal, agate, red pearl and carnelian. They represent the seven power of faith, perseverance, sense of shame, avoidance of wrongdoing, mindfulness, concentration and wisdom.

Siddham

Blessed, endowed with supernatural faculties. This same term refers to the Sanskrit alphabet also and is, likewise, transliterated as His-ta in Chinese.

Siddhanta

The four siddhanta. The Buddha taught by (1) mundane of ordinary modes of expression; (2) individual treatment, adapting his teaching to the capacity of his hearers; (3) diagnostic treatment of their moral diseases; and (4) the perfect and highest truth.

Siksamana

A lay-disciple who maintains the eight precepts, either temporarily or as preparation for leaving home.

Sila

Moral precepts. These number 5,8,10.250 or 350. Also, one of the Paramitas.

Six Directions

North, South, East, West, above and below, i.e., all directions. In the Avatamsaka Sutra, they are expanded to include points of the compass in between and are referred to as the Ten Directions.

Six Dusts

See "Dusts."

Six Organs

The six indriyas, or sense organs: eye, ear, nose, tongue, body and mind.

Six Planes of Existence (Six Paths)

The paths within the realm of Birth and Death. Includes the three Evil Paths (hells, hungry ghosts, animosity) and the paths of humans, asuras and celestials. These paths can be understood as states of mind. See also "Evil Paths."

Sixth Patriarch

Hui Neng (638-713), the Sixth Patriarch of the Chinese Zen school and author of the Platform Sutra.

Skandhas

As taught by the Buddha, the skandhas are the components of the human so-called entity that is constantly changing. They are: 1. Name/form; 2. Feeling; 3. Conception; 4. Impulse; 5. Consciousness.

Skillful Means

See "Expedient Means."

Small Vehicle

See entry under Hinayana.

Spiritual power

Also called miraculous power, Includes, inter alia, the ability to see all forms (deva eye), to hear all sounds (deva ear), to know the throughts of others, to be anywhere and do anything at will.

Sramana

Lit., labourer; applied to those who wholeheartedly practice toward enlightenment; root word of the designation for novice monk.

Sramanera

A novice monk holding the 10 precepts.

Sramanerika

A novice nun holding the 10 precepts.

Sravakas

"Lit., 'voice-hearers': those who follow [Theravada] and eventually become arhats as a result of listening to the Buddhas and following their teachings" (A. Buzo and T. Prince.) See also "Arhat."

Sudhana (Good Wealth)

The main protagonist in the next-to-last and longest chapter of the Avatamsaka Sutra. Seeking Enlightenment, he visited and studied with fifty-three spiritual advisors and became the equal of the Buddhas in one lifetime. Both his first advisor and his last advisor (Samantabhadra) taught him the Pure Land path.

Suddhodana

Pure Rice King, the father of Shakyamuni, ruled over the Sakyans at Kapilavasthu on the Nepalese border.

Sudra

The lowest of the four Hindi Castes at the time of Shakyamuni. They were peasants, slaves and serfs.

Sumeru

Lit., exalted, excellent; mythical "world mountain" that rises through the center of a Buddhist universe.

Surangama Sutra

Also called Heroic Gate Sutra.

The "Sutra of the Heroic One" exercised a great influence on the development of Mahayana Buddhism in China [and neighbouring countries]. It emphasizes the power of samadhi, through which enlightenment can be attained, and explains the various methods of emptiness meditation through the practice of which everyone ... can realize ... enlightenment ä (Shambhala Dictionary of Buddhism and Zen.)

Sutra

An aphorism; a thread of suggestive words or phrases summarizing religious and philosophical instruction. In buddhism, it refers to a discourse by the Buddha or one of his major disciples. The Sutra collection is one of the three divisions of the Buddhist scriptures.

T

Tao

Path or Way. The Sanskrit equivalent to this Chinese term is marga.

Tathagata

Usually translated as "Thus Come One."

He who came as did all Buddhas, who took the absolute way of cause and effect, and attained to perfect wisdom; one of the highest title of a Buddha (Charles Luk).

Ten Directions

North, South. East, N-F, N-W, S-F, S-W, Zenith and Nadir.

Ten Evil Acts (Ten Evil Deeds, Ten Sins)

1. Killing; 2. stealing; 3. sexual misconduct; 4. lying; 5. slander; 6. coarse language; 7. empty chatter; 8. covetousness; 9. angry speech; 10. wrong views. See also "Ten Precepts."

Ten Great Vows

The famous vows of the Bodhisattva Samantabhadra in the Avatamsaka Sutra. These vows represent the quintessence of this Sutra and are the basis of all Mahayana practice. Studying the vows and putting them into practice is tantamount to studying the Avatamsaka Sutra and practising its teachings. See also "Samantabhadra."

Ten Precepts

Include an expanded version of the Five Precepts of body and mouth (not to kill, steal, engage in illicit sex, lie, or take intoxicants) with the addition of the virtues of the mind (elimination of greed, anger and delusion). See also "Five Precepts," "The Evil Acts."

Ten Stages of a Bodhisattva's Progress

The are the following: (1) Joy at having overcome former difficulties and at now entering the path to Buddhahood; (2) Freedom for all possible defilement, the stage of purity; (3) The stage of further enlightenment; (4) Glowing wisdom; (5) Mastery of the utmost or final difficulties; (6) The open way of wisdom that is beyond purity and impurity; (7) Proceeding afar, above the concept of "self" in order to save others; (8) Attainment of calm imperturbability; (9) Achievement of the finest discriminatory wisdom; knowing, expediently, where and how to save; possessing the ten powers; (10) Attainment of the fertilizing powers of the Law Cloud.

Ten Virtues

The virtuous modes of behaviour, which are the positive counterparts to the Five Precepts.

Theravada

Lit., the School of the Elders; one of the two main forms of Buddhism known in the world today; practised chiefly in south-east Asia; has the Pali Canon for textual foundation; this tradition advocates the Arahantship.

Third Lifetime

In the first lifetime, the practitioner engages in mundane good deeds which bring ephemeral worldly blessings (wealth, power, authority, etc.) in the second lifetime. Since power tends to corrupt, he is likely to create evil karma, resulting in retribution in the third lifetime. Thus, good deeds in the first lifetime are potential "enemies" of the third lifetime. To ensure that mundane good deeds do not become "enemies the practitioner should dedicate all merits to a transcendental goal, i.e., to become Bodhisattvas or Buddhas or, in Pure Land teaching, to achieve rebirth in the Pure Land—a Buddha land beyond Birth and Death.

In a mundane context, these three lifetimes can be conceived of as three generations. Thus, the patriarch of a prominent family, through work and luck, amasses great power, fortune and influence (first lifetime). His children are then able to enjoy a leisurely, and, too often, dissipated life (second lifetime). By the generation of the grandchildren, the family's fortune and good reputation have all but disappeared (third lifetime).

Thirty-seven Limbs of Enlightenment

These are: *(a)* the four mindfulnesses; *(b)* the four right efforts; *(c)* the four bases of miraculous powers; *(d)* the five roots; *(e)* the five powers; *(f)* the seven factors of enlightenment; and *(g)* the eightfold noble path (G.C.C. Chang).

Three Bodies of the Buddha (Skt. Trikaya)

1. Dharmakaya: The Dharma-body, or the "body of reality", which is formless, unchanging, transcendental, and inconceivable. Synonymous with suchness, or emptiness. 2. Sambhogakaya: the "body of enjoyment", the celestial body of the Buddha. Personification of eternal perfection in its ultimate sense. It "resides" in the Pure Land and never manifests itself in the mundane world, but only in the celestial spheres, accompanied by enlightened Bodhisattvas. 3. Nirmanakaya: the "incarnated body" of the Buddha. In order to benefit certain sentient beings, a Buddha incarnates himself into an appropriate visible body, such as that of Sakyamuni Buddha.

The incarnated body of the Buddha should not be confused with a magically produced Buddha. The former is a real, tangible human body which has a definite life span, The latter is an illusory Buddha-form which is produced with miraculous powers and can be withdrawn with miraculous powers (G.C.C. Chang).

Three Evil Paths

See "Evil Paths."

Three Jewels (Three Precious Ones, Three Treasures)

In Sanskrit, Rathatraya. Buddha, Dharma and Sangha; sometimes referred to as the Teacher, the Teaching and the Taught.

Three Karmas

The three conditions, inheritances or karmas, of which there are several groups, including the karmas of deeds, words and thoughts.

Three Poisons

Craving, aversion and delusion; also, these are termed the three root-stains or the three roots of unskillfulness.

Three Pure Land Sutras

Pure Land Buddhism s based on three basic sutras:

(a) Amitabha Sutra (or Shorter Amitabha Sutra, or Smaller Sukhavati-Vyuha, or the Sutra of Amida);

(b) Longer Amitabha Sutra (or Longer Sukhavati-Vyuha, or the Teaching of Infinite Life);

(c) Meditation Sutra (or the Meditation on the Buddha of Infinite Life, or the Amitayus Dhyana Sutra).

Sometimes the last chapter of the Avatamsaka Sutra ("The Practices and Vows of the Bodhisattva Samantabhadra") is considered the fourth basic sutra of the Pure Land tradition. Note: in Pure Land, the Longer Amitabha Sutra is considered a shorter form of the Lotus Sutra.

Three Realms (Triple Realm, Three Worlds)

The realms of desire (our world), form (realms of the lesser deities) and formlessness (realms of the higher deities). The Western Pure Land is outside the Triple Realm, beyond samsara and retrogression. See also "Pure Land."

Three Refuges

Taking refuge and possessing confidence in the Buddha's Awakening, in his Teaching and in the Sangha of enlightened disciples.

Three Vehicles

The yanas of Sravakas, Pratyekabuddhas and Bodhisattvas.

T'ien T'ai (Tendai) School

A major school that takes the Lotus Sutra as its principal text. Historically, it has had a close relationship with Pure Land. See also "Lotus Sutra."

Tolerance of Non-Birth

"Tolerance" (insight) that comes from the knowledge that all phenomena are unborn. Sometimes translated as "insight into the non-origination of all existence/non-origination of the dharmas."

> A Mahayana Buddhist term for the insight into emptiness, the non-origination or birthlessness of things or beings realized by Bodhisattvas who have attained the eight Stage [Ground] of the path to Buddhahood. When a Bodhisattva realizes this insight he has attained the stage of non-retrogression. (Ryukoku University.)

The Pure Land School teaches that anyone reborn in the Pure Land attains the Tolerance of Non-Birth and reaches the stage of non-retrogression, never to fall back into samsara. See also "Non-Birth."

Transference of Merit

The concept of merit transference, or sharing one's own merits and virtues with others, is reflected in the following passage:

> Some of us may ask whether the effect of [evil] karma can be... [changed] by repeating the name of Kuan-Yin. This question is tied up with that of rebirth in Sukhavati [the Pure Land] and it may be answered by saying that invocation of Kuan-Yin's name forms another cause which will right away offset the previous karma. We known, for example) that if there is a dark, heavy cloud above, the chances are that it will rain. But we all know that if a strong wind should blow, the cloud will be carried away somewhere else and we will not feel the rain. Similarly, the addition of one big factor can alter the whole course of karma
>
> It is only by accepting the idea of life as one whole that both Theravadins and Mahayanists can advocate the practice of transference of merit to others. With the case of Kuan-Yin then, by calling on Her name we identify ourselves with Her and as a result of this identification, Her merits flow over to us. These merits which are now ours then counterbalance our bad karma and save us from calamity. The law of cause and effect still stands good. All that has happened is that a powerful and immensely good karma has overshadowed the weaker one. (Lecture on Kuan-Tin by Tech Eng Soon – Penang Buddhist Association, c. 1960. Pamphlet.)

Triloka or Trailoka

See "Threee Realms."

Tripitaka

Lit., three baskets: The earliest Buddhist canonical text consisting of three sections: 1. Buddha's discourses (sutras), 2 Rules of Discipline (Vinaya), 3. Analytical and explanatory texts or commentaries (sastras); usually referreed to as the Pali canon.

Triple Jewel

See "Three Treasures."

Two Truths

1) Relative or conventional, everyday truth of the mundane world subject to delusion and dichotomies and 2) the Ultimate Truth, transcending dichotomies, as taught by the Buddhas.

> According to Buddhism, there are two kinds of Truth, the Absolute and the Relative. The Absolute Truth (of the Void) manifests "illumination but is

> always still," and this is absolutely inexplicable. On the other hand, the Relative Truth (of the Unreal) manifests "stillness but is always illuminating," which means that it is immanent in everything. (Hsu Heng Chi/P.H. Wei).

Pure Land thinkers such as the Patriarch Tao Ch'o accepted "the legitimacy of Conventional Truth as an expression of Ultimate Truth and as a vehicle to reach Ultimate Truth. Even though all form is nonform, it is acceptable and necessary to use form within the limits of causality, because its use is an expedient means of saving others out of one's compassion for them and because, even for the unenlightened, the use of form can lead to the revelation of form as nonform" (David Chappell). Thus to reach Buddhahood, which is formless, the cultivator can practice the Pure Land method based on form.

Tzung

A term originally used to mean "sect", but later appropriated by the intentional school known as Ch'an (Japanese, Zen) for use in special contexts.

U

Unconditioned (Transcendental)

Anything "without outflows," i.e., free of the three marks of greed, anger an delusion. See also "Conditioned."

Upasaka/Upasika

Buddhist lay disciple (man/woman), who formally received five precepts or rules of conduct.

V

Vaidehi

The Queen of King Bimbisara of Magadha, India. It was in response to her entreaties that Buddha Shakyamuni preached the Meditation Sutra, which teaches a series of sixteen visualizations (of Amitabha Buddha, the Pure Land ...) leading to rebirth. In the Land of Ultimate Bliss.

Vaidurya

A precious substance, perhaps lapis lazuli or beryl.

Vairocana

The main Buddha in the Avatamsaka Sutra. Represents the Dharma Body of Buddha Shakyamuni and all Buddhas. His Pure Land is the Flower Store World, i.e., the entire cosmos.

Vaisravana

One of the four maharaja-deva graudians of the first or lowest devaloka on its four sides. Vaisravana guards the north.

Vaisya

The third of the four Hindi Castes at the time of Shakyamuni. They were merchant, entrepreneurs, traders, farmers, manufacturers, etc., but not well-educated.

Varuna

God of the sea and of the waters; guardian of the western quarter of the compass.

Veda

True or sacred knowledge or lore; name of celebrated works which constitute the basis of the first period of the Hindu religion.

Vimalakirti Sutra

Also called Vimalakirti Nirdesa Sutra. A key Mahayana sutra particularly popular with Zen and to a lesser extent Pure Land followers. The main protagonist is a layman named Vimalakirti who is the equal of many Bodhisattvas in wisdom, eloquence, etc. He explained the teaching of Emptiness in terms of non-duality ... "The true nature of things is beyond the limiting concepts imposed by words." Thus, when asked by Manjusri to define the non-dual Truth, Vimalakirti simply remained silent.

Vinaya

Disciplined conduct, referring specifically to the monastic rules for the disciples who have left home; also, one of the three divisions of the Buddhist scriptures.

Vipasyana

Discernment; also, insight, correct perception or view.

Virtue

See "Merit and Virtue."

Virya: Energy

The energy necessary to maintain and progress in spiritual development. Also, one of the Paramitas.

Visualization

See Meditation Sutra for explanation.

> The visualizations [in the Meditation Sutra] are distinguished into sixteen kinds [shifting from earthly scenes to Pure scenes at the third Visualization]: (1) visualization of the sun, (2) visualization of water, (3) visualization of the ground [in the Pure Land], (4) visualization of the trees, (5) visualization of the lake [s], (6) unified visualization of the [50 billion] storied-pavilions, trees, lakes, and so forth, (7) visualization of the [lotus throne of Amitabha Buddha], (8) visualization of the images of the Buddha [Amitabha] and Bodhisattvas [Avalokitesvara and Mahasthamaprapta], (9) visualization of the [Reward body of Amitabha Buddha, i.e., the form in which He appears in the Pure Land], (10) visualization of Avalokitesvara, (11) visualization of Mahasthamaprapta, (12) visualization of one's own rebirth, (13) [see below], (14) visualization of the rebirth of the highest grades, (15) visualization of the rebirth of the middle grades and (16) visualization of the rebirth of the lowest grades. (K.K. Tanaka. The Down of Chinese Pure Land Doctrine.)

The 13th Visualization has been summarized as follows:

> If one cannot visualize the [Reward body of Amitabha Buddha], focus on the small body, which is sixteen cubits high (the traditional height of Shakyamuni while he dwelt on earth); contemplate an intermingling of the [Reward] and small bodies. (loji Okazaki, p. 52.)

Visualizations 14-16 refer to the nine lotus grades (or rebirth), divided into three sets of three grades each.

W

Way (Path, Tao)

The path leading to Supreme Enlightenment, to Buddhahood.

Wisdom-life

The life of a Buddha or Bodhisattva, which is sustained by wisdom, just as the life of an ordinary being is sustained by food.

Y

Yama

In the Vedas, the god of the dead.

Yana

Sankrit term, commonly translated as vehicle; means spiritual vehicle, path or career.

Yasodhara

The wife of Siddhartha Goutama. Later become a nun.

Yogacara School

Another name for the Mind-Only school, founded in the fourth century by the brothers Asanga and Vasubandhu.

Z

The First Discourse of the Buddha
By Rewata Dhamma; foreword by Ajahn Sumedho
Boston: Wisdom Publications, 1997

MEDITATION AND PRACTICE IN GENERAL

The Myth of Freedom and the Way of Meditation
By Chogyam Trungpa
Boston: Shambhala Publications, 1976

Vision and Transformation:
An Introduction to the Buddha's Noble Eightfold Path
By Sangharakshita
Glasgow: Windhorse Publications, 1995

Transforming Self and World
By Sangharakshita
Birmingham: Windhorse Publications, 1995

Buddhism in Practice
Edited by Donald S. Lopez, Jr.
Princeton: Princeton University Press, 1995

When Things Fall Apart
By Pema Chodron
Boston: Shambhala Publications, 1996

Still Point: A Beginner's Guide to Zen Meditation
By John Daido Loori
Mt. Tremper, NY: Dharma Communications, 1996

Breath by Breath: The Liberating Practice of Insight Meditation
By Larry Rosenberg with David Guy; foreword by Jon Kobat-Zinn
Boston: Shambhala Publications, 1998

THE THERAVADA TRADITION

Ethics in Early Buddhism
By David J. Kalupahana
Honolulu: University of Hawaii Press, 1995

Living Dharma: Teachings of Twelve Buddhist Masters
By Jack Kornfield: forewords by Chogyam Trungpa and Ram Dass
Boston: Shambhala Publications, 1996

Buddhist Ethics
By Hammalawa Saddatissa; introduction by Charles Hallisey
Boston: Wisdom Publications, 1997

Mindfulness in Plain English
By Bhante Henepola Gunaratana
Boston: Wisdom Publications, 1993

Eight Mindful Steps to Happiness
By Bhante Henepola Gunaratana
Boston: Wisdom Publications, 2001

THE ZEN TRADITION

Tracing Back the Radiance: Chinul's Korean Way of Zen
By Robert E. Buswell, Jr.
Honolulu: The Kuroda Institute and University of Hawaii Press, 1983

The Collected Works of Chinul
Translated and introduced by Robert E. Buswell, Jr.
Honolulu: University of Hawaii Press, 1983

The Zen Monastic Experience: Buddhist Practice in Contemporary Korea
By Robert E. Buswell, Jr.
Princeton: Princeton University Press, 1992

Ch'an and Zen Teaching, volumes I-III
By Charles Luk
York Beach: Samuel Weiser, 1993

Master Dogen's Shobogenzo
Translated by Gudo Wafu Nishijima and Chodo Cross
Woods Hole, MA: Windbell Publications, 4 vols., 1994-1997

Zen Mind, Beginner's Mind
By Shunryu Suzuki
New York: Weatherhill, 1998

THE VAJRAYANA (TIBETAN) TRADITION

The Life of Milarepa
Translated by Lobsand P. Lhalungpa
New York: Penguin Books, 1979

The Tantric Distinction: An Introduction to Tibertan Buddhism
By Jeffery Hopkins
Boston: Wisdom Publications, 1992

A Flash of Lightning in the Dark of Night:
A Guide to the Bodhisattva's Way of Life
By the Dalai Lama; translated by the Padmakara Translation Group
Boston: Shambhala Publications, 1994

The Tibetan Book of The Dead:
Liberation Through Understanding in the Between
Translated by Robert A. F. Thurman
New York: Bantam Books, 1994

ENGAGED BUDDHISM AND BEYOND

Dharma Gaia: A Harvest of Essays in Buddhism and Ecology
Edited by Allan Hunt Badiner; foreword by the Dalai Lama
Berkeley: Parallax Press, 1990

Buddhism and Ecology: The Interconnection of Dharma and Deeds
Edited by Mary Evelyn Tucker and Duncan Ryuken Williams
Cambridge, MA: Harvard University Center of the Study of World Religions, 1997

The Wheel of Engaged Buddhism: A New Map of the Path
By Kenneth Kraft
New York: Weatherhill, 1999

Dharma Rain: Sources of Buddhist Environmentalism
Edited by Stephanie Kaza and Kenneth Kraft
Boston: Shambhala Publications, 2000

The Man Who Planted Trees
By Jean Giono
Chelsea, VT: Chelsea Green Publishing, 1985

The Snow Leopard
By Peter Matthiessen
New York: Viking Press, 1978

Wildlife in America
By Peter Matthiesses
New York: Viking Penguin, 1987

Tigers in The Snow
By Peter Mattiessen; introduction and photographs by Maurice Hornocker
New York: North Point Press, 2000

The Back Country
By Gary Snyder
New York: New Directions Books, 1971

The Practice of the Wild: Essays by Gary Snyder
By Gary Snyder
San Francisco: North Point Press, 1990

No Nature: New and Selected Poems
By Gary Snyder
New York: Pantheon Books, 1992

Left Out in the Rain: New Poems 1947-1985
By Gary Snyder
New York: North Point Press, 1995